W9-BWS-251

"Understanding and appreciating the power of situations gives you a leg up in life, and *Situations Matter* is the best place to start investigating this challenge. It is excellent, entertaining reading for anyone interested in classic human questions about morality, conformity, and the real differences between men and women."

—Tyler Cowen, professor of economics, George Mason University, and author of *Create Your Own Economy* and *The Great Stagnation*

"It can be easy to overlook how ordinary situations shape behavior. It might seem like Sam Sommers is brilliant for choosing to write a book on this important topic, but he'd probably just explain that circumstance drove him to it. Still, we're all lucky he did."

—Leonard Mlodinow, author of *The Drunkard's Walk* and coauthor of *The Grand Design*

"I loved *Situations Matter*. True, I read it while sitting on my comfortable couch, but I bet I would have loved it no matter the situation, even if I read it submerged in ice-cold water. Sam Sommers shows us the surprising extent to which humans are influenced by external factors. It's a fascinating read, and one that will improve your life in many ways, whether dealing with road rage, choosing a spouse, or trying to handle your boss."

—A. J. Jacobs, author of *The Year of Living Biblically* and *My Life as an Experiment*

"This book is a true eye-opener. From the boardroom meeting to the dining room table, from why we love to why we hate, you'll never look at the ordinary world around you in exactly the same way again."

—Wray Herbert, author of *On Second Thought: Outsmarting Your Mind's Hard-Wired Habits*

SITUATIONS MATTER

Understanding How Context Transforms Your World

SAM SOMMERS

RIVERHEAD BOOKS
New York

RIVERHEAD BOOKS
Published by the Penguin Group
Penguin Group (USA) Inc.
375 Hudson Street, New York, New York 10014, USA
Penguin Group (Canada), 90 Eglinton Avenue East, Suite 700, Toronto, Ontario M4P 2Y3, Canada
(a division of Pearson Penguin Canada Inc.) • Penguin Books Ltd., 80 Strand, London WC2R 0RL,
England • Penguin Group Ireland, 25 St. Stephen's Green, Dublin 2, Ireland (a division of Penguin
Books Ltd.) • Penguin Group (Australia), 250 Camberwell Road, Camberwell, Victoria 3124, Australia
(a division of Pearson Australia Group Pty. Ltd.) • Penguin Books India Pvt. Ltd., 11 Community
Centre, Panchsheel Park, New Delhi—110 017, India • Penguin Group (NZ), 67 Apollo Drive,
Rosedale, Auckland 0632, New Zealand (a division of Pearson New Zealand Ltd.) • Penguin Books
(South Africa) (Pty.) Ltd., 24 Sturdee Avenue, Rosebank, Johannesburg 2196, South Africa

Penguin Books Ltd., Registered Offices: 80 Strand, London WC2R 0RL, England

While the author has made every effort to provide accurate telephone numbers and Internet addresses at the
time of publication, neither the publisher nor the author assumes any responsibility for errors, or for
changes that occur after publication. Further, the publisher does not have any control over and does not
assume any responsibility for author or third-party websites or their content.

First Riverhead hardcover edition: December 2011
First Riverhead trade paperback edition: January 2013
Riverhead trade paperback ISBN: 978-1-59448-620-3

The Library of Congress has catalogued the Riverhead hardcover edition as follows:

Sommers, Sam.
Situations matter : understanding how context transforms your world / Sam Sommers.
p.   cm.
ISBN 978-1-59448-818-4
1. Context effects (Psychology)   2. Decision making.   I. Title.
BF714.S66   2011   2011039695
155.9—dc23

PRINTED IN THE UNITED STATES OF AMERICA

10 9 8 7 6 5 4 3

For my colleagues, from Allport to Zimbardo,
for work so engaging that its story almost tells itself.

For Saul and Steve, for introducing me to that story
with such enthusiasm and accessibility.

And, mostly, for the enduringly lovely Sommers Ladies, M, A, & S,
for providing distractions unfailingly enjoyable,
regardless of the convenience of their timing.

CONTENTS

SITUATIONS MATTER

PROLOGUE

MAMA SAID THERE'D BE DAYS LIKE THIS. BUT SHE failed to mention that mine would keep happening at the Newark airport.

We were on our way from Michigan to Massachusetts for a wedding. Still graduate students, my wife and I were blessed with a flexible schedule but burdened by a fixed income. In other words, we were the perfect guinea pigs for one of those travel websites that offers low fares in return for your relinquishing control over airlines and flight times. So I had typed in our travel dates, agreed to the terms and conditions, and hoped for the best.

Instead, I got Newark.

To be fair, I have nothing against the city proper—my only visits have come in the form of airport layovers. And I suppose my repeated experiences of long lines, longer delays, and inexplicable cancellations have had more to do with the airlines I've flown than the airport itself. But it sure feels like every time the word *Newark* pops up on my itinerary, the fates conspire against me in new and creatively malevolent ways.

On my previous visit, misfortune had arrived in the form of a last-minute cancellation followed by two equipment-related delays. I ended up on the floor of an overcrowded gate for hours, squeezed between a dozen Hasidic Jews who passed most of their time in prayer. The only silver lining was my corresponding reassurance that God would never let anything bad happen to the plane once it did take off, my own spotty record of synagogue attendance notwithstanding.

But that was then. This time, my problems started with a website itinerary that left just forty minutes to make our connection in Newark. High winds that had briefly delayed our first flight narrowed this time window even further. And, of course, our airline just had to be the one to spread out its gates over multiple terminals, forcing us through a gauntlet of monorails, food courts, and moving walkways on the way to our second flight. When it became clear that the success of the mission might hinge on mere seconds, I decided to dash ahead of my wife, determined to get to the gate and hold the plane for us before the agents closed the boarding door.

Because, as we all know, once they close that door, there's no going back. No, that's nonnegotiable and irreversible. To reopen that door—that modern incarnation of Pandora's box—would be unthinkable. Doing so would undermine the very fabric that holds our society together, not to mention disrupt the space-time continuum as we know it. Clearly, you can't reopen that door under any circumstance. Not even when the plane is still parked right outside and it's eight minutes until the posted departure time and there isn't another flight from Newark to Boston until late the following morning right around the same time as that wedding you're supposed to attend.

It was demoralizing to see our plane through the window but hear that we were too late to board. Still sweating from my impromptu sprint, I waited for my wife to arrive and then we both dragged ourselves over to the airline's customer service desk along with the other aggrieved passengers who'd also stumbled on a surprise New Jersey overnight. Exhausted, our focus shifted from irritation to simply wanting to find out how to get to the hotel where the airline would be putting us up for the night.

But we were in for another surprise. Things in the customer service line weren't going so well, either. The first passenger to the desk was a heavyset man with sunglasses perched backward on his enormous shaved head. As his conversation grew increasingly animated, the glasses staring back at the rest of us began to bob up and down rhythmically. He became apoplectic—the glasses speeding up to a discolike tempo—when he learned that there'd be no hotel voucher because the delays to his first flight had been caused by weather. He stormed off in a huff, still cursing under his breath as he headed toward the bar.

Next up was a well-dressed woman who seemed just a bit too made-up for the airport. She related her tale of woe, voice trembling with tearful sincerity. She needed to get to Boston to see her sister before surgery, her plans were now ruined, and she demanded a hotel room as well as a full refund. No dice. Marta, as the desk agent's bewinged name tag read, wasn't biting, not even when the passenger's quiet sniffling devolved into a full-fledged tantrum. After continued hysterics, she finally moved to the side and began furiously punching buttons on her cell phone.

Now it was my turn. Obviously, I needed a different strategy. Yelling wasn't working with Marta. Neither was crying. My wife had grown so discouraged that she had already left the line for the comfort of a nearby bench, taking out a magazine from her carry-on to pass the time.

And that's when I saw the light.

Right at that moment, it dawned on me that I was uniquely equipped to figure out how to successfully navigate this interaction. After all, this is what I'd been studying as I worked toward my Ph.D.: the nature of situations. Of course, not this exact situation, involving angry passengers or stoic airline agents—then, as now, my research examined the ways in which we think and act differently in contexts that are racially diverse, as well as how people make decisions in legal settings like the courtroom. But the basic principle still applied to this, the most mundane of circumstances:

To understand human nature, you must appreciate the power of situations.

I took a figurative step back from the counter to assess as objectively as I could the context I was in, something that I'm pretty sure sunglasses guy and makeup lady hadn't done. They simply saw Marta as the enemy—the flesh-and-bones representation of the faceless airline that had screwed us. And make no mistake: the airline *had* screwed us. They knew that a dozen of us were in the airport, making our way to the gate from another terminal. They knew this was the last flight out. Yet they still closed the boarding door ten minutes before the posted departure time, and then had the nerve to tell us we were on our own for the night.

So I understood my fellow passengers' anger, and I could see why, in their minds, Marta deserved our wrath. Who else was there to take it out on?

But I also knew there was more to this situation. And besides, the whole righteous indignation bit didn't seem to be working too well. The setting called for more than just a knee-jerk emotional response. This was a social puzzle waiting to be solved.

From the wide-lens view of the situation, Marta didn't look to me like a heartless automaton. In her mid-to-late thirties, she wore a wedding band and a heart-shaped locket—at least *some*body *some*where found her lovable. She looked haggard; she had probably spent a full day being berated for gate decisions she hadn't made and policies she hadn't created, and the job was becoming even more difficult as the night grew long and the passengers more agitated. She was the airline's sacrificial lamb, designated to stand there and absorb our abuse so that the rest of the company didn't have to. Accordingly, she eyed me warily, resigned to the verbal and emotional onslaught that I would inevitably bring as the next person in line.

I recognized that I needed to shake things up, to exaggerate the contrast between my approach and that of the passengers before me. I started by acknowledging the unpleasant circumstances in which we both found ourselves. "Hi, how are you?" I asked in the friendliest voice I could muster. "Look, I know that this isn't your fault and that you're having just as long a night as we are."

Marta blinked, unmoved. She said nothing.

"But put yourself in my shoes, too," I continued. "The airline gave us an itinerary with a tight connection. They knew our first plane was a few minutes late and that this was the last flight out, and they still made a conscious decision not to hold the plane. Fine. I get that."

Marta's eyes widened just a bit. She looked confused by the direction the conversation was taking.

"I really do," I said calmly. "It costs money each minute the plane is at the gate, so it's cheaper to pull away than to wait for a handful of passengers. We came out on the short end of the financial analysis, and I can live with that. But now the airline has to deal with those of us on the short end, right? I'm not asking for a refund. Just a hotel room. It's the right thing to do and the airline still comes out ahead."

"Mr. Sommers," Marta interjected as if on cue, "the issue is that we can't provide a hotel because your first flight's delay was weather-related."

"I understand that policy," I responded in as rational a tone as I could. "And it even makes sense to me in most cases. But what happened tonight was a little different, no? Our first plane was only a couple of minutes late. We got to the gate here before the scheduled departure time. The airline just didn't feel like waiting for us, and weather really had nothing to do with it," I offered.

Marta had softened a tad, but she remained unbowed, sticking to her script: "I'm sorry, sir, but that's our policy. My hands are tied."

Methodically, I probed further. "Well, there must be *something* you can do. You must have *some* discretion. I can't believe you're going to make the older woman behind me spend the night in the airport," I argued, conveniently overlooking that this purported concern for my elders hadn't been enough to compel me to offer said woman my spot at the front of the line.

"Well, we make exceptions in special cases, of course. If you were in a wheelchair or were ill, I could give you a voucher," she admitted. "But you don't seem ill, Mr. Sommers," she said with the knowing smile of someone who realizes that she's winning the argument.

I smiled back. I wasn't ill. But I did now have a better grasp of the situation. Marta wasn't hard-hearted or even unreasonable. In fact, I was even starting to like her a little. In a different setting— next to her on the bus or at the grocery store—I would have found her to be pleasant or at the very least innocuous. But tonight she was an employee toeing the bottom line. She was just following procedure. And our civil conversation had gone on long enough to reveal one of the loopholes in that procedure.

"No, I'm not sick," I agreed. I took a deep breath and then plunged forward. "My wife, however . . ." I said, pointing to the bench where she was now waiting with our bags. "She's . . . two months pregnant," I stammered, my voice now in a near whisper.

Marta blinked twice, processing this new development.

"I probably shouldn't be telling you this," I continued, in what I suppose was an instinctual effort to fill the silence.

"We haven't even told our family yet," I rambled on.

"Actually, you're the first person to know," I added, now picking up steam. "Well, other than our obstetrician. Oh, and the guy at the pharmacy who sold us the pregnancy test—I'm pretty sure he has his suspicions."

Marta started typing, which I took as a sign to shut up. Good move, too, because had I kept talking, I might have gone on to promise to name our firstborn after her. After a few moments, she silently held out a green hotel voucher. Then, for good measure, she threw in tickets for breakfast the next morning.

My wife greeted me with a mixed response. Ecstatic that we had a hotel room, she also cautioned me that any future pregnancy complications would be chalked up to my having violated our superstitious agreement to keep all such talk private until we reached the second trimester.

"How do you feel about Marta for a girl's name?" I asked her.

I STUDY SITUATIONS for a living. It's the greatest job in the world, teaching people about the power of context and examining it in my own research. As I detail in this book, the world around us is constantly pulling our strings, coloring how we think and guiding how we behave. And yet we rarely notice.

My hope is that this book will force you to notice. Its aim is to prompt you to appreciate the influence that different situations have on your daily tendencies and experiences. Ordinary contexts of all types—where you are, who you're with, what you see around you—transform how you act and, indeed, what kind of person you appear to be. By coming to grips with this idea, we gain a deeper understanding of ourselves and the other people in our lives.

What does the science of situations teach us? That many of our intuitions about human nature are wrong. Though we come to believe at a young age that we have a pretty good handle on what makes people do what they do, many of these assumptions turn out to be misplaced: individuals' personalities—yours and mine included—are not as stable as we think they are. We're more influenced by those around us than we'd like to believe. Even our private sense of identity is highly context-dependent.

This book will take you down a less-traveled, often surprising, and sometimes disconcerting road of human experience, refocusing your attention on the ordinary situations that have extraordinary effects on how we think and act. Research shows us that context impacts even the most intimate aspects of our lives, and this conclusion offers to those who embrace it insight as well as competitive advantage.

Now, I'm not promising you that reading this book will make you a better person. After all, I opened with a story about reneging on a marital agreement and shamelessly exploiting the miracle of pregnancy—all in the name of a free hotel night in New Jersey. So a self-help book this isn't.

But I will promise that this book will alter the way you think about human nature, thereby making you a more *effective* person. It will do so by improving your ability to predict how others around you will react to a wide range of situations: by training you to step back and assess more dispassionately the contexts in which you find yourself and the social dilemmas you encounter; by making you acutely aware of how situational factors can be manipulated to sway others and how you can deflect similar efforts to unduly influence you. In short, if you want to maximize success in professional ventures such as sales, politics, litigation, marketing, negotiation, and teaching—not to mention more generally refine your "people skills"—you have to start studying up on the science of situations.

Admittedly, there was nothing all that scientific about my performance in Newark. I didn't draw on specific research findings to figure out how best to demonstrate voucher-worthiness. Rather, I just followed a more general principle: when we look at situations objectively, detaching ourselves from the emotion and bias that often cloud our vision, we're better able to pick up on the clues that allow us to understand other people and achieve the outcomes we seek.

However, the science of situations also offers more concrete lessons about navigating our social universe. The chapters that follow explore human nature across a variety of dimensions, relying on empirical research as well as daily observation, drawing from scientific theory as well as *Seinfeld* episodes. And this is what makes studying situations so useful as well as so captivating: it requires attention to both scientific method and mundane detail; it appeals to both the behavioral researcher and sitcom fan lurking within each of us.

Because, in the end, situations of all types are important, from the unexceptional to the profound. Consider that the very same principles at work in my routine airport interaction with Marta can be found in settings with far graver consequences. As one example, according to a recent book by pseudonymous intelligence officer Matthew Alexander, U.S. interrogators weren't particularly successful in obtaining useful information from alleged terrorists captured during the first few years of the Iraq war.[1] The reason, suggests Alexander, was the default tendency of most interrogators to view their suspects as incorrigible evildoers who'd only respond to domination, threat, and fear—much like the fruitless strategies pursued by many customers with service representatives. And if you think this analogy strains credulity, well, clearly you've never

seen the residents of my grandparents' retirement community interacting with the dining room waitstaff during dinner.

The turning point in Iraq, writes Alexander, came when interrogators changed strategies, abandoning the harsh tactics of
belittlement in the name of cultural respect and rapport building. It's not that they started taking detainees out for pizza and ice
cream—distortion of reality, false hope, and good, old-fashioned
lies became essential ingredients of the new game plan. But the key
was a shift from brutality to brains, as Alexander calls it.

The suspect is a father with young kids? Then pretend you're a
dad, too—all the better to bond over parenting stories. The interrogators' goal became to find out as much as possible about the
detainees, to suss out as many details as they could regarding the
context in which this tense interaction was taking place, and then
to spin those details to their own advantage.

From airports to Abu Ghraib, from small talk to life-or-death
decisions, situations matter.

By the end of this book, my hope is that you'll appreciate this
conclusion and recognize the many ways in which context shapes
human behavior and daily experiences—even your own. These are
life lessons with the potential to pay dividends both personal and
professional, in the short term as well as the long run. Because even
when we aren't bartering for hotel rooms or questioning terrorists,
who among us doesn't spend more time than we'd like to admit
trying to anticipate the behavior of the people we live and work
with? Devising strategies for making a better first impression? Pondering whether the saleswoman really has a thing for me or just
tells everyone who tries on that shirt that he looks good in it?

We come to better answers to questions like these—regarding both the mundane and sublime aspects of our social world—when we take into account the power of situations. So think of this book as a primer on what really makes people tick. Consider it your guide as you start down a new path toward a deeper understanding of the true nature of human nature.

For the record, the saleswoman works on commission, hotshot. She says that to every customer.

1.

WYSIWYG

THE RIDDLE OF THE SPHINX. RUBIK'S CUBE. FERMAT'S Last Theorem. The popularity of NASCAR. To this pantheon of inscrutable puzzles, permit me to add another entry: the Conundrum of the Game Show Host.

Imagine, if you will, the following scenario. You're looking to hire a tutor. Maybe your fourteen-year-old is struggling with early European history; maybe *you're* struggling with early European history. Either way, the school year is well under way, and all the experienced tutors are booked for the foreseeable future. However, as a result of the economic downturn, you're able to dig up a few surprising applicants interested in the position. Your three finalists have no teaching experience whatsoever, but their names are familiar: Pat Sajak, Ryan Seacrest, Alex Trebek.

Remember, this is a vitally important choice. The grade point average of a loved one hangs in the balance. So take a moment.

Seriously. To the extent that your mental library of game show host images permits it, visualize each of these men as you mull over the question of whom to hire as a history tutor: the host of *Wheel of Fortune*, *American Idol*, or *Jeopardy!*

All set? Decision made? As yet another host would ask, is this your final answer? Then continue reading.

Most of you picked Trebek, of course. With Sajak a distant second. Why? Because *Jeopardy!* is the most intellectually challenging of the shows on which these men appear. We therefore assume that Trebek must be an intelligent guy in order to host it effectively— after all, *he* always knows the answer. While "European History" has been a category on his program, I don't recall Simon and Randy (or, for that matter, J.Lo and Steven Tyler) ever discussing the Hundred Years' War between *Idol* auditions. Perhaps Trebek retained some relevant information through osmosis? And at the very least, you're confident that he's going to know how to pronounce "Charlemagne."

But is this a wise decision? Maybe Trebek isn't the best choice after all. Would it surprise you to learn that Seacrest majored in history at Yale? That Sajak began a Ph.D. in European literature before turning to a career in television?

OK, it would surprise them, too, because I just made all that up.

What *is* true, though, is that you and I have no idea how intelligent these men are. For all we know, each is bright, well-read, and would make an adequate tutor. But for all we know, they're nothing more than glorified spokesmodels who read well from cue cards and make good small talk with strangers. Even though the only information we have about these three individuals has been gleaned from the sanitized, edited context of syndicated television, we still feel like we have some idea of the type of people they are.

Therein lies the puzzle. Logically speaking, being asked to choose the wisest game show host should lead us to throw up our hands and plead ignorance. But Trebek is the consensus choice. Rationally, I have little more basis for this conclusion than I do for thinking that Patrick Dempsey or any other TV doctor could give me at least *some* useful insight regarding my grandmother's blood pressure medication. But try telling that to my neighbor down the street with the faded "Martin Sheen Is My President" bumper sticker. You see, the Conundrum of the Game Show Host isn't *which* of these three gentlemen you'll choose as your tutor, but rather the question of *why* the vast majority of us is so quick to pick the same guy.

The phenomenon isn't limited to Trebek. Our tendency to attribute wisdom to game show hosts emerges even when perfect diction and a certain Canadian bonhomie—mustachioed or not—isn't part of the picture. Consider a research study conducted with pairs of college students at Stanford.[1] At random, one member of each pair was assigned to the role of quiz show host, or "Questioner." The other became the "Contestant." The Questioner was given several minutes to compose a list of ten challenging questions on any topics, the only requirement being that she had to know the right answer to each one. Once the list was complete, the Questioner then proceeded to quiz the Contestant, whose job, naturally, was to answer the questions correctly.

The student body at Stanford is an impressive group. These are really smart people. But on average, Contestants answered only four out of ten questions correctly. After all, even the most accomplished of scholars is challenged when asked to match the idiosyncratic knowledge of another bright person. Just think about your friends and their varied interests, experiences, and expertise. When you're a gourmet chef who's into fantasy football and your buddy the entomologist can quote every episode of *Star Trek* by heart, stumping each other with trivia isn't too hard. Finding common ground to talk about when you get together for drinks? That seems more challenging, but hey, he's your friend, not mine.

Imagine how much greater this variability in expertise is for strangers with no shared history. In the quiz show task, unless the Contestant lucks into a partner who just happens to mirror exactly her own areas of interest, she'll be stumped before too long. Take, for example, the eclectically well-rounded expertise exhibited by one of my former students during an in-class demonstration of this study:

1. Name all 5 members of NSYNC.

2. Who was the only President to serve on the Supreme Court?

3. Name all 5 members of the Backstreet Boys.

Maybe you're equally proficient in judicial political history and pop music boy bands. For most people, though, this combination of disciplines poses a challenge.

Knowing all this: knowing that the Contestant's job is quite difficult, that the Questioner is pulling topics out of thin air, and that the random draw to determine roles could easily have gone the other way, how would you evaluate the quiz show participants? The researchers asked this question by getting neutral observers of the study—the "studio audience" for the quiz show—to rate the general knowledge of both the Questioner and the Contestant on a scale of 1–100.

On average, they rated the Questioner an 82.

They rated the Contestant a 49.

In other words, despite knowing that the Contestant was at a pronounced disadvantage in this situation, observers drew internal conclusions about the pair as they watched them play the game. The Questioner must be the one with the greater wealth of knowledge, they inferred. The Questioner is the one they'd expect to do well on a real game show, and presumably the one they'd hire as a tutor. The Contestant, they determined in a resounding majority, was dumber.

SEDUCED BY CHARACTER

So much of how we see and interact with the social universe around us is shaped by our immediate context. As the chapters in this book detail, seemingly trivial aspects of daily situations determine whether we keep to ourselves or get involved in the affairs of others, whether we follow a group or stake out an independent path, why we're drawn to certain people and away from others.

But as the game show examples demonstrate, we rarely appreciate this robust power of situations. We look right past them, hidden in plain sight. Just like the museum visitor pays little heed to the painting's frame, we fail to notice the impact of outside influences on our innermost thoughts and instincts. But frames *do* matter. Though you won't find them highlighted in a museum's catalogue, they catch the eye and accentuate aspects of the paintings within. You might not realize it, but your experience at the museum wouldn't be the same without them.

The frame of social context has a similar impact on how people behave. When we overlook it, we produce an oversimplified picture of human nature, clinging as we do to the belief that *what you see is what you get*. Computer programmers have adopted this phrase, complete with a fun-to-pronounce acronym, to refer to an interface that allows the user to see what the final product will look like while a document is being created. In daily life, even when we should know better, we endorse this idea of WYSIWYG (or wizzywig, if you prefer) when we assume that the behavior we observe of another person at a particular point in time provides an accurate glimpse of the "true product" within.

The waiter who screwed up our order? We label him incompetent. The colleague who won't return our e-mails? She's inconsiderate. The actor who delivers the knockout soliloquy? He's articulate. WYSIWYG leads us to conclude that these actions result from underlying, consistent character—and we expect this personality to emerge reliably anytime, anywhere. So the waiter was an idiot before you showed up for lunch, the coworker is a jerk even on her day off, the actor would be the perfect commencement speaker, and Alex Trebek will help me pass history once he wraps his shooting schedule.

In essence, we're most comfortable seeing each other the same way we watch sitcoms, expecting to encounter familiar characters who act much the same from episode to episode. Even in exotic locations, like a vat of grapes or a cursed Hawaiian vacation, we look for the familiar dispositions of our TV friends to shine through. When you think about it, although we call these shows "situation comedies," they depend on stable personalities, and stock ones at that.

Developing a sitcom? You might want to include a nosy or wacky neighbor. Or even better, a nosy *and* wacky neighbor. Perhaps an overbearing mother-in-law or world-weary grouch with a hidden heart of gold. It only takes a few minutes at www.small time.com/dictator to confirm this notion of standard-issue sitcom characters. The website uses binary trees created by user input— essentially a flowchart of yes-or-no questions—to guess the sitcom character or world dictator you're thinking of (clever site tagline: "whether you're Gilligan or Fidel stuck on that island").

The program needed thirty-four questions to figure out that I was thinking of Pol Pot. For Cliff Clavin, the mailman from *Cheers*, it only took eleven.

The recent emergence of "reality TV" isn't much different. These shows consistently promise the manipulative villain, the flirtatious schemer, the carefree soul just there to have a good time. These "characters" are often the products of creative editing (or even intentional staging), but viewers don't seem to mind. Clearly, the producers of such programming also realize the appeal of easily identifiable personalities to those of us watching at home.

Back to the *real* real world, it's true that every so often life redirects our attention to the power of situations, snapping us out of our default WYSIWYG mode. Maybe we discover our inept waiter at a nightclub playing a proficient guitar and learn that his incompetence is context-specific. We find out that our unresponsive coworker has been battling a computer virus and never received our messages. Our favorite thespian gives a stilted, hackneyed graduation speech and we realize that he isn't particularly well spoken when the words are his own and he hasn't had rehearsal.

Or we catch a glimpse of a more subversive, self-referential sitcom. Like the episode of *Seinfeld* when, through a typically convoluted tangle of plotlines, the giant neon chicken sign outside Kramer's window prompts an apartment swap with Jerry. After just one night in a noisy, distraction-filled bedroom, suddenly it's Jerry who's frazzled and jumpy, recounting 3:00 a.m. phone calls from oddball friends and eating straight out of the ice cream carton. And the soothing effects of just one good night's sleep allow Kramer to emerge as the all-knowing yet sarcastic voice of reason around whom the group gathers for perspective on their own neuroses. The comedic premise works because the audience is familiar with each character by this point in the show's run. We immediately get the joke that the sleep-depriving physical space of Kramer's apartment (and the relative lack of chaos across the hall at Jerry's) could be all that separates one character's recognizable quirks from the other's.

But by the end of the half hour, status quo has returned. And in real life, too, while unfamiliar situations can push us beyond WYSIWYG, the general tendency lingers on: we encounter new people, we observe new behaviors, and we instinctively draw new conclusions regarding character and personality. Just ask the patient chagrined to see his doctor outside her realm of expertise, struggling to, say, parallel park. Or the surprised student who once ran into me at a bar and asked, "Isn't it strange for professors to go out and see people from class?" While I realize that I continue to exist outside the lecture hall, she seemed genuinely shocked to learn that I could survive, much less enjoy myself, in a room without a dry-erase board.

We're easily seduced by the notion of stable character. So much of who we are, how we think, and what we do is driven by the situations we're in, yet we remain blissfully unaware of it.

LAST SUMMER, I got a first- (and second-) hand refresher course in just how blind we tend to be to situations. It came just days after I discovered that I am a marvel of modern medicine. Or, at least, that's what a bemused emergency room physician told me when I showed up one night with two broken fingers, one on each hand.

How did I hurt myself? As I trudged through the next several weeks with matching splints, I had ample opportunity to answer this question. My response varied by mood. Sometimes I'd get creative and say I was injured pulling orphans from the rubble of an earthquake. Other days I'd stick to the truth and admit that the damage came from the knob of a slippery softball bat that flew out of my hands during a rainy slow-pitch game. It didn't really matter whether or not I was honest: either way, no one—including multiple orthopedists—seemed to believe me.

One of the fractures went into a joint, which meant I needed surgery. But the morning of the procedure, I really wasn't nervous. In fact, I was much less anxious than my wife, who was still juggling sympathy with (completely justified) irritation at how I had suffered the injury. Had I really been saving orphans, I would've gotten a pass, but my decision to ignore her prescient warnings against playing softball during a downpour didn't sit well.

At the hospital, I was left alone in a small room to change into a plastic-wrapped gown, or "johnnie" as those in the know apparently call it. When I asked for clarification, I was informed that, yes, I did have to remove every last article of clothing before embarking on a thirty-minute outpatient procedure on the tip of my right middle finger.

So here's the scene: I'm alone in a dark waiting room that seems to double as a storage closet for outmoded Soviet computer equipment, nothing but a paper-thin gown between me and the rest of the world. And I can't keep the damn thing closed because it has the one fastener I can't navigate in my current state: a tie drawstring. The nurse returns to ask me questions, but I'm barely listening—I have to constantly attend to the unraveling knot in back of my johnnie, desperate to ensure that our interaction remains entrenched in the nurse/patient category without devolving into that of artist/nude model.

Suddenly, the "anesthesia team" descends upon me in S.W.A.T. formation. I had no idea it would take an entire squadron to dull my pain. They brief me on my options:

I can get a local finger block, but they're not convinced it'll be strong enough if the surgeon needs to insert screws.

Wait a minute, who said anything about screws?

I can get a block on the entire arm, the most common side effect of which is permanent nerve damage.

Ah, it's not like I really needed nerves in both *arms, right?*

I can "go under" altogether, with or without a breathing tube.

Oh, and while we're on the topic, do I have any dental work they should be aware of in case things deteriorate—*deteriorate?!*—quickly and said tube needs to be inserted in a hurry?

By the time they start asking about a health-care proxy, I'm officially freaking out. What's next, brochures for hospice care? A "Do Not Resuscitate" order? Because I don't think I'm cut out for a coma.

I know that they're all just doing their jobs, and in a thorough and courteous manner at that. But this situation now has me totally spooked. I'm in an unfamiliar place, consulting with people I've never met before, getting a crash course on medical issues about which I know very little. And I'm still essentially naked. I figure everyone in the room is picking up on my discomfort and anxiety by now. It must be written all over my face. So I wait for the inevitable pep talk from my doctor or nurse.

It never comes.

As I take a few deep breaths and look around the room, I realize that for the hospital staff, there's nothing remarkable about this situation or my reaction to it. Two medical residents stand at the foot of my bed, bemoaning a new hospital requirement of additional paperwork, the same way my university colleagues and I might chirp about unwelcome changes in course registration procedure. At the side of my bed, a nurse shares with a colleague her recipe for vegetarian chili. Off in the corner, a conversation broaches the pressing topic of vacation plans.

To everyone around me, it's just another day at the office and I'm just a regular patient. In their eyes, there's nothing noteworthy about this situation. It's just business as usual. An ordinary Friday morning.

So I took a deep breath to calm myself, consulted with my wife, and decided to go with the finger block.

Our typical obliviousness to the power of situations emerges because most of our daily existence takes place in familiar environments, within the confines of well-worn routine. It takes the jolt of the unfamiliar to remind you just how blind you are to your regular surroundings. Only after traveling abroad do you start to note the unwritten rules guiding social interactions back home. Not until you move out of the house you grew up in do you realize, upon return visits, that it has a distinct smell and sound. And so on.

But our default tendency remains to look right past situations. Take, as a case study, my dear wife. This is a loving woman and doting mother to two young daughters. For that matter, she's the indisputable hero of the saga of the softball-broken fingers. She showed up at the ER that night, boxed pizza in tow, having called a short-notice babysitter so that I wouldn't go hungry or need a cab home. She gave up any semblance of free time the rest of the summer, forced as she was to do everything around the house from paying bills to opening pickle jars to washing my hair for me in the shower.

Still, lurking within this nurturing woman is the same capacity for unabashed animosity possessed by all of us (more details in this book's final chapter), and it arises from the very tendency to jump to conclusions about personality. There's one group in particular that inspires her wrath, one category of humanity toward which she harbors a gut-level antipathy along the lines of how cats feel about dogs, Hatfields about McCoys, and Democrats about Joe Lieberman. Why, city bus drivers, naturally.

She's convinced that these drivers are aggressive, reckless, sadistic individuals who choose their area of employ for the sole purpose of carrying out their evil schemes. She tangles with them often on the streets of our urban neighborhood, what with our house literally situated on Main Street. To drive anywhere nearby is to jostle for space with the forty-foot-long behemoths of the Massachusetts Bay Transportation Authority.

To little avail, I try to convince her that there may be more to these people than first glance suggests. That navigating a bus through the streets of Boston requires an assertiveness and fearlessness rarely demanded of civilians during peacetime. Faced with dense traffic, narrow streets, and notoriously impatient motorists, bus drivers on a rigid schedule have little choice but to pull back onto the road blindly, assuming that cars will scatter much in the way that pigeons do for the rest of us. They're really just doing their job, I argue. They're simply reacting to the environment around them.

She doesn't buy it. To her, the situation is irrelevant. *She'd* never cut people off like that, she says. To my wife, the drivers are just dispositional jerks, as any one of them who's had the gall to infringe upon her car's personal space can attest. Because, unlike me, she has no trouble with full extension of her middle finger.

WYSIWYG ON MADISON AVENUE

The implications of WYSIWYG go beyond how we watch TV or react to bad driving. Consider the following scenario. You're asked to read a high school student's essay. You're told that his assignment was to evaluate U.S. policy in Afghanistan, taking any stance he wanted. The essay starts as follows:

> While there have been bumps in the road, overall the mission in Afghanistan is moving in the right direction. The people of Afghanistan now have a share in their government and are demonstrating their approval by their tremendous response to the trials of building a new society from the wreckage left by previous leaders.

Knowing nothing else about the student, what do you think his personal attitude about the war is? Use a scale of 1–7, where 1 means he's very much opposed to U.S. involvement in Afghanistan and 7 means he's very much in favor. What number do you choose?

A 6 or 7, right? In the 1960s, two researchers at Duke University, Ned Jones and Victor Harris, conducted a similar study using essays about Castro's Cuba.[2] The second sentence in the paragraph above actually comes almost word for word from their study. The average response of participants back then to the same question I just posed to you was a 6: readers believed that the personal beliefs of the essay writer were fairly pro-Castro.

This makes sense. The student was able to choose which side of the issue to take, and the coherent opinions expressed in his essay are reasonably interpreted as indicators of his personal attitudes. The same thing happened when a different set of participants read an anti-Castro essay; their ratings of the writer's true attitudes averaged between a 1 and 2. Again, a perfectly reasonable response: the student chose to write an anti-Castro essay because he himself is anti-Castro.

But now imagine that I give you the same excerpt with a different context. Once again, it's from an essay by a student asked to write about U.S. policy in Afghanistan. But this time he was *assigned* to advocate for the pro-war position. Now I pose to you the same question on the same scale of 1–7: Having read the passage, what do you think are the writer's true attitudes regarding the war?

Maybe this time a 5? Or 4? Because now the student *has* to write in favor of the war, so we recognize that his essay tells us less about his personal feelings. In the 1960s, those who read a pro-Castro essay averaged a more neutral rating of 4.4 when they believed the writer was assigned to his position. Participants who read an anti-Castro essay showed a similar tendency, moving from a 1.7 for the free-choice version to a less extreme 2.3 for the supposedly assigned version.

But take a closer look at those numbers.

For an assigned pro-Castro essay, the average rating was 4.4.

For an assigned anti-Castro writer, it was 2.3.

In other words, even when respondents believed that the students had no choice in their position, they still thought of the anti-Castro writer as less of a sympathizer than the pro-Castro writer. Two points less sympathetic, in fact—a substantial difference on a 7-point scale. Readers found it difficult to resist the temptation to draw inferences about the writer's underlying beliefs, despite the clear situational factors at play. This would be like attending a debate competition, watching the coin toss to determine which side of the abortion issue each team will defend, and then leaving convinced that the debaters on one side of the stage are truly pro-life and those on the other side are pro-choice.

That's how strong WYSIWYG is. Even in the face of compelling evidence to the contrary, we turn to internal explanations for the behavior of others. Researchers aren't the only ones who know this. Many commercials, for instance, work only if advertisers can count on you to overlook the obvious situational explanation (*they're paying this guy to say how great their razor is*), turning instead to a more internal, dispositional interpretation of what you see (*hey, this guy really likes his razor!*).

Sometimes they accomplish this with testimonials by "ordinary people." Other times it's a purported expert who tells you how well a detergent cleans or a sports drink rehydrates. Like the recent Sharp commercials, in which a white-haired gentleman of apparent distinction intones that it "Seems like you need to be a physics professor to choose the right TV. Luckily, I am one." Yes, how fortunate are we to have access to such groundbreaking science! Of course, I've yet to meet a tenure-track astrophysicist with a product endorsement deal. Not to mention that we have no way to know whether his alleged degree comes from the same mail-order school Sally Struthers used to shill for, the one that offered diplomas in animal husbandry and TV/VCR repair.

Perhaps the most striking example of how WYSIWYG plays into the hands of advertisers is the celebrity endorser. The hope here is that we're so asleep at the switch that we'll think a famous person's proficiency in one area bleeds into another: *Michael Jordan was a great basketball player; I suppose he knows what he's talking about when it comes to underwear as well.* Come on, do any of us really think that Jordan conducted a careful product analysis before determining that Hanes was the way to go? Has William Shatner ever really bid online for nonrefundable coach airfare? Had Martha Stewart ever stepped foot in a Kmart, much less actually shopped there?

Sure, there's more to this advertising strategy than I'm letting on. The celebrity spokesmodel draws attention to the product, and that alone may be worth a company's money. The most recent development appears to be the celebrity narrator, whom we never see and who never even offers an explicit endorsement. *Hey, this voice-over sounds familiar—is that Gene Hackman? I like Gene Hackman. I don't know what these Oppenheimer Funds are that he's talking about, but I guess I should like them, too.*

The bottom line remains that ad executives count on you to look past the power of the situation. They trust that you won't dismiss out of hand what the endorser says just because you know she was paid to say it. Rationally, though, we should. It's an admittedly extreme analogy, but paid endorsements—like student essays with an assigned position—tell us little more about an individual's true beliefs than would the confession of a detainee with a gun pointed at him. The endorser simply wants to make money, the essay writer wants a good grade, and the suspect just wants to see the light of another day. Speaking of which . . .

COMPELLED CONFESSIONS, COMPELLING EVIDENCE

On an autumn morning in 1988, a wealthy Long Island husband and wife were discovered by their son in pools of blood on opposite sides of their bedroom. Arlene Tankleff, fifty-four, had been bludgeoned and stabbed to death. Seymour Tankleff, sixty-two, was fighting for his life but soon slipped into a coma and died a

month later. With no sign of forced entry, the police quickly settled on the seventeen-year-old son, Marty, as chief suspect, bringing him in for immediate questioning. Hours later, when the
teenager's lawyer learned of his client's location and called the dis-
trict attorney to stop the interrogation, it was already too late:
Marty had confessed.

A jury convicted Tankleff on two counts of murder. In addition
to the confession, the prosecution presented witnesses who testified that Marty was surprisingly emotionless at the crime scene but
had been observed arguing loudly with his father in public just
days earlier. The judge sentenced Marty to no less than fifty years
in prison, seventeen of which he served before his release in 2007.[3]

Why did Tankleff serve only one-third of his minimum sentence? Because he didn't kill his parents. He'd been duped into a
confession, then spent almost two decades trying to convince the
State of New York what had happened. And much of what went
wrong can be chalked up to WYSIWYG.

In retrospect, the evidence against Marty Tankleff was never
very compelling.[4] According to the police statement, Marty confessed to committing the attacks between 5:30 and 6:00 with a
barbell and fruit paring knife. But forensic analysis placed Arlene's
time of death hours earlier and neither household item tested positive for blood. Defensive wounds on Arlene's body indicated a
struggle with her assailant, but Marty had no scratches or bruises.
Immediately after the attacks, an estranged business associate who
had been at the Tankleff house that night for a poker game and
who owed a half million dollars to Seymour—a man whom Marty
immediately named to detectives as a probable suspect with a

grudge to bear—suddenly shaved his beard, skipped town to California, and checked into a spa under an assumed name.

Still, the prosecution based its case, and the jury its verdict, on four words uttered by Marty at police headquarters, mere hours after he had found his parents: "Yeah, I did it."

And for good reason, right? After all, who would ever confess to something he hadn't done? Sure, by trial Marty had recanted his confession, claiming that he was coerced while in an unstable state. But isn't that what guilty people do once they lawyer up? As Morgan Freeman's Red says in *The Shawshank Redemption*, "Everyone in here is innocent, you know that?"

It was this mentality—*confessions always come from internal causes, from people who know they're guilty*—that prompted prosecutors to charge Marty, the jury to convict him, and a judge to send him away for fifty years for crimes he didn't commit. It was WYSIWYG, an automatic assumption that no external forces could ever lead an innocent person to confess. And let's be fair: we probably would have come to the same conclusion had we been on the jury. Everyone thinks that they'd never confess to something they didn't do.

But suspend your automatic disbelief for a moment. Ponder more carefully Marty Tankleff's situation. He's seventeen. Having just stumbled upon his parents' bodies, he's literally in shock. The police haul him in for questioning without a lawyer and grow increasingly aggressive as they press him to explain why he isn't crying more. Then they start fabricating evidence in the effort to box Marty in. They tell him they found clumps of his hair in his dead mother's hands. They say that something called a "humidity test"

proves he showered right after the attack, not the night before as
he claimed.

What's that, you say? The police can't just make things up? Oh
yes, they can. They can't present it at trial—it is false evidence,
after all. But during an interrogation, the police can spin tales far
and wide. They can give you a lie detector test and say that you
failed. They can say your fingerprints were found on the murder
weapon. Or that the doctors injected your nearly dead father with
adrenaline, rousing him from his coma just long enough for him
to finger you as his attacker.

For Marty, this last gambit was the straw that broke the camel's
back. Wracked with grief and exhausted from the police interview,
he let down his guard for just a moment when they told him his
father had identified him. In the wake of this bombshell, he wondered aloud if he could've blacked out and committed the crimes.
After being asked the same question dozens of times, Marty
Tankleff finally succumbed to the situation around him. Just to
make his world stop spinning, just to get some breathing room so
he could try to wrap his head around that morning's incompre-
hensible events, he replied, "Yeah, I did it."

So the police drafted a statement with their version of events,
reflecting their theory for the case. It was a theory that the forensic
tests would soon reveal to be impossible. And it was a statement
that Marty would never sign, as he would almost immediately
come to regret and withdraw his so-called confession.

Marty Tankleff wasn't alone. By some accounting, the Suffolk
County Police Department had a 94 percent confession rate in
homicide cases in the 1980s, an obscenely high percentage un-
matched by surrounding jurisdictions. I mean, 94 percent is the

return on Madoff investments or Ahmadinejad elections, not homicide investigations—you just don't get all but 6 percent of murder suspects to confess unless something fishy is going on. A few
juries may have seen past this slew of purported confessions, correctly determining that the defendant in their case hadn't confessed
of free will and clear mind. Unfortunately for Marty, his wasn't one
of them.

Like it or not, you and I probably would have judged Marty's
case the same way. Legal researchers at Williams College once asked
mock juries to evaluate the summary transcript of an interrogation
in which a detective obtained a murder confession by yelling and
waving his gun in a threatening manner. Respondents said that the
confession wasn't voluntary. They reported that it wouldn't affect
their judgment of the trial. They claimed that they'd disregard it
entirely. And then, when asked to render a verdict, they were still
four times more likely to think the defendant was guilty than were
other mock juries never told about a confession.[5]

The problem isn't confined to Long Island, either. The Inno-
cence Project is a national consortium of attorneys and other legal
professionals dedicated to overturning wrongful convictions. Over
the past two decades, it has succeeded with more than two hundred exonerations through DNA testing, proving, for example,
that the semen of a man convicted of rape didn't match that left
by the rapist at the crime scene. In over 25 percent of these DNA
exonerations, a false or coerced confession played a major role in
the original conviction. This means that more than one-quarter of
these innocent men and women who were sent to prison had, at
one point, offered some sort of admission of guilt.

Contrary to intuition, there's a surprisingly wide range of situations that can drive an innocent person to confess. Overt threats. Intoxication. Ignorance of the law: *The police can't just make up evidence, can they?* A prolonged interrogation leading to physical deprivation, emotional exhaustion, and thoughts like, *I'll say whatever they want so I can get out of here and get some sleep—it'll all get sorted out in the morning.*

Marty Tankleff's morning was more than seventeen years in the making. That's the uphill battle you face when going up against WYSIWYG.

THE INVISIBILITY OF SITUATIONS

So what drives us to explain other people's behavior in internal, character-driven terms? To forsake the power of situations for the allure of personality? The answer lies in how we think as well as how we feel.[6] That is, this tendency results from the way our minds take in information and also because thinking this way makes our world a reassuringly predictable place.

People are easy to see. They're tangible. Context is harder: it's an abstract, nebulous concept, a backdrop that can be downright invisible. In this sense, our social lens is set to shallow focus. We see the world with limited depth of field, blurring the background and accentuating in sharp contrast the action up front. Just like most cinematography in pre–Orson Welles Hollywood. Or sports magazine photos of bikinied supermodels on beaches. At least, that's what they tell me—I only made it through the first twenty minutes of *Citizen Kane*.

Precisely because situations are difficult to see, effort is required to recognize their influence. So we're particularly likely to stick to internal explanations for behavior when we don't have the mental energy to consider the alternatives. When we're tired, busy, or under time pressure, our cognitive resources are otherwise occupied and we can't summon the mental strength necessary to mount the challenge to WYSIWYG.

As an example, in one research study at the University of Texas, respondents evaluated a woman in a videotaped conversation.[7] She always appeared nervous, though in one version of the video her anxiety had an obvious situational cause: she was asked to discuss her sexual fantasies. In the other version it was less clear why she was nervous, as she was only talking about her passion for gardening. After both versions of the video, participants rated her personality as more anxious than average, but this was particularly the case after the gardening discussion. While her nervous appearance made sense when she was discussing sex, why was she so anxious when talking about hydrangeas?

However, a different outcome emerged for the next group of viewers. They were instructed to watch the video and *simultaneously* remember a list of words. For these observers, personality ratings didn't vary by conversation topic. They thought the woman was an anxious type when she talked about gardening, and they saw her as just as anxious when she talked about sex. So caught up in rehearsing the memory list, these respondents were too cognitively drained to exert the mental effort necessary to recognize the power of her situation. They lost sight of the fact that sharing fantasies with strangers would make anyone uncomfortable outside of a late-night Cinemax movie.

When our mind is occupied by other tasks and concerns, we're even less able than usual to see situations. Much of the time, our default tendency is an automatic leap to WYSIWYG, and sometimes we're powerless to override it.

THERE'S ALSO ANOTHER, more strategic reason for the pull of WYSIWYG. Quite often, we simply don't *want* to recognize the influence of context.

Natural disasters strike without warning. Financial markets go into free fall. The Red Sox win the World Series. Twice. The world can be a nutty, unpredictable place, so some semblance of consistency in the personalities of our fellow man and woman gives us one less thing to worry about. It makes us feel more in control.

After all, it's not just *any* internal explanations we jump to when evaluating the behavior of others. In particular, we cling to the notion of stable character. In the Stanford quiz show study, the idea that the Questioner looked so smart because he's the smarter person is the most appealingly simple explanation for what the audience observed.

Our false confidence that we can predict the behavior of others is reassuring, and it leads us to resist evidence to the contrary. It's comforting to think that our neighbors are capable of nothing worse than the sins we observe: leaving the lids off garbage cans and parking too far from the curb. But how many times have we seen the news report in which the coworker, ex-roommate, or fiancée says, "I know him and he couldn't hurt a fly"? And then the evidence emerges to prove that the suspect was, indeed, capable of insecticide and then some.

The motivation to ignore situations is even stronger when the actions in question are distasteful. It's reassuring to label bystanders who fail to help in an emergency as chronically apathetic. That's what we think when we hear about the patient who collapses and dies in the waiting room, in full view of hospital staff who do nothing to assist him for more than an hour. Or the woman attacked within earshot of dozens of her neighbors, none of whom intervene, yell out the window, or even call the police. Our immediate reaction to these stories is *What's wrong with these people?* We cling to the belief that we would have risen to the occasion. However, as detailed in chapter 2, this thought process overlooks a wide range of circumstances under which everyone—you and me included—is likely to keep going about our business, failing to come to the rescue of a fellow citizen in need.

WYSIWYG allows us to see the world as a stable place and view ourselves in a positive light. It enables us to resist the idea that were we to find ourselves in the same situation, we might act the very same unappealing way. Perhaps you experienced just this sort of resistance as you read this chapter. Have you been thinking that you would've been the exception in the quiz show study, the observer who rated Questioner and Contestant as equally intelligent? That you're too savvy to be swayed by paid endorsements? That you would've gone all *12 Angry Men* on your fellow jurors, holding out and Henry Fonda-ing them into an acquittal to save Marty Tankleff?

Maybe you're right. I'll admit, I often find myself thinking this way. But the research says otherwise. Other than the fact that my mother and Mister Rogers always told me I was unique, what's the basis for thinking that I'm somehow the exception? At the end of the day, while my mom may have been more judicious in her praise, I'm pretty sure Mister Rogers was telling all the other kids in the neighborhood that they were special, too.

DON'T THINK, THOUGH, that the message of this chapter is that seeing others in dispositional terms is inevitable. Is this tendency pervasive? Absolutely—sometimes we're almost powerless to avoid it. But totally unavoidable? No.

We don't *always* draw inferences about personality. For one, we often recognize the impact of situations when we think about people we already know well.[8] We've seen our friends and family in a variety of settings. This reservoir of memories reminds us that our roommate isn't always a lousy tipper and that Uncle Barry has a gentle side in addition to the obnoxious one currently on display.

You're also more likely to recognize the influence of situations when you're the actor in question. Unlike the other people waiting for the restroom, I have access to the information that I only cut the line because I was holding a preschooler with a time bomb for a bladder. I know that I'm not socially awkward; there just wasn't anyone at that party worth talking to. In short, there's a huge difference between being an observer and being the one involved in the action.[9]

You don't view yourself through the lens of WYSIWYG because, for better or for worse, you're stuck with yourself all the time. You've seen how you act differently across different contexts. Moreover, as I'll explore in more detail a few chapters from now, we tend to be overly generous when evaluating the self, so we're particularly motivated to explain away our own negative behavior in situational terms.

Still another way to think about the inevitability question is to consider whether there are individuals who don't fall victim to WYSIWYG in the first place. While some behavioral scientists have labeled it a fundamental human tendency,[10] more recent research suggests that the failure to take note of context is particularly pronounced in American, European, and other Western cultures.

Take, for example, the scene below.

Photo courtesy Taka Masuda

How would you describe it? If you grew up in the United States or Western Europe, your response would probably be something like, *There are fish swimming around.* Or, *The fish in front are moving to the left.*

But the same image shown to Japanese students elicits very different responses.[11] Japanese talk about the fish in front but often in terms of their relationship to the rest of the scene. Unlike Americans, they mention the plant formation on the left, the inert animals in the background, and the color of the water. In other words, they seem to notice and consider context in a way that many Westerners don't. They literally see more of the situation than Americans do.

This study teaches us that the tendency to look past situations and focus on the action up front is not some sort of universal given. Rather, cultural experiences and priorities shape our default tendencies for how we see the world. In particular, it's Westerners who are most likely to be hard-core disciples of the doctrine of WYSIWYG, a mind-set that's a natural offshoot of traditional Western values such as rugged individualism, self-reliance, personal uniqueness, and self-actualization. These ideals translate easily into a social focus on the specific individuals around us and what their behavior has to say about their underlying character.

Japanese respondents, however, attend more to backdrop and context in looking at the fish scene. Cultural psychologists and anthropologists would suggest that this reflects the more holistic, situationally sensitive way of thought prevalent in Asian societies, a worldview dating back to ancient China's emphasis on social obligation and collective harmony.[12] Indeed, the Chinese were contemplating the relatedness of all things while early Greek philosophers touted the unique properties inherent to every object. While Eastern medicine emphasized a harmonious balance of forces throughout the body, Western medicine experimented with surgery, solving health problems by excising the individually problematic body part. And while Beijing opened its Olympics with 2,008 drummers performing in stunning synchronization, the Atlanta opening ceremonies a decade earlier were highlighted by the inimitably unique properties of one Celine Dion.

Plato would have been so proud.

You could write an entire book exploring the roots of these cultural differences. And feel free, because this is not that book. For our purposes, the paragraphs above suffice, illustrating as they do that we are not born with brains hardwired to look past context. In comparisons of how children in Western and Eastern cultures write about the behavior of others, mostly similarities emerge. It's the adults who have evolved to see things differently, with Americans turning to personality-based explanations for others' actions (e.g., "He's just a self-absorbed person") and Indians offering more context-sensitive accounts (e.g., "He's unemployed and not in a position to give that money").[13] Situations don't have to be invisible, but many of us grow up in cultures that teach us to focus on the individuals up front, to think about what makes a fish or object or person unique as opposed to considering how it fits into the surrounding environment.

So make no mistake—personality and character do exist. Some people really *are* more helpful or more aggressive or more outgoing than others. But the way we tend to view one another, especially in the West, is out of balance. We put all our eggs in the basket of personality, overlooking context.

Fortunately, this also means that you can train yourself not to do this—or at least not all the time. And that *is* what this book is about.

REDISCOVERING CONTEXT

Days after my finger surgery, once the haze of anxiety and pain medication lifted, I recounted my experiences to my father-in-law, an accomplished physician himself. He told me that whenever he addresses graduating medical students, he always tells them that the best thing that can happen to them is to get sick. Nothing serious, of course. Just enough for them to struggle to book a timely appointment, haggle with their insurance carrier, sit in waiting rooms—a refresher course on what it's like to be a patient.

It's great advice. And it's one concrete strategy you can use to break free from the WYSIWYG mentality, from the complacency of looking past context: force yourself to see familiar situations from unfamiliar perspectives. Every day, make yourself walk the proverbial mile in the proverbial shoes of others.

If you teach for a living, then attend the classes of other teachers once in a while, sitting quietly in the crowd to rediscover what separates the riveting lecture from the one that sends the audience scrambling for the sudoku puzzle. If you're a customer service representative, wait on hold while the recording assures you that your call is important. If you're an airline attendant, fly coach.

This prescription works in the other direction as well, applying to service consumers as well as providers. If you're a student irritated that two hours have passed without an e-mail response from your professor, stop to consider that your ninety-nine fellow classmates might be making simultaneous requests for attention. If you're a traveler at the lost luggage desk, remind yourself that this clerk isn't the one who personally sent your bags to St. Petersburg instead of St. Louis. If you're a patient nearing the end of your third hour in the ER, recognize that, painful though they may be, your two broken fingers don't require prompter medical attention than the asthma attack of the seven-year-old who just arrived by ambulance. Even if you are pretty sure that the kid's a big faker.

Assuming the perspective of others is one way to make sure that you don't lose sight of the small factors that have huge impacts on the people with whom you interact. And rediscovering the power of situations will do more than make you a more patient human being—it'll improve your ability to navigate social settings and make you better at your job to boot.

Who knows, by learning to appreciate that situations matter, you might even manage to save the world one day. Indeed, breaking free from WYSIWYG was critical to resolving one of the most tense international crises of the nuclear era. An oft-cited chapter of the 1962 Cuban Missile Crisis is that of the competing Khrushchev letters.[14] On Friday, October 26, at the height of the conflict, Nikita Khrushchev sent a private letter to his American counterpart, John Kennedy. It rambled through thirty-one conciliatory paragraphs, promising to withdraw Soviet missiles from the area in return for American assurances that Cuba wouldn't be invaded.

But the next day, October 27, relations went downhill. The Soviets shot down a U-2 reconnaissance plane over Cuba, killing its American pilot. Kennedy received a second letter from Khrushchev, this one released publicly and taking a tougher stance. Once again, Khrushchev insisted on a promise not to invade Cuba, but now he also demanded that the Americans dismantle their missile sites in Turkey. Suddenly, in both word and deed, the Soviet leader seemed to be escalating the conflict. Kennedy and his advisers faced a quandary: Which letter to respond to? Did the first offer still stand? Or did the public second missive irreversibly up the ante?

As the tale is told, Kennedy, influenced chiefly by the lobbying of his brother Robert, decided to respond only to the first letter, ignoring the second. The story goes that the Americans rightly attributed the more strident tone of the second letter to public posturing in an effort to appease Kremlin hard-liners. Whether this is an accurate depiction of the events in question is a debate I leave to historians. If it is, then the Kennedys' recognition of the situational pressures shaping Khrushchev's public words would certainly constitute a momentously important example of how effective leadership can be facilitated by going beyond WYSIWYG.

But even if the story of the Khrushchev letters is oversimplified legend—after all, U.S. removal of missiles from Turkey was part of the final agreement, so the second letter wasn't really ignored—the peaceful resolution of this seemingly intractable conflict would still owe much to the ability of both leaders to envision themselves in their rival's position, to see each other as more than "personality types." This was, after all, the same Khrushchev who six years earlier banged his shoe as he promised, "We will bury you." It would have been easy and understandable for Kennedy to see his adversary as a dispositional aggressor, bent on destruction of the United States and incapable of negotiation. But he held off on such a conclusion, at least for as long as he could.

A similarly generous evaluation can be made of Khrushchev. I'm not suggesting that the Soviet premier's original motivation in setting up missile sites was one of altruistic concern for Cuba's sovereignty. Hardly. But once the crisis hit its apex, Khrushchev, too, kept his eyes on context. His own translated words, from his first letter to Kennedy, reveal as much: "You can regard us with distrust, but, in any case, you can be calm in this regard, that we are of sound mind and understand perfectly well that if we attack you, you will respond the same way. . . . This indicates that we are normal people, that we correctly understand and correctly evaluate the situation."[15]

At this most consequential of moments, at a point in time when our civilization stood as close to full-out nuclear war as we've ever been, Kennedy and Khrushchev were able to sidestep calamity, in large part by resisting the urge to jump to conclusions about predisposition. In the words they exchanged, they even went so far as to assure each other that they appreciated the power of the situation. One envisions a much more sobering outcome to the crisis had either man insisted on seeing the other as a barbarian or evildoer or any other descriptor from the lexicon of WYSIWYG.

BUT AT THE RISK of repeating myself, let me be clear: my argument is not that embracing the influence of situations inevitably makes us better people. Sure, that would be a feel-good message, and I admit that there's some support for it. For example, research suggests that romantic couples are happier when they refrain from blaming negative outcomes on their partner's internal characteristics.[16] Recognizing the effects of context can make you a happier mate and better lover. And, more generally, many of us would be more patient, forgiving, and understanding citizens of the world if we didn't automatically draw conclusions about personality type.

The real moral of this book, however, is that recognizing the power of situations gives us a leg up in a range of endeavors. This competitive advantage may be accompanied by the side effect of "being a better person," but just as often it isn't. Consider the effective salesperson. Success in sales is often achieved by those who best appreciate the role of framing on consumer preference, who figure out how to make the same item more appealing just by pitching it differently. Toward this end, salespeople have honed dozens of techniques that take advantage of context to influence consumers' thoughts and behaviors.[17] Few of them have anything to do with striving to be a good person.

Want to tack on a service plan your customer doesn't really need? First offer the more expensive three-year contract so the shorter one seems like a bargain. Want to make a pedestrian product seem more valuable? Turn it into a scarce commodity available for a limited time only. Indeed, the sales pitch at every health club I've ever joined has ended with my discovery that I can take advantage of a special offer expiring later that day—an offer that just so happens to have only one spot remaining.

Perhaps I was just born lucky, though the physique that drives me to the gym (and, at least once in a while, the emergency room) suggests otherwise. No, I ain't no fortunate son. And these salespeople aren't paragons of sympathy and morality. Rather, they're professionals who have learned to harness the power of situations, to appreciate the contexts that frame how people think and act.

You can, too.

In fact, once you start learning about the effects of context on human nature, you'll have little choice. Once you attend to those situational influences that used to be hidden in plain sight, there's no going back. Like learning the secret to a magic trick or optical illusion, it becomes impossible to revert to old assumptions and see things the way you used to, through eyes that are blissfully but misleadingly naïve. In short, one of the best ways to combat WYSIWYG is simple awareness that it exists in the first place.

Accepting that what you see isn't always what you get will allow you to navigate your social universe more shrewdly, whether the biggest challenge on your to-do list is negotiating nuclear prolif-eration or finding a new gym. For example, the next time you're in the midst of a political argument or heated negotiation, take time out before angrily concluding that you're butting heads with a zealot or hopeless curmudgeon. Instead, force yourself to see the discussion from your opponent's point of view—even if fleetingly. Not because it will make you a kindler, gentler person, but because it'll make you more likely to win out in the end.

The next time you read about, say, the webcam suicide that went unreported for hours by the rest of the chat room, pause before you make blanket assessments regarding the demise of com-passion in the modern era. Take a moment to at least briefly con-sider the impact of physical detachment and anonymity across various walks of life. Then gird yourself for a more proactive re-sponse when you next encounter a situation in which everybody seems to be waiting for someone else to take action.

And remind yourself not to assume that the brief snippets of public behavior you observe in others—whether through your own eyes or the media's—tell you everything you need to know about what someone "is capable of." How gullible are we to think that press conferences, paid endorsements, and talk show appear-ances allow us to get to know the type of person someone is? Yet we fall for this trap over and over again. It's high time to stop being surprised by the politician's philandering, the actor's bigoted rant, the athlete's steroid use, and the international golfing icon's . . . well, whatever the hell you want to call what he did.

The chapters that follow continue to flesh out lessons like these in specific detail, examining the overlooked impact of ordinary situations on a wide range of human experiences. We'll take a look at the contextual considerations that shape our private sense of self, that color our notion of the differences between men and women, that determine who we love and who we hate. We'll start by examining the circumstances that dictate when we're heroic and when we're cowardly, with particular focus on the very situational notion that when surrounded by others, we become very different people than when we're on our own.

2.

HELP WANTED

SHORTLY AFTER 3:30 ON A FEBRUARY AFTERNOON IN 1993, a security camera at the Bootle Strand Shopping Centre outside Liverpool, England, captured an image that would have been, in any other circumstance, eminently forgettable. The recorded scene was pedestrian, by both meanings of the word. Shoppers in winter coats carried bags in various directions. In the center of the frame, backs to the camera, a toddler reached up to hold the hand of a taller, older boy. A mundane image, yes, but also one approaching the staged cuteness of a greeting card, what with the older, faceless child standing *exactly* twice the height of his younger, also anonymous dependent.

Less than two days later, this photograph was the talk of England for the most unfathomable of reasons. Literally a picture of tranquillity, this still frame had captured two-year-old James Bulger moments after he was lured away from his mother at the Strand and just two hours before his death. James's companion was not an older brother shepherding him through a busy shopping mall but rather one of two ten-year-olds who would later admit to abducting and torturing the young boy before leaving his body on train tracks in the hope that the death would be deemed accidental.

The nature of the crime and, of course, the age of its perpetrators, both horrified and captivated a nation. Wrenching questions emerged instantaneously. What could drive two children to terrorize and kill another child? What does such barbarism say about morality in the modern era? What punishment could ever do justice to both the youth of the perpetrators and the heinousness of their actions?

These aren't the questions addressed in this chapter.

James Bulger's killers spent more than two hours with him before their final act of violence, a time during which they covered two miles, alternately accompanying, carrying, and dragging the boy through public thoroughfares. We know this because at trial the prosecution called thirty-eight witnesses who had seen the threesome together that afternoon. Thirty-eight ordinary citizens who—in the midst of daily routine—observed some aspect of James's terrifying ordeal, but none of whom intervened and helped him.[1]

Some of the thirty-eight testified that they saw James crying. One witness observed the defendants drag the boy and kick him in the ribs. Another saw the older boys shaking James angrily. A few bystanders approached to find out what was going on: in one instance, the older children explained that James was their brother and they were bringing him home; in another, that they found the boy wandering on the street and were taking him to the police station. But none of the bystanders accompanied the threesome to these purported destinations. Not a single one phoned the police just to be safe.

While it feels easy to dismiss James's killers as subhuman, to label them as monsters whose abnormal conduct falls outside the realm of typical human capacity, the thirty-eight witnesses to his abduction appear to be unavoidably and disturbingly ordinary. By all accounts, they were regular people like us. But that's difficult to accept. When we hear their story, who among us doesn't think, *no, not me?* *I* would have done something to help. *I* would have insisted on walking with the boys to the police station or maybe even picked up James and carried him there myself.

We're quick to pass judgment on the character of these bystanders, in the WYSIWYG manner described in the previous chapter. We search for some abiding character flaw to explain their inaction: *What's wrong with these people anyway?* Why was poor James doubly cursed—first, the happenstance encounter with ten-year-old sociopaths, then the misfortune of being paraded around a neighborhood inhabited by the indifferent and the apathetic? If only this had been a different city with different witnesses, we think.

But the story isn't that simple.

I DON'T DISPUTE THAT James Bulger might have met a less tragic fate if even one of the bystanders he encountered had been of a particularly attentive or assertive disposition. But chalking up James's death to the personalities of thirty-eight witnesses—to the idea that there are helpful and unhelpful people in the world and James's ultimate misfortune was crossing paths with the latter—

misses the big picture. Such a conclusion may be comforting, allowing us to feel a bit better about ourselves and our own neighborhoods, but it deflects focus from the true power of situations.

Indeed, one of the most dramatic demonstrations of how situational factors transform our behavior turns out to be this very influence of context on bystanders. Our decisions to help (or not help) those in need are the perfect place to begin the effort to catalogue the impacts of situations on human nature. Because in spite of our instinct to label as chronically apathetic the witnesses to James Bulger's ordeal, there are circumstances under which all of us become less likely to help—or even notice that there's an emergency in the first place. One of the most compelling illustrations of this conclusion is a now-famous study conducted at Princeton University by John Darley and Daniel Batson.[2]

In this experiment, students were asked to give a brief oral presentation in another building on campus. On their walk to this second location, handwritten map in tow, they passed a shabbily dressed actor slumped over in a doorway. Per the researchers' script, this actor kept his eyes closed, moaned, and coughed twice as each participant passed. Overall, only 40 percent of the students made any sort of effort to assist him.

But the more striking finding has to do with the factors that dictated who stopped to help and who didn't. The critical determinant of helping behavior wasn't some aspect of the participants' personalities—which the researchers had assessed before sending them on their walk—but rather the most mundane of situational considerations: whether or not the students were in a rush.

When told that they were running ahead of schedule, 63 percent stopped to tend to the actor in the doorway. Among those told to hurry because they were late, only 10 percent helped.

Why is this noteworthy, you might ask? Is it *that* surprising that when in a rush, we're less likely to get involved in the affairs of others? Well, the most remarkable result from the study was that of all the potential determinants of helping behavior examined by researchers, time pressure was the single *strongest* influence. This ordinary experience of being in a hurry was a much better predictor of helping than was personality type. Time pressure was even more influential than the assigned topic of the oral presentation— all the more surprising a conclusion given that half of the participants were heading across campus to give a talk about . . . the parable of the Good Samaritan!

And I haven't even mentioned the really ironic finding yet. In evaluating the various impacts on helping behavior, the researchers had actually stacked the deck against situational factors. That is, they chose participants you'd expect to be particularly likely to assist others, regardless of context. You see, the participants in this study weren't just any Princeton students—they were *seminary* students.

It isn't a group that you'd expect to turn a blind eye to the suffering of others. I mean, we're not talking Wall Street brokers or Baltimore Ravens linebackers or even FEMA administrators. These were men and women studying to join the clergy. Yet dozens of them just walked right by a stranger in need. In fact, when running late, a full 90 percent failed to give any sort of assistance, in some instances literally stepping around a semiconscious man en route to discuss the Good Samaritan.

This triumph of context over personality—of situation over occupation—is more than just ironic. There are few better demonstrations of the transcendent power of ordinary situations.

Time pressure isn't the only mundane consideration that shapes helping. In a study of much lower-stakes helping, researchers went up to 116 people at an American shopping mall and simply asked for change for a dollar.[3] A male researcher always approached the male shoppers, and a female researcher approached the females. In front of a Cinnabon or Mrs. Fields Cookies—locations that even the novice shopper can tell you are the best-smelling storefronts at the mall—60 percent of the respondents agreed to make change. But fewer than 20 percent of the individuals in front of clothing stores helped when asked. Follow-up questions revealed that the sweet smells of food court bakeries put mall denizens in a better mood, and people are more helpful when they're happy.

Just ask the waitress who leaves mints along with your check— she knows exactly what she's doing, and it has nothing to do with your after-dinner breath. Statistical analysis indicates that average gratuities rise from 15 percent to 18 percent when candy is included with the bill, and climb even higher if customers get to choose their own piece.[4] Free candy puts us in a good mood, but the strategy also works because we're more likely to help those who have previously helped us. There's a reason the guy on the street corner hands you a small flag or trinket before hitting you up for a donation—the same reason you get agitated when your chivalrous gesture to another driver doesn't elicit so much as a thank you wave. The notion of reciprocity, the obligation to return a favor, also pushes us toward helping.

Taken together, various studies indicate that context plays too important a role to permit us the reassurance of classifying the world's citizenry in terms of the dispositionally helpful versus the chronically unhelpful. The same person who, one day, interrupts her leisurely stroll to give directions to the lost tourist may very well, the next morning, drive right by you in the parking garage because she's in no mood to give a jump start.

How does any of this help us understand the Bulger witnesses? It doesn't really, at least not directly. We've yet to touch on the contextual considerations that might have been at play that afternoon in Liverpool. Sure, some of those thirty-eight witnesses may have been under time pressure like the students at Princeton Seminary, but others were just idling in parked cars, waiting for a friend, or taking a smoke break from their delivery route. And mood doesn't seem particularly relevant to our analysis, either.

No, to more fully understand the "Liverpool 38," as the British press dubbed them, we need to dig deeper. We have to ponder perhaps the strongest situational influence of all: the effect of being around other people.

THE POWER OF CROWDS

I spend hours each week in front of crowded lecture halls. It's a familiar context that I take for granted as part of my routine. But I still remember my first time in this situation more than a decade ago. Almost instantly, the experience brought with it two realizations.

The first was that no matter the content, the simple act of clicking to my next lecture slide inevitably sets in motion scores of synchronized, scribbling pens. I learned very quickly that there's a devoted contingent of the audience intractable in its goal of writing down every last word projected during class. Midlecture, it dawned on me that I could have put on the screen, say, dirty limericks, and many a dedicated student would have kept on writing long after "Nantucket."

The second epiphany was that I owed some of my former teachers an apology. Actually, a lot of them. Turns out that you're not as anonymous sitting in the crowded classroom as you think you are. While teaching, I could hear two students on the left trade wisecracks throughout the entire class. I could see the woman a few rows in front of them surreptitiously reading a magazine. And, of course, in the far corner of the room was Sleepy Guy, drifting in and out of consciousness with the soothing regularity of the tides.

Damn, I thought to myself. My history professor must have known I was just pretending to take notes on the antebellum South as I actually pondered the more stimulating nature of 11-across. And, while I'm coming clean, same with linear algebra. Intro to Religion and art history, too.

But you *think* you're anonymous in the lecture hall. You certainly feel like you are. How else to explain why—when I'm busy setting up before class—students in the front row feel free to share other audible nuggets like, "I haven't even started the paper for Wednesday. Think he'll give me an extension?"

It takes every bit of my willpower not to interject, "You know, *he* is just twelve feet away. And, since you asked, that'd be a 'no' on the extension." As fun as that would be, blowing my cover would cost me a valuable means of counterinsurgent surveillance.

This feeling of anonymity in crowds affects our tendency to

help as well. To illustrate, I sometimes bring to class a sheaf of scrap paper on the day we discuss helping behavior. In the midst of my preclass maneuvers, I "accidentally" drop the pile in the front of the room—I've gotten pretty good over the years at maximizing paper dispersion. Though more than one hundred people are watching, it's rare that any one of them so much as asks if I need help picking things up, even though the title slide from my lecture is already writ large on the projection screen: "HELPING BEHAVIOR, PART I."

The power of being in a crowd shines through in my students' reaction (or lack thereof). The presence of others is more influential than any anticipation they have regarding that day's topic; it's a better predictor of how they will act than any personality type. Remember, these are intelligent and personable young people. Sitting across my desk on a solo visit to office hours, they'd help me if I dropped something. For that matter, in such a highly individualized context, they might agree to mow my lawn and pick up my dry cleaning. I am the one who assigns final grades, after all.

But in a large group, they stay bolted to their seats and watch while I turn my back to them, embarrassingly get down on all fours, and crawl around picking up my pile of meaningless papers. It's not a pretty sight, I assure you—but think of it as just punishment for their apathy. And consider yourself lucky that the publisher nixed my plans for a photo insert for this book.

REMARKABLY, WE'RE SO used to feeling anonymous and detached in crowds that simply asking people to imagine being surrounded by others is enough to make them less helpful. In one creative set of studies, researchers instructed participants to visualize themselves in a crowded movie theater or out to dinner with thirty friends.[5] After answering several unimportant questions—like, what room temperature would they prefer in the theater—participants moved on to an ostensibly unrelated charity survey.

Having just pictured themselves in a crowd, respondents pledged smaller donations compared to participants who had earlier been instructed to visualize an empty theater or more intimate dinner for two. In a follow-up study, the same researchers gave a new set of respondents a word categorization task. Participants who had been asked to imagine a crowd showed quicker reaction times to words like "unaccountable" and "exempt." Even being with imaginary people shapes how we think about helping.

You can understand why we get used to feeling this way in crowds. Take the movie theater example. You pony up six dollars for popcorn to go with the thirteen-dollar tickets. But then you just sit there passively when the projector goes out of focus. You don't want to miss anything, so you assume that some other sucker will report the problem. It's easy to skirt responsibility with dozens of viable candidates around to pick up the slack. And if that phrase sounds familiar, it's because the U.S. Securities and Exchange Commission apparently adopted it as their official motto during the pre–bank bailout era.

Over time, we learn to associate these two ideas: on the one hand, being in a crowd, and on the other, relinquishing responsibility.

Crowd. Lack of responsibility.

Crowd. Someone else will take care of this.

Make the connection enough times, and eventually the mere

thought of a group of people is enough to trigger passivity. It's all very Pavlovian, but with detachment and disengagement instead of dogs and drooling.

Again, though, what about the case of James Bulger? It's one thing to feel apathetic in movie theaters, restaurants, and lecture halls—it's another altogether to remain on the sidelines when a child is in danger. Is the effect of a crowd strong enough to shape our responses to actual life-and-death emergencies?

Unfortunately, yes.

Consider the following scenario: An undergraduate signs up for a research study requiring her to discuss with peers her adjustment to college life. To ensure that she's willing to speak freely about personal issues, the researchers place her—and each of the other students—in her own cubicle with an intercom. The researchers won't be listening in on the conversation, she is assured, and none of the group will ever see each other or learn the names of their conversation partners.[6]

The intercoms are set up so that students each have two minutes when their microphone is the only one on. So one student speaks while the others listen, then another student has a turn, and so on. The conversation begins without incident. One student confesses, say, her difficulty getting used to an urban campus after growing up in a small town. Another reluctantly mentions a health problem that leaves him prone to seizures when under stress, a condition that particularly concerns him during finals week.

In the second round, though, things take an unexpected turn. When the student who had mentioned a health problem comes on the air again, he quickly grows distressed. Stuttering loudly, he suggests that he could use "a little help." With choking sounds interfering with his speech, he becomes increasingly incoherent until all that is audible are words like "seizure," "die," and of course, "help." Then, radio silence.

Having read about the Good Samaritan study, you've probably guessed that no one was in real danger in this scenario. The other intercom voices—including that of the seizure victim—were prerecorded for our undergraduate's listening displeasure. But she doesn't know that. In her mind, she's listening in on a fellow student in the midst of a serious medical emergency. How will she respond? As you also might have guessed, it depends on how many other people she thinks are in the group with her.

When participants in this study believed they were in a two-person conversation with the victim, 85 percent left their cubicle to alert the researcher to the ongoing emergency. When they thought they were in a three-person conversation, the number dropped to 62 percent.

But what about respondents who thought they were part of a six-person group? Who believed that there were four other individuals with the same opportunity to help? Only 31 percent left their cubicle. More than two-thirds of these students stayed put and stayed quiet for a full six minutes after the apparent seizure had begun.

Being in a crowd altered their behavior. Gender didn't predict who helped and who didn't. Personality type didn't, either. No, it was the mundane situation to which they were randomly assigned that guided their reactions. It was sheer group size that played the biggest part in whether ordinary college students assumed the role of hero or remained mere bystanders, just like when I drop papers in my classroom.

THE INERTIA OF INACTION

In crowds, we're simply less likely to see emergencies for what they really are.

Many an emergency doesn't seem so emergent while it's happening. Passersby see three unsupervised youngsters on the street as an unfortunate but innocuous example of inattentive parenting. Apartment residents used to having sleep interrupted by drunken antics respond indifferently to late-night screaming. Sean Hannity views the unprecedented melting of glacial ice as simply reflecting the "natural ebb and flow" of global temperatures, not to mention a boon for waterfront condo developers in Nebraska. Et cetera.

Situations, even emergencies, can be ambiguous. At the time, we often don't know that they're emergencies. So we use the people around us as guides. We gauge their reactions so that we may calibrate our own responses. If no one else seems alarmed by what's going on—when everyone goes about business as usual—we assume that all is well. We see no reason to forsake inaction for action.

The 1999 death of Ignacio Mendez received widespread attention. The reason? Mendez died on a New York subway, but no one noticed for more than three hours, giving him enough time to complete two round-trips from the Bronx to the Staten Island Ferry. Many viewed the circumstances surrounding Mendez's death as an indictment of the very character of the city's inhabitants. As his nephew suggested, "At 8:30 in the morning there's a million people on the train, and nobody saw he was dead? It makes me feel that New York doesn't have a heart. The people care only about themselves."[7]

His reaction is understandable. Most of us would be outraged by the unceremonious death of a loved one. And you can add to his case against New Yorkers the fact that similar incidents have occurred in the city since then.

But a sweeping indictment of the New York personality isn't persuasive to me. It's just WYSIWYG all over again. What if you or I had boarded the number 1 train that morning at 9:30, taking a seat across from this large man who was sitting upright with his eyes closed and, by some reports, smelled of alcohol? How likely would you have been to shake his shoulder or whisper in his ear to make sure he was OK?

As a transplanted New Yorker who grew up in the Midwest, I vividly recall my first visit back to the city, as well as my first subway ride as a child, which came complete with parental instructions regarding eye contact. I don't remember the exact details of what they told me, but I'm pretty sure that they didn't give a green light to poking nonresponsive passengers seated nearby.

If you had boarded Mendez's subway car at 9:30, you would have looked around to see fellow passengers caught up in the ordinary activities of their daily commute. Maybe you would have paused when catching a glimpse of Mendez, but no one else seemed concerned, so why should you be? Other passengers had been on the train longer than you—it would be logical to figure that they knew more about what was going on. Maybe they had seen him alert and awake just moments earlier.

The assumption that everyone must know something you don't—in this case, that there's no emergency—is a reassuring one to fall back on. When no one in the crowd seems concerned by what's going on, each of us feels more comfortable with the status quo, contributing to a cycle of inaction that only continues as new individuals enter the scene. You don't know that it's an emergency, so your calmness in the face of the unconscious subway rider assuages any concerns of the 9:45 commuters, and their subsequent indifference does the same for the 10:00 passengers. And so on.

We attribute a certain wisdom to crowds, and not just in helping situations. In fact, chapter 3 explores this idea in more detail, pondering the ways in which being in groups sometimes leads to unusual forms of *action* rather than *in*action. But our tendency in ambiguous situations to use other people's responses to guide our own has clear implications for when and why we fail to help others.

In a demonstration of this, the same two researchers from the seizure study described above arranged for vaporlike smoke to seep in from a wall vent while students were in the midst of completing a written survey.[8] When this happened to respondents seated in a room by themselves, 75 percent of them quickly got up to report that there was some sort of problem. But of those students seated in a room with two actors who had been instructed *not* to respond to the billowing smoke, just 10 percent took action.

That's right, extraordinarily, nine out of ten respondents seated with a group stayed put as the room filled with smoke. Barely able to see the papers in front of them, they fanned the fumes away and kept at their questionnaire, sometimes through coughing fits. Persuaded by their colleagues' apparent indifference, these students determined that the smoke wasn't *that* unusual and certainly didn't call for action. It was probably just steam, they suggested in post-experiment interviews. Or maybe some sort of air-conditioning leak.

In crowds, emergencies transform into ordinary affairs right before our eyes.

EVEN WHEN WE DO realize we're witnessing an emergency, being in a crowd still leaves us less likely to get involved. Crowds diffuse responsibility. Look no farther than the ubiquitous mass e-mail to catch this process in action. In fact, just such a message popped into my inbox literally minutes before I wrote this paragraph. Sent by a well-intentioned administrator in my department, it read as follows:

> *Dear Faculty,*
>
> *This student (please see attached message) was hoping someone could help her with advice regarding a summer internship. Do you have any ideas or recommendations for her?*
>
> *Thanks,*
> *Well-Intentioned Department Administrator*

It took me all of five seconds to file this message under "D" for Delete.

Why? Because I'm busy. Because I don't know the student in question. Because I'm well aware that any one of the other seventeen members of my department can answer her questions as well as I can. And because I know there will be no serious consequences to my inaction. To be brutally honest, there are plenty of minor, irritating costs to my getting involved in this exchange, with few tangible benefits to outweigh them.

Of course, I'd feel very differently if the student had contacted me directly. Or if our administrator had forwarded the e-mail to me individually, with some explanation for why I'd be the ideal person to respond. In those cases, I'd seem (and feel) like a jerk if I didn't send a reply, even if only to say, sorry, I don't have any suggestions.

Being in a crowd—even a virtual, cyberspace one—permits inaction. The crowd works like a release valve on the pressure to help. A direct e-mail request would have placed 100 percent of this pressure squarely on me, making failure to respond an uncomfortable course of action (although I, like you, have some coworkers apparently impervious to such discomfort, not to mention friends who never seem to mind letting others pick up the check). A mass e-mail request, however, spreads out that sense of responsibility, distributing evenly across eighteen of us the pressure to respond. Shrugging off 5.5 percent of the responsibility is easy. And my guess is that each one of my colleagues will do just that, leaving this student with no choice but to go it alone or contact someone directly.

In other words, crowds allow us the luxury of shirking obligation. An engineer named Max Ringelmann discovered this a century ago when he had groups ranging from one to eight people pull together on a rope. Though the total force exerted increased as teams got bigger, the per-person average decreased. One person pulling alone generated 63 kilograms of force. A team of three produced 160 kilograms, translating to just 53 per person. A team of eight produced 248 kilograms of force, or only 31 per individual rope puller. So eight people didn't come close to exerting eight times the force on the rope that one person did alone. And it wasn't that they were getting in one another's way: even when their fellow group members were actors just pretending to pull, individual participants still gave less effort when they were part of a team.[9]

This is the same social loafing exhibited by the deleter of mass e-mail requests, the project team member who never steps up to take the lead, or the student who greets nonrhetorical questions during class with silence—and, sometimes, the charade of flipping through notebook pages pretending to look carefully for the answer but really just avoiding eye contact until the teacher calls on someone else. (Yes, we do realize that's what you're doing; we used to do that, too.)

Responsibility diffuses in groups. Chemists talk about diffusion in terms of molecules spreading from areas of high concentration to low concentration. The same thing happens to feelings of obligation and responsibility in a crowd.

What about in emergencies, though? Sure, workers jump at the chance to avoid extra, unpaid responsibilities, and most of us outgrow the desire to pull as hard as we can on ropes after fourth-grade summer camp. But how about when another person is in need?

Well, there are potential costs to helping in an emergency, too. Physical danger. The time commitment of involvement. Embarrassment if your efforts prove unsuccessful or unnecessary. And in an increasingly litigious society, the risk of being sued because your life-saving Heimlich maneuver left an ungrateful beneficiary with fractured ribs.

Sometimes we're willing to assume these risks. Like when they're outweighed by potential benefits of offering assistance. Or when the costs of *not* helping are even greater—you're on a first date and want to make a good impression or you're just not sure how you'll soothe your conscience later if you don't lend a hand. But we're less inclined to take such risks when people are around to pick up the slack. Why should I assume the burden when others are just as capable? There are cost/benefit analyses underlying our decisions about helping, even if we don't compute them consciously.

Having already offered an unsophisticated chemistry allusion, allow me to introduce some Half-Assed Physics (trademark pending). Helping is all about inertia. Objects at rest remain at rest unless newfound force is applied. Bystanders in emergencies are, by definition, uninvolved in the proceedings, and it takes a compelling force to change this as well. Being in a crowd pushes us toward passivity, leaving the path to helping all that steeper an uphill climb. Thus, the inertia of inaction only grows stronger when we're in the presence of others.

38 NOT-SO-SPECIAL

Recognizing this power of crowds leads to the surprising conclusion that James Bulger's ultimate misfortune may not have come in the form of *who* witnessed his final hours but rather *how many* witnesses did so.

To be fair, there were far more than thirty-eight people who observed some portion of his ordeal. For starters, take the oblivious shoppers captured in the security footage at the Strand; also, those who crossed paths with the threesome but to this day don't realize that they did. It's a safe bet that there were additional witnesses afraid of coming forward, who therefore never took the stand at trial or assumed their place in James's tragic legacy. But the name "Liverpool 38" was catchy and specific and it stuck.

Can the power of crowds account for their inaction? A closer look at the thirty-eight reveals little in the way of abnormal personality or individual idiosyncrasy that would otherwise explain their behavior:

David Keay, a thirty-three-year-old taxi driver parked outside the shopping center, saw the older boys pull a recalcitrant James by the arms and assumed Bulger was playing the part of stubborn toddler, refusing to walk as many a two-year-old will do during a shopping outing.

Kathleen Richardson, forty-five, was on a bus when she observed the older boys through the window, swinging James into the air as they walked. She recalled asking aloud what type of parents allowed a child that young to be out on his own, even with older siblings.

Mark Pimblett, a driver for a dry-cleaning company, saw one of the older boys kick James. He took note but later explained that it never dawned on him that a kidnapping was in progress since "it's usually grown-up fellas who do that kind of thing."

Elizabeth McCarrick, having just picked up her own seven-year-old, overheard the boys talking to a woman about how to get to the police station. When they walked off in the wrong direction, she called them back. The older boys explained that they had found James at the Strand and were taking him to the police. Confused as to why they were so far from the shopping center— not to mention why they had walked the wrong way after getting directions—she took James's hand and said she'd accompany them. She only relented when one of the boys insisted that they'd handle things on their own.

Quite simply, there is little extraordinary about the Liverpool 38. They're men and women, young and old—a fairly representative cross section of a fairly unremarkable community. Reading their testimony, their reactions to what they saw start to sound reasonable. You can understand why someone would have assumed the children were brothers walking home—too young to have been left on their own, sure, but not in any immediate danger requiring intervention.

If we permit ourselves, their testimony conjures up memories of times when we, too, have been less than proactive in investigating the true nature of events going on around us. Like the loud argument that we assumed was a private domestic squabble under control. Or the disoriented man on the park bench about whose fate no one else seemed the least bit concerned. Maybe, as we suspected, those weren't emergencies. But maybe they were.

At the playground with my daughters not long ago, I sat passively while a ten-year-old jumped repeatedly from the top of a fifteen-foot climbing structure. He emerged unscathed, even if his inability to stick the landing on dismount would have cost him points with the Romanian judge. The whole endeavor looked unnecessarily dangerous to me, but who was I to interfere? His parents were somewhere nearby, I figured.

To be honest, I can easily imagine myself as one of the Liverpool 38, walking by James Bulger and his abductors without getting involved in their lives. Can't you?

THE "LIVERPOOL 38" was more than a catchy nickname; the sobriquet was also reassuring. It grouped these witnesses into a single, apathetic collective, confining them to a particular locale and a finite quantity. *We* didn't fail James that day—rather, it was a fixed number of people from a specific town in England. The name conjures up the image of three dozen broken souls slinking off en masse to an outpost where they can live out their lives in ignominy.

But we've seen that there was little remarkable about these individuals. And further investigation reveals that their inaction was hardly a uniquely Liverpudlian response. That is, for the Liverpool 38 to remain the paragon of apathy, their dubious performance needs to stand out as a glaring aberration of time and place.

It doesn't.

Early one morning in October 2007, Constable Christopher Worden of the Royal Canadian Mounted Police was on patrol in a small town in the Northwest Territories. Upon observing suspicious behavior, Worden called out to three men, two of whom were already seated in the back of a taxi. The third man, standing outside, panicked and ran into the woods. Worden chased after him on foot. Seconds later, gunshots rang out.

Three women in front of a house nearby told police that they saw the officer run into the woods, heard shots, and did not see anyone come back out. A man asleep inside an adjacent building was awakened by gunfire and scrambled to his window to catch a glimpse of a civilian fleeing the area. The taxi driver, too, saw the chase unfold, assumed that the shots came from the officer's gun, then decided to go ahead and drive his remaining passengers to their destination elsewhere. All told, at least seven people heard shots and saw parts of the chase. Not one of them called the police. Two hours later—only after the dispatcher became concerned that Worden wasn't answering his radio—a fellow officer found him bleeding in the woods. He died later that night.

A year earlier, in West Melbourne, Australia, thirty-five-year-old computer store employee Juan Zhang was reported missing by her fiancé. Zhang had left a retail location earlier that evening to follow her nightly routine of driving to the regional office to deliver cash earnings—a total of $9,000 on the day in question. She never arrived. The next morning, police found Zhang's eyeglasses in a pool of blood in the staff parking lot behind the store. Days later, her body was found across town in the trunk of her car.

Investigators determined that a coworker had waited for Zhang in the parking lot so he could rob her. She resisted, resulting in more than sixty defensive stab wounds: twenty-two to her hands, ten to her neck, and thirty-four to her head. Zhang's killer confirmed that she had put up a lengthy struggle, including repeated cries for help. In fact, he confessed to throwing her in the trunk and driving to a side street to wait for her screams to stop before going home to clean up. Police located at least eight witnesses who heard "blood-curdling" screams from the parking lot. Not one so much as picked up the phone while Zhang bled to death in the trunk of her own car.

It is true that, unlike the Liverpool 38, the bystanders in these cases witnessed an ongoing violent confrontation. They might have feared for their own safety, and that shock could have short-circuited any natural inclination to get involved. But just as real-life bystander inaction isn't confined to a particular nation of origin, it also extends beyond the realm of violent crime. Consider Eric Steel's 2006 documentary *The Bridge*, which examines suicides at San Francisco's Golden Gate. Shot on location throughout 2004, the film depicts nearly two dozen different suicides. Some are shown in long focus, where a barely visible splash is the only indication that you've just witnessed an actual death. Others are shown via close-up, with the audience given an uncomfortably intimate glimpse into the last tormented moments of another person's life.

Part of what makes the film so jarring (and what enabled its creation in the first place) is that the suicides occur in public, in the midst of tourists, bikers, and commuters. The close-ups create a surreal juxtaposition of one individual's death with the mundane routine of everyone else on the bridge. Kevin Hines, one of the lucky 2 percent to have survived his jump, describes the intersection of these two worlds. A depressed nineteen-year-old at the time, he spent forty minutes on the bridge before jumping. "Crying my eyes out" as hundreds of people walked by, he found it odd that no one thought to check on him, given his obvious distress in a popular suicide spot.

Finally, a passerby stopped. She wanted him to take her picture.

In the film, Hines describes his thoughts at that moment: "Wow, I'm going to kill myself. What is wrong with you? Can't you see the tears pouring down my face? But she couldn't. She was on her own hype."

Hines snapped the photo, as requested. Then he returned the camera, climbed to the top of the railing, and jumped.

LOCATION, LOCATION, LOCATION

Crowds inhibit helping, leading to the counterintuitive conclusion that you may be better off running out of gas on a lightly traveled road than on a busy highway. In the latter case, the hundreds of other cars around give each motorist a good excuse to drive right by. The lone driver encountering your stopped car on a quiet side street enjoys no such luxury. Thus, location makes a big difference when it comes to getting help.

It might be tempting, therefore, to pigeonhole bystander apathy as a uniquely urban phenomenon—a problem that rears its ugly head on city streets, on crowded bridges, and in busy shopping centers but not elsewhere. Indeed, when researchers visited thirty-six U.S. cities to assess where people were most likely to help pick up dropped items or assist a blind pedestrian across the street, they observed less help the more densely populated a location was.[10] Planning an old-fashioned American cross-country road trip? Try to squeeze the car problems into the middle portions of the journey, because it's easier to find help in Chattanooga and Kansas City than in Philadelphia and Los Angeles.

One explanation for this finding is that having more people around translates into more opportunities for seeing emergencies as nonurgent and relinquishing responsibility to others. There's also a more basic perceptual process at play: cities are cognitively demanding. For a moment, forget about failing to interpret events as emergencies or shirking responsibility—in crowded settings we're just less tuned in to everything around us.

There's so much going on in the city: masses of people, honking car horns, flashing lights, kamikaze taxi drivers, peculiar odors of uncertain origin, and then some. Perceptually, it's impossible and inadvisable to take it all in. Faced with sensory overload, urbanites have to prioritize by determining what must be attended to and what can be ignored. The experienced city dweller adapts by developing sensory blinders, focusing on the immediate goal at hand and blocking out everything else.

This urban tunnel vision allows for efficient navigation of city life, but it brings with it side effects. For one, it comes at the expense of attention span and memory, such that a walk through a park or nature reserve actually has been found to have restorative qualities for cognitive functioning. In a recent study at the University of Michigan, respondents completed a task that required them to repeat a series of number sequences in backward order.[11] Individuals who had just walked through an arboretum performed better than did those who had just walked down a busy urban street and, presumably, still had their figurative blinders on.

Another side effect of cities is that people become less likely to notice others in need of help. City University of New York psychologist Stanley Milgram—about whom you'll read much more later, and whose research may very well constitute the most famous scientific demonstrations of the power of situations—described this urban sensory process as follows: "There are practical limitations to the Samaritan impulse in a major city. If a citizen attended to every needy person, if he were sensitive to and acted on every altruistic impulse that was evoked in the city, he could scarcely keep his own affairs in order."[12]

But I also must warn you against reading too much into these conclusions about cities. Understanding helping isn't the same as investing in real estate—it's not only location, location, location. Consider, once again, the refrain that New Yorkers are chronically unhelpful. To the contrary, I, for one, have had many helpful suggestions yelled at me while trying to read street maps in busy Manhattan crosswalks. And though most are either unfit for publication or anatomically impossible, one—offered while a friend and I were having what we believed to be a private conversation about lunch plans—led me to find my favorite bagel place in the city, at Fifty-first and Third.

So there.

And keep in mind that the examples on the previous pages came from all over the map: England, Canada, Australia, and California. The potential for inaction knows no geographic or cultural boundary. For every story about urbanites who fail to come to the aid of one of their own, there's a comparable tale like Constable Worden's, the Mountie left bleeding in the woods in a town of four thousand. For every report of dead subway riders, there's the New Yorker who risks his life to save a child who's fallen on the same set of tracks. Locations influence our thoughts and actions, but they do not define us.

Well, then, can we at least reconcile bystander inaction as the product of a specific time period? The examples I have cited occurred in the past two decades, in an era when technology has shrunk the figurative distance between communities but has also made it easier than ever to disengage from the outside world. In today's waiting rooms, elevators, and commuter trains, you see more pairs of headphones than conversation partners, more people thumbing iPhones than making eye contact. Maybe our hyper-technological culture produced the Liverpool 38 and its progeny? Would a return to the more communal days of yore rekindle concern for our fellow citizens?

Alas, bystander inaction is no more easily confined to era than to culture or region. Probably its most notorious example occurred almost fifty years ago, in front of an apartment building in Queens, New York. Just after three o'clock that March morning in 1964, an assailant grabbed Catherine "Kitty" Genovese from behind and stabbed her before fleeing. Genovese screamed for help and staggered toward her apartment. Unable to make it, she entered a different building and collapsed in the lobby. Ten minutes later, emboldened by the lack of a police response, her assailant returned and continued his attack for another half hour. Not until 3:50 did police arrive, having been summoned, finally, by a concerned neighbor at least thirty-five minutes after the attack began.

Genovese died en route to the hospital. The *New York Times* article about her murder opened as follows: "For more than half an hour thirty-eight respectable, law-abiding citizens in Queens watched a killer stalk and stab a woman in three separate attacks." That's right, by the wonder of numerical coincidence, Liverpool wasn't the first city to boast a notoriously apathetic collective of thirty-eight.

It turns out that much of the reporting on the murder, including the original *Times* piece, was somewhat misleading.[13] Investigators actually located only a dozen witnesses who admitted hearing or seeing part of the attack, and few if any observed the entire incident. It wasn't true, as the article implied, that thirty-eight neighbors stood silently at their windows for half an hour, leering as if watching a slasher film. Several had no idea a crime was under way; apparently, it was not unusual to hear early-morning commotion on the streets below, given their proximity to several bars. Many of the witnesses gave rational if naïve explanations for their failure to intervene, just as their British contemporaries would nearly thirty years later.

Though reports on Genovese's murder quickly devolved into more exaggerated parable than historical documentation, the well-known incident still demonstrates that the inaction of bystanders transcends community, continent, and era. The Liverpool 38 was no aberration of personality, no tragic fluke of time and place.

LESSONS LEARNED

The situational influences on helping are varied in number and nature. Many revolve around being in a crowd, an experience that informs our sensory perception, relieves feelings of responsibility, and ups the stakes for the action we take. Crowds make us less likely to realize there's an emergency. Moreover, trying to rouse the semiconscious subway passenger or intervening in a couple's loud, but intimate argument always carries risks, but doing so in front of an audience adds the threat of public embarrassment. Inaction is usually the safest bet.

This very notion that there's something approaching a cost/benefit analysis underlying decisions to help is unpalatable to many. And the more general conclusion regarding the context dependence of helping can seem disconcerting as well. We prefer our morality as we do the daily newspaper—in black and white, and not teetering on bankruptcy. But the modern reality is more challenging for both halves of the analogy.

This realization presents an opportunity more so than a rude awakening, however. Understanding that helping isn't just about personality opens new doors in the effort to combat apathy. I'm not alluding to anything as formal as legislation—in the wake of Princess Diana's death in 1997, you may recall the upsurge in interest regarding "Good Samaritan" laws among politicians as well as sitcom writers.[14] But many European countries, including France where the crash occurred, already had on the books at the time of Diana's death a legal duty to rescue in the case of emergencies.

Rather, I'm talking about the more individualized epiphanies experienced when we learn about our tendencies for nonintervention. Consider the following e-mail from one of my students:

> *Not 20 minutes after the end of your lecture today, I witness someone's food fall over at [dining hall] & I felt so bad for her. I thought to myself, what would Professor Sommers do?! Haha, but really, after that lecture there was no way I could not help her. I brought her a new cover for her food & I was even willing to help her clean up (even though as a vegetarian I'm kind of uncomfortable touching food with meat).*

Or, on the more severe end of the continuum, another e-mail from a former student:

you probably don't remember me, but i took your class 4 years ago. i have a story for you. late last night, around 2:00 am, i'm driving home and the car in front of me starts to swerve off the road. i figured he's pulling over to sleep or go to the bathroom or whatever, but after i passed, i started thinking about what we learned about people driving by emergencies. so i turned around . . . the guy didn't look good. when i knocked on the window he didn't move, so i called 911. they wound up taking him away in an ambulance . . . honestly, i haven't thought about any of my college classes in a while (no offense ☺), but i just couldn't keep driving when i realized i was doing the exact same thing we read about.

Learning about the true influences on human nature can be a life-changing experience. The impact of situations usually hides right in front of you, so once your attention is drawn to it, it's hard to revert to old habits. Whether or not my students expected it, their newfound understanding of apathy and helping stuck with them and influenced how they saw the world from that point forward.

That'll teach Sleepy Guy to doze through my lectures.

I've had similar epiphanies, though admittedly on a less dramatic scale than witnessing a car wreck. Much to my wife's chagrin, I no longer sit patiently when the film goes out of focus; I jump up to report it, then run back to my seat so as not to miss too much of the movie. And much to my wife's amusement, I insist on calling city hall when the light overhanging our densely populated street burns out. I'm not trying to win a merit badge for citizenship—I've just learned too much to assume that anyone else is going to notice, much less report these problems. These days, I have a hard time letting the pressure to act diffuse to others, even with a crowd around. After reading this chapter, I hope you will, too.

So lest anyone suggest that this situational analysis is a misguided effort to excuse those who fail to help, remember my students' e-mails. This chapter's objective has not been to *exonerate* the passive bystander, but rather to better *understand* what leads all of us to exhibit indifference and inaction. Through this investigation, we gain a deeper understanding of human nature, yes, but we also disabuse ourselves of the naïveté and mistaken assumptions that contribute to the inertia of inaction in the first place. The more we understand about the situational obstacles to helping, the better we're able to avoid them; knowing about bystander apathy makes mindless passivity less likely.

In other words, good luck remaining uninvolved the next time you cross paths with someone in obvious need. Now you know too much to rest comfortably in your own inaction.

EMBRACING THE POWER of situations does more than make us socially conscious, however. There are also strategic and even selfish objectives accomplished by learning about the real nature of helping. Understanding the factors that combat nonintervention pays dividends for any effort to nudge people from indifference to action. So reading this chapter can also make you more persuasive and resourceful when you're in crowds.

How can you prevent apathy in those around you? How can you motivate audiences, employees, students, and consumers to override basic tendencies and take action? For starters, avoid the mass e-mail phenomenon, in cyberspace as in person. I always make the effort to learn the names of every student in my classes, even the lecture courses with enrollment for more than one hundred. I don't have a secret memory trick or clever mnemonic—I just rely on sheer persistence and rote repetition. Why bother? Because my knowing their names undermines the pacifying effects of sitting in a large audience.

My goal isn't to increase the likelihood that these students will leap to my rescue in case of a real midlecture emergency. That's a lost cause. After my paper-dropping performance—not to mention their hearing about study after study with fake seizures and smoke-filled rooms—I'm pretty sure that I could suffer a real heart attack in front of the class and they'd all just stare at me, comfortable in the assumption that it's just a ruse being recorded via hidden camera.

No, the reason I learn their names is to ward off any temptation toward apathy in the more mundane, nonemergency aspects of the class. I want my students to feel accountable for their performance, both to me and to themselves. It's far too easy to blow off assigned readings or sit there passively during discussions when you feel anonymous. It's much more difficult to stay on the sidelines when you realize that your teacher knows who you are and will notice if you disengage. I've found that the fear of being called on with nothing to say is unparalleled in its capacity to motivate.

The way I see it, there are bigger costs to *not* knowing my students' names. There's an urban legend in teaching circles about the student who dares to ignore a stern warning not to turn in the final exam so much as one minute late. When he finally walks to the front of the room with his test, the professor smugly explains that he won't even grade it. As the story goes, the student replies, "Do you know who I am?" Flummoxed, the professor says nothing, so the student asks again, "Do you even know my name?" When the apocryphal professor admits that he does not, the student deadpans, "Didn't think so," shoves his exam in the middle of the stack on the desk, and walks out. This is one less problem I have to worry about when teaching.

Outside the classroom, there are also lessons to be learned concerning how to manage situations to get the help you need. The key, as you now know, is to break through the barriers of anonymity and ambiguity that come with crowds. The next time you're desperate for assistance, your best bet is to ask for it specifically and directly. Simply looking needy won't cut it, and generic requests aren't enough, either. Arizona State University psychologist Robert Cialdini provides a great example in his book *Influence*, an endlessly useful and entertaining compendium of how to get people to do what you want them to, culled in large part from his observations of experts like car salesmen and advertising execs. Here's Cialdini's prescription for getting emergency help:

> [I]solate one individual from the crowd. Stare, speak, and point directly at that person and no one else: "You sir, in the blue jacket, I need help. Call an ambulance." With that one utterance . . . he should now understand that emergency aid is needed; he should understand that he, not someone else, is responsible for providing the aid; and, finally, he should understand exactly how to provide it.[15]

You can see this advice in action in those *other* Sally Struthers commercials, the charitable ones asking viewers to sponsor an individual child for a low daily rate. The ads make an unambiguous case that assistance is needed. They tell the individual donor that she can actually make a difference. Then they show her precisely how to do so, right down to the exact dollar amount. Each of these factors renders helping a more reasonable, realistic course of action offering concrete benefits.

But perhaps the shrewdest aspect of these pleas is that they present the allure of a specific recipient who will benefit from the assistance. The ads promise photos and personal information from the sponsored child, and in some cases even an opportunity to exchange letters. The charities know that it's easier to maintain indifference toward a nameless, faceless crowd than toward a particular person. How else to reconcile our relative numbness to the abstract numbers of mass casualties with our more emotional response to individualized human-interest stories? Taken together, the tactics of these sponsorship charities are quite successful: the Save the Children group Struthers has pitched for recently took in over $240 million in annual private donations.

The concrete lesson here is that our mental calculations regarding helping are colored by whom it is that we're supposed to help. We're more apt to assist those who are attractive. Or who are smiling. And—in a research finding that will do little to reassure your faith in the notion of altruism or the basic goodness of humanity—male drivers in Europe are more likely to offer a ride to a female hitchhiker who has a large bust size.[16] If you're surprised to hear that this is the type of scientific research finding published in an academic outlet titled *Perceptual and Motor Skills*, well, then, clearly you've never seen the journal's annual swimsuit issue.

What, pray tell, is the practical lesson for you of such research?

Again, it's that the best way to solicit help isn't by trying to forecast who around you will be the most helpful person. Rather, it's managing the situation. Like any other attempt at persuasion, when you're looking for help, it's all about the sales pitch.

Why do organizations feature photos of children in solicitations? Because kids are cute, vulnerable, and seem deserving of our help. Deeming someone worthy of assistance is enough to tip the balance of an observer's calculations toward helping. In evaluating a fictitious individual with AIDS, for example, respondents show more sympathy when the disease was contracted through blood transfusion than through unprotected sex or drug use.[17] In the former case, they see the target as deserving of help; in the latter, they hold him responsible for his own fate. In short, the characteristics of the helpee are more important than those of the helper. Instead of focusing on the types of people most likely to offer you assistance, you should spend your energy framing the person(s) who needs help in the most sympathetic light possible.

So whether you're trying to raise consciousness for a humanitarian crisis or get someone to help you change a flat tire, remember that situations matter. From neighborhood to time of day, from group size to bra size, a wide range of contextual considerations feed into our calculations about helping and determine whether or not we even notice the need for assistance in the first place.

When you need help, be direct. Target specific individuals. Paint yourself in the most empathetic light possible. Do whatever it takes to stave off the potential of anonymity and diffusion of responsibility to overwhelm your call to aid.

And when you're out and about, take off the blinders once in a while. Look into curious noises or suspicious activity. Don't just figure someone else will take care of it or that if no one else seems alarmed by the unprecedented rates of return, then it can't be a Ponzi scheme. We're all better off if you err on the side of the unnecessary 911 call rather than relying on the blind assumption that *I'm sure everything is OK.*

These are conclusions that aren't available to you when you hew to the party line of WYSIWYG. None of these lessons emerge unless you're willing to give up thinking of people in the oversimplified terms of helpful and unhelpful predisposition, no matter how reassuring such a stable worldview might be. You now know better: at the end of the day, you don't have to wait for the right tribe to come around—if you manage the situation right, you can turn almost anyone into a Good Samaritan.

3.

GO WITH THE FLOW

CAMERON HUGHES IS THE CROWD WHISPERER.

According to a litany of popular books and television shows, we're now living in the golden age of "whispering." Supposedly, there's a wide range of self-taught experts out there able to regularly commune with horses, dogs, babies, and even ghosts. Well, Cameron Hughes has a unique skill set, too. He speaks the secret language of adult humans of a less-than-supernatural variety. The wild, unpredictable beasts that he's learned to "read" and bend to his will are crowds of people.

Hughes makes his living—and a nice one at that—riling up spectators at sporting events. He's had paying gigs at close to a thousand games over the past decade, serving at the pleasure and on the payroll of big-name, big-league clubs like the Los Angeles Dodgers, Cleveland Cavaliers, and New Jersey Devils. At the 2010

Winter Olympics, organizers hired him to whip crowds into a frenzy at the men's and women's ice hockey venue. For two weeks, Hughes's schedule was booked solid: when he wasn't cheering and clapping through one of thirty games, he was scouring drugstores for throat lozenges and websites for Finnish cheers.

Published profiles of Hughes invariably refer to the affable Canadian as a "superfan" or "professional sports fan." But these descriptions don't do justice to his craft. Hughes is practiced at the art of pulling a crowd's strings. He's an expert at manipulating situations to shape group behavior.

Like so many discoveries, Hughes stumbled upon his expertise through trial and error dashed with a pinch of serendipity. That, plus a fair amount of alcohol. In attendance at an NHL game in Ottawa fifteen years ago, he was frustrated by the staid demeanor of his fellow Senators fans and emboldened by more than a few plastic cups' worth of Molson. The result was a maniacal, impromptu piece of performance art in the aisle, comprising equal parts dance, step aerobics, and cheerleading. In retrospect, Hughes simply describes what he did as "going crazy." The crowd responded in kind, its quiet detachment transformed, almost instantly, into rollicking enthusiasm.

Exhausted, Hughes plopped back into his seat. When team officials with walkie-talkies approached, he figured he had earned himself an ejection from the arena. Instead, they offered him a few hundred loonies to come back and do it again the next week.

I talked with Hughes recently to learn more about what he does and why it works so well. From the outset of our conversation, it was clear that this is a man who takes his job seriously, even though much of his workweek is spent clapping, stomping, chanting, and preening. These days, there's no alcohol before performances, just careful planning and choreography, as well as a whole lot of stretching and ankle tape.

For example, though Hughes sees himself as an entertainer, he doesn't draw self-comparison to the Will Ferrells of the world. No, the surprising analogy he turns to is that of the symphony. That's right, Cameron Hughes is more Royal Philharmonic than Phillie Phanatic: "I've become an expert at being an orchestra leader," he told me. "What I do, it's . . . a calculated experience of how to move people to action."

Our conversation revealed to me three specific keys to Hughes's success. First, he's able to turn the power of crowds upside down. Hughes changes the experience of being in a mass of people from one that inhibits action to one that promotes it. The previous chapter focuses on this former notion, the inertia of inaction that ensues when we observe the complacency of those around us. However, crowds can also lead us to act in ways we ordinarily wouldn't. In groups, we can get caught up in the flow of action, not just inaction, as demonstrated by your average bachelor party reveler or stay-at-home mom at a Jimmy Buffett concert.

Sometimes it takes but a single person to set into motion this type of social influence—just one individual to alter a group's sense of what's expected and acceptable. Of course, being the first to take action isn't easy, but that's where Hughes comes in. "The phenomenon of being in a crowd is that once one person does it, you know, it becomes contagious," he explained to me. "It's like everybody is waiting for someone else to do something . . . it's like everybody is waiting for permission to cheer."

In other words, Hughes's strategy is to spring the first leak in the levee. Once he does, a tidal wave of conformity surges behind him. He makes following his lead as easy as possible by taking his own act to the absolute height of frenzied non-self-consciousness: compared to the multishirt striptease that's now a staple of his oeuvre, a little bit of rhythmic clapping doesn't seem like such a big deal to the fan two rows down. Essentially, Hughes is a disciple of the jackass school of influence, as in, *If this guy can make such a jackass of himself, I guess I can at least stand up and cheer.* As he admitted to me, "What I do at games is *so* not normal. It's just not."

But if I may beg to differ with my fellow student of situations, it is precisely *because* he seems so normal that Hughes is so successful. Indeed, this is the second key to his effectiveness: he looks like an average, ordinary fan. This isn't some costumed mascot or a superfan with a mask and cape. Hughes is dressed like everybody else at the game (but for the aforementioned baker's dozen of T-shirts lurking underneath; it's no wonder the cool environs of the ice hockey rink are his preferred work locale).

Much of the power of Hughes's performance lies in the fact that most in attendance think he's a fellow fan, not an employee of the home team. Cheerleaders and mascots are expected to act like this; regular spectators are not. Hughes is able to get people to follow his lead because the fans view him as one of their own, as part of the group. In fact, some in his inner circle have cautioned him not to give interviews because he might "let the cat out of the bag" and attract too much attention to his position on the payroll.

In the end, Hughes realizes that much of his appeal derives from his Everyman persona. After all, his endearing calling card remains the partial striptease that even grandma can enjoy, performed in decidedly unerotic fashion by a six-foot three-inch redhead, who, per his own description, is no "svelte model type." He's not Chris Farley in that old *Saturday Night Live* Chippendales sketch, but he ain't early-1990s Patrick Swayze, either.

The third key to Hughes's effectiveness is that he's a master of situations, in precisely the manner alluded to throughout this book. As he started on his unique career path, his apprenticeship involved going to arenas and studying people. He paid attention to which attempts at firing up a crowd worked and which fell flat; he learned the right time to start the wave and the right time to sit back and leave the focus on the game. "With crowds, you've got to read them and you've got to feel out when they need it and when they're ready," he told me. "There's nothing worse—even for me, and I do this for a living—than starting a cheer and no one responds."

Throughout his entire routine, whether channeling Richard Simmons or Little Richard, Hughes is busy, in his own words, "reading people." Their body language, their subtle nonverbals, the cues that many of us fail to pick up on in daily interactions. He uses this information to determine when to push a little bit more and when to pull back, whether a particular fan is fair game for more needling or whether he should steer his antics in a more self-deprecating direction. He spends his work nights gauging the reactions of individual fans but also the temperament of the crowd at-large.

Cameron Hughes doesn't view the world through the lens of WYSIWYG. It doesn't matter to him who's in attendance—he's confident that he'll get through to them. Of course, other people still see *him* as having a stable predisposition. Many a fan running into Hughes outside the arena is surprised to find him acting normally, just waiting in line patiently at the Home Depot like everyone else. It's as if people expect him to start dancing right there in the paint section: "You get invited to a lot of parties. . . . People expect you to be like that more often than not. But what I do is exhausting." Just imagine how they'd react upon learning that little Cameron was "pretty shy as a kid. I used to cry just going to school."

At the end of our conversation, I asked Hughes about one of the major themes of this book, the idea that appreciating the power of situations gives you a leg up in life. Specifically, I wanted to know whether his ability to "read" people comes in handy outside of sports arenas. Is he adept, say, at sweet-talking the customer service rep, getting out of speeding tickets, or picking up women at bars? "Um, yeah, I'm pretty good at it," he responded with a chuckle, confirming that while reading crowds and individuals isn't the same art form, it is a crossover skill. He said he'd prove it if I stopped my tape recorder, which I did. Off the record, he named some of the famous women he has dated.

Take my word for it: Cameron Hughes's mastery of situations has helped him compile a little black book just as impressive as his professional résumé.

WE'RE NOT ALWAYS THE freethinking, independent-minded individuals we think we are. This chapter explores why even though you fancy yourself the master of your own destiny, the people around you still have a dramatic impact on how you think and act. The previous chapter touches on this tendency to go with the flow, focusing as it does on the contagion of inaction. But as the fired-up sports fan knows all too well, being in a group also has the power to goad individuals into action, often in ways we'd never dream of when on our own.

There's a silly, albeit innocuous side to this social influence—for example, the sudden fashionability of men's capri pants or babies named after states or boroughs. Then there are the notoriously reckless things college students do in groups, like fraternity initiations or spring break escapades fueled by peer pressure, hormones, and alcohol. (Or so I hear—in the social circles in which I traveled in college, it was a bunch of us switching off the freezer in the dining hall soft-serve machine, then watching as student after student pulled the lever to get sprayed by melted ice cream. Good times.)

However, let's also consider a more troubling side of our tendency toward conformity: namely, its role in poorly conceived political decisions, military atrocities, and even mass murder. We're quick to dismiss such behavior as the result of aberrational personality—the misguided handiwork of a select few bad apples. But that's WYSIWYG talking. That's just letting ourselves off the hook from having to consider the broader contextual and institutional pressures that contribute to such malfeasance. In reality, often the apples aren't hopelessly bad—the barrel itself is rotten.

Because for every Cameron Hughes out there using the power of crowds for wholesome fun, there's the cult leader or dictator who has learned to manipulate the same principles out of less admirable motivations. Our propensity for conformity helps keep society running smoothly, but it fuels more nefarious and destructive plots as well. As we've learned from the movies, even when it comes to crowds, the force always has a dark side.

UNWRITTEN RULES

Much of daily life is governed by norms. They're the societal expectations that determine appropriate behavior—the unwritten rules we follow to remain community members in good standing. As the frequent traveler can attest, specifics vary by culture, but all cultures have them in one form or another. Norms are what dictate how we behave in large audiences. How we react to the gaudy Father's Day present that we know will never see the light of day. How much personal space we give an intimate other, an unacquainted conversation partner, or the person in front of us at the ATM.

The better you are at recognizing norms, the more smoothly you navigate social settings and the better you are able to manipulate them. For example, Cameron Hughes makes his living rewriting the rules of group conduct, emboldening his fellow sports fans to break through the restraints that typically guide public behavior. So to truly understand the human tendency for conformity, first we have to understand the ubiquity and consequences of norms.

Despite their pervasiveness, we don't talk about norms all that much. They're usually relegated to the province of social commentators or the comedian who poses rhetorical "Did you ever notice . . ." questions. Entire entertainment dynasties have been built on the simple idea that the exploration of norms is uncharted territory. At its minutiae-focused best, *Seinfeld* was a twenty-three-minute weekly discourse on social norms: After how many dates are you obligated to break off a relationship in person? Which special occasions do and don't require gifts? Which calls are too important to be made via cell phone? What's the appropriate way to dip a chip? And so on.

This wasn't a "show about nothing," as its creators, critics, and fans touted. It was an analysis of the ins and outs of daily interaction, of the mundane social experiences rarely deemed worthy of exploration in front of a mass audience. It was a show about norms, not nothing.

More recently, *Seinfeld*'s cocreator, Larry David, has taken this theme even further on HBO's *Curb Your Enthusiasm*. *Curb* is all about what happens when we violate norms. The violations are almost always perpetrated by the show's protagonist—the eponymous David playing an exaggerated version of himself. In one episode, Larry declines a tour of a friend's house, saying, "I get it . . . it's bedrooms, bathrooms . . . you don't need to walk me around." In another, he withholds candy from adolescent trick-or-treaters because they aren't in costumes and, to his mind, are too old for Halloween.

The comedy derives from Larry's willingness to do what most of us wouldn't dare. But you have to admit, his responses carry a certain appeal. I mean, how many tours can you take before houses all start to look the same? As Larry suggests before pondering the prospect of forty-year-olds on the prowl for candy, "There's got to be some kind of cutoff, shouldn't there be, for Halloween?" But unwritten rules dictate that we accept all tours when offered and we reward all trick-or-treaters. Violation of these norms carries clear consequences—in Larry's case, an expletive-laden ejection from the untoured house and the November 1st toilet-papering of his property.

In real life, the repercussions of breaking with norms range in severity from simple awkwardness to social exclusion. Consider the small talk of daily conversation. By adulthood, most of us have learned that the casual acquaintance who asks "How's it going?" does so in the way of simple greeting, not as a request for an annotated response. The range of appropriate replies is quite narrow, spanning from "OK" to "good" with a midpoint of "fine." The respondent who launches into a long-winded answer risks a quizzical reaction, a strained interaction, and—in all likelihood—no more than a silent wave the next time paths cross.

Conversational norms have more important lessons to teach us as well. The first time I ever testified in court as an expert was at a murder trial in Cape Cod, Massachusetts, in 2008. The crime had received national media attention: Christa Worthington, a white fashion writer from a wealthy family, had been discovered stabbed to death, her two-year-old daughter clutching her lifeless body.[1] Several years later, Christopher McCowen, a black garbage collector with an IQ below 80, was convicted of the murder.

I testified in a post-trial hearing examining allegations of racism against several of the deliberating jurors. The potentially biased statements were, on their surface, descriptive in nature. One white juror, in referencing the extent of the victim's injuries while deliberating, had allegedly exclaimed that this is what happens "when a two-hundred-pound black guy beats on a small woman." Another had voiced anxiety at sitting so close to this "big, black guy" in the courtroom. But race was more than a mere descriptor in these statements, contrary to the claims of the prosecutor and the jurors themselves. Understanding social norms is what allowed me to testify to that.

The norms of conversation dictate that we include in our statements that information which we deem relevant to the point we're seeking to make.[2] We typically avoid stating the obvious or dwelling on details that everybody already knows. In the McCowen case, no one in the jury room was confused about the accused's race—there was no need to differentiate him from another defendant. So why did the jurors say "black" when talking about how dangerous McCowen was? For the same reason they said "big": they saw his race as relevant to this conclusion about danger, regardless of their willingness to admit as much to the judge or even to themselves. Otherwise, why mention the obvious?

These jurors' statements are little different from, say, a complaint about Hillary Clinton's diplomatic performance phrased as follows: "This is what happens when you send a female secretary of state to the Middle East." Everyone already knows that Clinton is a woman, so "female" is no innocuous descriptor—our hypothetical critic must see gender as relevant to Secretary Clinton's on-the-job effectiveness.

The McCowen jurors' violation of conversational norms revealed something about their personal attitudes. Similarly, the prosecutor's decision to begin my cross-examination with the unexpected question "Doctor, do you mind if I ask how old you are?" betrayed his motivations—namely, to rattle me and impugn my expertise. I don't think either goal was accomplished: I said that I didn't mind the question as long as I could ask him the same one in return; the judge then implored us to move beyond the issue of age by interjecting that the surgeon who had examined his knee the week prior looked to be fresh out of high school. Then again, the judge did ultimately side with the prosecution after the hearing, so who knows?

The bottom line is that whether parsing sitcom dialogue or murder trial transcripts, norms and their violations shed light on human nature. We don't take lightly this breaking with unwritten rules. Doing so carries a variety of costs, from embarrassment to stilted interactions to pariah status. And recent neuroscience research indicates that the experience of being ostracized in a group—even something as trivial as not having the ball thrown to you enough during a game of catch—triggers activity in the very regions of the brain associated with the sensation of physical pain.[3]

Norm violation and its ensuing rejection hurts, sometimes literally. Going with the flow—conformity—is often the least painful course of action. As a learned expert once told me, there's nothing worse than starting a cheer and no one joins in.

ASCH'S LINES

Take a look at these lines. Which of the three on the right—A, B, or C—matches the solitary one on the left? Easy, right? C. And more than 98 percent of people tell you so when you ask them. (The other 2 percent? They become NBA referees.)

Now change the situation.

Instead of judging these lines on your own, in private, imagine that you're seated at a table with five other people. Shown a series of line charts like this one, the group goes around giving responses aloud. For the first few charts, everything proceeds as expected. But on the chart above, a funny thing happens. The first person says, "A." You blink. Maybe you chuckle to yourself and figure she just didn't take a good look.

But then the second person also says, "A."

And the third and the fourth, too.

Now it's your turn. What do you do? Do you stick to your guns and break with the group, giving the answer you know to be right? Or do you just go along with everyone else—you know, why bother ruffling feathers?

I know, I know. You'd give the right answer, you say. You're not afraid to think for yourself.

But I don't believe you. Or, more precisely, I don't believe three-fourths of you. Because when Swarthmore College psychologist Solomon Asch conducted this very study decades ago, recruiting actors to assume the roles of the myopic fellow group members, a full 75 percent of participants went along with the wrong answer at least once.[4]

In a nutshell, that's the pull of conformity. Our tendency to go along with the precedents others establish is ingrained enough that three-quarters of us would give answers that we know to be incorrect before we'd go against the clear consensus of the group. Being wrong is easier than breaking rank.

You might be thinking that there are aspects of the task Asch created that make it a unique situation. That's true. There isn't much at stake here for participants—there are no real repercussions to giving the wrong answer or saying one thing but believing another. Respondents may have just decided that life is too short to spend part of it arguing with strangers about lines.

Fair enough. But this tendency toward the path of least resistance is not without problematic consequences in real life. When we give in to the group just to make life easier, we sacrifice personal preference in the name of group consensus. We forsake comfort for fashion. We take up risky behaviors and reckless habits that we'd otherwise steer clear of on our own.

And don't underestimate the strength of the social pressures even in a low-stakes setting like Asch's study. Photos of the participants depict expressions of perplexed wonder—they seem to find the task fairly stressful. Moreover, a few paragraphs ago, when I asked whether you'd give an incorrect response in this study, think about how confident you were that you would not. Even without direct consequences, few of us are comfortable with the idea of making obviously inaccurate statements in public (insert your own politician joke here). But this is precisely what most of Asch's respondents opted to do, demonstrating just how powerful the pressures to conform are.

It turns out that our tendency to go with the flow is not limited to situations where we want to avoid making waves. Sometimes people around us shape not only public behavior but also our private thoughts. Like when you *don't* know the right answer. Say you're asked to estimate not lines but rather the length of the Mississippi River. If you have no idea how long it is, but everyone around you gives confident, converging answers, it would be logical to adjust your response accordingly. In fact, even if others' responses are all over the place, using them to guide your own calculations makes sense. This is the thesis of James Surowiecki's *The Wisdom of Crowds*, namely that the averaged estimates of groups tend to be more accurate than those of individual experts.[5] As Surowiecki suggests, it's why contestants on *Who Wants to be a Millionaire* typically do well to poll the studio audience and go with majority opinion.

In this manner, there's also an informational component to conformity. Sometimes we use other people as a source of knowledge, just as we do when we encounter the ambiguously prostrate passenger in the crowded subway car. None of the other commuters are alarmed? Then it must not be an emergency. Everyone at the table says that the Mississippi is at least two thousand miles long? Then I'd better tweak my own estimate of five hundred, no matter how big a fan of Mark Twain I fancy myself.

In an experiment in this vein, individuals were seated in a completely dark room for what they were told was a vision test.[6] Several feet in front of them, a small point of light shone for a few seconds. Their task was to estimate how far the light moved. Some said as much as nine or ten inches; others thought just one inch. In reality the light didn't move at all, but without any reference points in the dark room, it sure *seemed* like it moved. So participants' estimates reflected their subjective take on a visual illusion.

Over the next few days, researchers brought these same students back to the dark room, but this time in groups of three. Asked to complete the same task—judge how far the light had moved—participants gave their answers out loud, one by one. Over time, responses converged within groups. Before long, everyone in the group was in general agreement that the light was moving somewhere in the neighborhood of two to four inches. Absent a visual marker to orient their perception, individuals turned to a different, more social reference point: the people around them.

SO CONFORMITY CAN ALSO come from a desire to gather accurate information. But that's not what happened in Asch's study. There was nothing ambiguous about his lines, yet respondents still went along with a wrong answer. Here, the conformity wasn't informational in nature but rather grew out of a simple motivation to fit in and adhere to group norms. These participants just wanted to avoid rocking the boat.

As you'll probably expect me to say by now, there was nothing remarkable about these participants. They weren't individuals particularly susceptible to conformity; it was the situation, not some sheeplike personality trait that dictated their actions. How do we know? Because when Asch varied aspects of his experiment—when he made just subtle changes to the context—respondents' behavior changed dramatically.

For example, much of the power of Asch's situation derived from the unanimity participants encountered. The finding that 75 percent of respondents conformed at least one time emerged when every last person around the table agreed on the incorrect response. When just one actor broke from consensus, participants felt liberated to do the same: suddenly fewer than 10 percent conformed. In fact, even when the lone dissenter voiced an incorrect response different from the wrong answer given by the rest of the actors, the participants' conformity rate still dropped.

Holding firm to our independent beliefs and tendencies becomes easier—or, at least, less difficult—with some semblance of an ally. It's empowering to see someone else go against the norm. It's liberating, actually, as arena acolytes of Cameron Hughes have discovered. A dissenter changes the culture of a group, reshaping its norms. Instead of being unthinkable or intolerable, disagreement becomes merely awkward.

Another crucial aspect of the context of Asch's study is that the respondents' decision was a public one. Participants committed to their responses aloud, permitting everyone else to immediately and unambiguously know whether they were adhering to the group consensus. Without such public accountability, conformity should drop dramatically, which is exactly what happened when Asch allowed participants to write down instead of voice their line-judging responses.

These variations on Asch's original study demonstrate the power of situations to dictate conformity. And though his research took place in the 1950s, the findings were hardly the product of a particular era: forty years later, *Dateline NBC* conducted the same study in front of hidden cameras and found conformity among more than half of the respondents. It's not an exclusively American tendency, either, as more than 130 variations of Asch's study have been conducted in at least seventeen different countries.[7] If anything, average conformity rates are *lower* among American and British respondents than among non-Western samples from Japan, Hong Kong, Ghana, and Zimbabwe. In other words, the conformity Asch observed emerged in spite of traditional American values like independence and individualism. In cultures with a more collectivist, communal orientation, the tendency to go with the flow can be even more pronounced.

Conformity is so ingrained that we often practice it without trying to, as when we mimic others' nonverbal behavior. In one study at New York University, individuals were paired with a conversation partner who made a habit of either shaking his foot or rubbing his head. Without realizing it, participants started to mirror this repetitive behavior.[8] There's good reason for this tendency, which the researchers labeled the "chameleon effect": in a follow-up study, they found that the more someone adopts our mannerisms during conversation, the more we end up liking her.

We get so used to conformity smoothing out our social interactions that we sometimes do it on autopilot. There's a scene in *When Harry Met Sally* when Billy Crystal's character relates to a friend at a football game his angst over his wife's decision to leave him. For a cinematic depiction of a platonic male friendship, it's an unusually intimate conversation. And right in the midst of this tête-à-tête, as Harry is sharing the most personal details of his emotional devastation, both characters stand up and sit back down mindlessly as the wave circles the stadium crowd. Three different times. Their conversation doesn't miss a beat.

Conformity also occurs on a societal scale, as with hairstyles and fashion. In fits and starts, we adjust our sense of the acceptable range of possibilities for how to get coiffed or dressed. Then, one day, sometimes much to our surprise, we realize that these standards—the norms—have changed. Our old yearbook photos are now fodder for amusement and embarrassment. Much of our closet is suddenly ready for the thrift shop. Honestly, in ten years don't you think we're going to have a hard time explaining to kids why grown-ups used to go out in public wearing plastic clogs with Swiss cheese holes?

Or take baby names. It's the shifting sands of normative conformity that accounts for how a name can go from the punch line of a movie joke—*the mermaid's so naïve she picked "Madison" off a street sign*—to the fourth-most popular girls' name in America less than three decades later. I suppose we should just count ourselves lucky that the screenwriters of *Splash* didn't have Daryl Hannah find herself on the other side of Central Park, on Amsterdam Avenue instead. In this case, all it took was one cinematic example to change prevailing norms, kick-starting the transformation of a name from comically unacceptable to utterly commonplace—not unlike how one book/movie about training horses can alter the common usage of the word *whisper.*

In short, conformity is all around us. Asch's lines provide a compelling demonstration of the extent to which we'll go along with the group even when a correct, alternative response is apparent. But life is often less straightforward—less black-and-white—and conformity becomes even *more* likely when we navigate the ambiguity of the real world. Like the Jew who finds himself in a Catholic church for the first time for a wedding, forced to spend the whole service following the lead of those around him. How else would he know when to stand and when to sit? That the cushioned stool was a kneeler? Or that those wafers weren't a midmorning snack to stave off low blood sugar?

Of course, the same Gentile friends who found my church performance so amusing were just as clueless later on when they arrived at the synagogue for *my* wedding. Life never fails to present us with unfamiliar social terrain to navigate. And it pays to recognize how useful other people can be for resolving these confusing situations.

CONFORMITY'S INVISIBLE HAND

So we're not as independent-minded as we think we are. Perhaps the most intriguing aspect of this tendency toward conformity is that it reflects an amazingly subtle form of social influence. That is, here's a process by which our thoughts and actions are drastically changed by those around us but without other people having to make any sort of direct appeal. In the end, it's an invisible hand that pulls our strings: this influence of those around us is all in our heads.

In the Asch study, no one *asks* participants to give wrong answers; the idea of breaking with the group leads to self-generated discomfort. And except for Joan Rivers and some obnoxious girls I knew in middle school, few people in your life make explicit suggestions about how you should dress or wear your hair, yet we as a society still converge toward a "look" that comes to epitomize an era or geographical region. The next time you have a few minutes to waste at work, upload your photo to www.yearbookyourself.com to explore how you'd look with the clothes and hairstyles of different decades. Conformity is the official psychological sponsor of this enjoyable break from office productivity.

So conformity is an internal process by which we sense a group's norm and adjust accordingly. But this isn't the way we usually think about social influence. What about intentional efforts to change someone's attitudes? Explicit appeals for assistance? The car salesman who wants you to add the rustproofing package for just $399? Well, our tendency to conform to unspoken rules also provides insight into compliance with more direct, external forms of social influence like these.

The success of many a direct solicitation also hinges on norms. For example, one time-tested strategy to get others to comply with your requests is to invoke the norm of reciprocity. As alluded to earlier, we feel obligated to return the favor to those who have helped us. Sometimes the return request is immediate, as when charities send free postcards, address labels, or other "tokens of appreciation" along with a donation card. Other people are content to bank return favors for use at a later date, à la Don Corleone on his daughter's wedding day. Because, really, you never know when a bad tollbooth stop will leave you in need of a good embalmer.

In one study of reciprocity, male college students were paired with a partner who either did an unexpected favor for him during the experiment—he went to buy a soda for himself and came back with two—or didn't.[9] Afterward, on their way out of the session, the partner asked if the participant would be willing to buy some raffle tickets he was selling for a fund-raiser. Students who had been given the free soda bought almost twice as many raffle tickets, even though the tickets were far more expensive than the drink they had received. Your small investment in reciprocity can pay handsome dividends.

Efforts like this one to elicit compliance draw on many of the same processes implicated in conformity, even as they include a direct, external request not found in, say, Asch's study. As with conformity, these compliance tactics don't apply heavy-handed pressure. Instead, they amount to behind-the-scenes orchestrations based on the assumption that once you activate someone's concerns about norms—like those regarding reciprocity—these concerns will apply all the force necessary to initiate action.

Another motivating consideration is commitment. Once we

agree to something, we don't like to go back on our word. As an example, consider that there are few notions more unpleasant to your average college student than waking up early. I teach a class that ends at 11:45 a.m., and on a recent course evaluation one student complained that we met "too early in the morning." Never mind that had the class ended fifteen minutes later, it literally wouldn't have been morning anymore.

Yet somehow, in one phone study, researchers were able to get 56 percent of the undergrads they called to agree to show up to a 7:00 a.m. experiment. How, pray tell, did they do this? By lowballing the students, only informing them of the start time *after* they had already agreed to participate.[10] Only 31 percent agreed to show up when they knew about the timing from the start of the call (and I can only assume that these were students who still planned to be awake from the night before anyway).

To be honest, boosting compliance doesn't even require that much creativity. Just as conformity can emerge as if on autopilot, so do people often respond mindlessly to direct requests. Consider the following scenario: You're at the library preparing to use the copy machine. Suddenly, someone approaches and asks if she can cut in front of you to make five copies because she's in a rush. A reasonable request, you figure, so you agree. Indeed, 94 percent of library patrons approached in this manner let someone go in front of them.[11] When the request was unaccompanied by an explanation—simply "Can I cut in front of you?"—agreement dropped to 60 percent.

A good reason for cutting in line—being in a rush—increases compliance by more than 30 percentage points. What about a lousy reason, though? What about "Can I cut in front of you because I have to make copies?" By any rational basis, this query shouldn't lead to any more compliance than the 60 percent rate observed absent an explanation. But it does. In fact, 93 percent of library patrons agreed to the empty request. Just hearing *any* explanation, even if it's meaningless, can be as influential as a good explanation.

It pays to remember that when it comes to the impact of others on how we think and act, both internal and external pressures are at play. Many of the same elements that explain our tendency to go with the flow also account for how we respond to direct requests: the impact of norms, the power of public commitment, mindless reactions to our surroundings. To be an expert of social influence, you have to draw upon all of these factors, capitalizing on the human tendencies toward conformity as well as compliance. Because, remember, the superfan asks people to get up and cheer, but he also sets the example through his own behavior. Do as I ask *and* as I do is the mantra of the successful crowd whisperer.

FOLLOW THE LEADER

Conformity is a glue that helps hold society together. It keeps crowded city sidewalks in synchronized lockstep during an otherwise chaotic rush hour. It's a compass for navigating unfamiliar situations, like those faced by the Jew in church or the straight guy at an Indigo Girls concert. But still, taking your cue from those in the know is only as effective as these other people are knowledgeable. Remember the participants in the dark room who had to judge how far a light had moved? They turned to fellow group members for guidance, but the information they gleaned was misleading: the light was actually stationary. Going with the flow can shepherd us through challenging situations, but it doesn't guarantee accuracy or even a positive outcome. For that matter, in some instances the consequences of conformity can be downright destructive.

In March 1997, thirty-nine bodies were discovered inside a rented house in Rancho Santa Fe, California. The dead were dressed identically: black sweat suits adorned by handmade arm patches, new black-and-white Nikes, and wallets with a five-dollar bill inside. We soon learned that the dead were members of a communal religious group called Heaven's Gate. Their mass suicide by way of a vodka-phenobarbital cocktail—timed to coincide with the approach of the Hale-Bopp comet, which cult members believed would be followed by a UFO—reminded many of the even larger mass suicide at Jim Jones's "Peoples Temple" in Guyana nearly two decades earlier. Though some of the more than nine hundred bodies found at Jonestown showed signs of gunshots or forcible injection, the vast majority had died after drinking a Kool-Aid-like drink laced with cyanide.

Conformity isn't limited to low-stakes situations—neither of these mass-suicide tragedies would have been possible without it. In fact, many of the details we've since learned about life in cults like these reflect tactics designed to create the very circumstances most likely to elicit conformity. They represent intentional efforts to manipulate situations: Uniform dress and the forsaking of given names reduce feelings of individuality. Communal living arrangements isolated from society heighten members' dependence on one another and exaggerate norms of reciprocity. Inside the Heaven's Gate house, investigators found labels indicating the function of every last shelf, cupboard, and light switch—the idea, apparently, was to facilitate mindlessness.

You don't have to look to the fringes of society to find groups that make use of conformity-boosting strategies. Nicknames and communal living? Uniform appearance and a mind-set to follow orders automatically? I could just as easily be talking about fraternities or the military. Of course, I'm not suggesting that these are cults, too. But many a group employs similar, cultlike tactics to promote cohesion and allegiance among its members—tactics that also make conformity that much more likely to occur.

Recall how after the Abu Ghraib prison scandal of 2004, many were quick to attribute the abuse to the aberrational personalities of a few U.S. servicepeople. The public face of these "bad apples" came to be that of Lynndie England, a twenty-year-old West Virginian who had been depicted in photos smiling and giving a thumbs-up as prisoners were sexually humiliated. She must have a sadistic streak, we assumed. At the very least, she and her fellow perpetrators had to be overly compliant individuals.

But no matter how closely you scrutinize the early years of England's life, there aren't red flags of personality. No stories of childhood abuse, either as perpetrator or victim. Her most egregious misconduct as a student apparently was passing notes that poked fun at a science teacher. And she was anything but a subservient wallflower, joining the military against her mother's objections and quitting a job at a chicken-processing plant because management had ignored her complaints about worker safety and health-code violations.[12] That's right—before becoming the poster child for military prison abuse, Lynndie England was a conformity-resisting whistle-blower.

Half a decade later, we've learned that the methods used at Abu Ghraib predated Lynndie England's arrival in Iraq and weren't confined to just one prison. Moreover, we've discovered that these actions weren't the creative inventions of individual service members but rather a response to clear directives issued by military superiors and modeled by intelligence officials. It may be difficult to fathom, but most of the personnel at Abu Ghraib had personalities little different from yours or mine:

> [T]he conclusions of researchers . . . hold that, although it is true that, in some situations, deranged and sadistic individuals have committed acts of torture for pleasure, in most cases in which torture is committed at the instigation of government officials, the torturers can best be described as normal individuals.[13]

England's own recollections read as if they had been lifted from a participant in a conformity experiment: "When we first got there, we were like, 'what's going on?' Then you see staff sergeants walking around not saying anything. . . . You think, 'OK, obviously it's normal.'"[14] This conclusion doesn't exonerate the perpetrators of abuse, but let's face it, no analysis of what went on at Abu Ghraib is complete without considering the dramatic impact of the situation. Once again, WYSIWYG is just a cop-out.

A UNIFYING THEME of the contexts of Heaven's Gate, the Peoples Temple, and Abu Ghraib was the presence of strong, persuasive leadership. In the cult examples, there were the group leaders Marshall Applewhite and Jim Jones. In Iraq, the military intelligence officers, as well as a general culture emphasizing chain of command. Indeed, while people will go with the flow in a wide range of settings, there are few better ways to fan the flames of social influence than by having a forceful leader.

Perhaps the most well-known demonstration of the power of situations on human nature examined this very idea of the easy impact of authority. In Stanley Milgram's 1960s obedience studies at Yale[15] participants were paired with a partner for what they thought was an investigation of how punishment affects learning. Through a rigged drawing, the participant was always assigned to the role of "Teacher" and the partner—actually an actor—became the "Learner." The setup was straightforward: the Teacher would read a list of word pairs and then test the Learner on them, administering electric shocks of increasing severity for each wrong answer. You know, sort of a cross between East German police interrogation and Japanese game show.

The shock panel had a long line of thirty switches. Each represented an increase of 15 volts from the one before it, up to a maximum of 450 volts. Descriptive labels appeared in increments of 60 volts, with 75 described as "Moderate Shock," 135 as "Strong Shock," and so on. At 375 volts, the label was "Danger: Severe Shock," and by 435 you were off the scale entirely—it simply and ominously read "XXX."

Of course, no one was actually on the receiving end of all this electricity. While participants believed that they were administering increasingly painful shocks to their partner each time he missed a question, the actor in the other room wasn't hooked up to the electrodes. The moans, complaints, and—eventually—screams heard through the intercom were all prerecorded.

Like this response to the 150 volt shock: "Get me out of here. I told you I had heart trouble. My heart's starting to bother me now. Get me out of here, please."

And at 180 volts: "I can't stand the pain. Let me out of here!"

At a shock of 300 volts, screams of anguish preceded the following: "I absolutely refuse to answer anymore. Get me out of here. You can't hold me here. Get me out."

By 345 volts, the Learner stopped responding altogether to the test questions or the shocks.

Before starting the study, Milgram famously asked dozens of psychiatrists to estimate what percentage of people would follow the instructions all the way to the end of the shock panel. On average, the psychiatrists guessed that one in one thousand—one-tenth of 1 percent—might be sadistic enough to keep administering shocks of apparently indescribable intensity to a partner who had become unresponsive.

Their prediction proved low when it came to participants left on their own to follow the study instructions. Closer to 3 percent of respondents proceeded all the way to 450 volts when left to their own devices.

In the presence of a lab coat–clad experimenter, however, a remarkable 65 percent went to the end of the shock panel. In fact, not a single respondent in the original study stopped before 300 volts.[16] And all the experimenter had to do was make innocuous comments like "Please go on" and "The experiment requires that you continue." The content of these words was no more informative than the library patron's request to cut the line because she "needs to make copies." But authority is inherently influential.

As Milgram emphasized, these participants were ordinary Americans: "postal clerks, high school teachers, salesmen, engineers, and laborers." It wasn't station in life, gender, or personality that predicted willingness to inflict harm. It was the situation. Sure, some people you know are less predisposed than others to conform to the masses or defer to authority—after all, every New England college campus has a guy who makes a point of wearing shorts and Birkenstocks each day, even in winter. Still, context plays a much bigger role than we give it credit for in determining whether we go with the flow.

Variations on Milgram's original study highlight this power of situations. When the research was moved from a university setting to an urban office building, fewer than 50 percent of the respondents went to the end of the shock panel. When the experimenter shed his lab coat—and, thus, some of his presumed authority—the rate fell below 20 percent. These are the factors that best predicted how respondents behaved, not their personality or profession or even the era when the research took place: in an updated version of the study in 2009, obedience levels were once again quite high.[17]

That authority could so drastically shape ordinary participants' behavior supports the notion that real-life atrocities like Abu Ghraib are often perpetrated by "normal people" in abnormal circumstances.[18] Milgram himself, in the very first paragraph of the first paper he published on the research, linked his investigation to the genocide of the Holocaust: "These inhumane policies may have originated in the mind of a single person, but they could only be carried out on a massive scale if a very large number of persons obeyed orders."[19] Once again, a profound human tragedy made possible by human tendencies like conformity, compliance, and obedience.

Simply put, Milgram showed us that all it takes to goad regular citizens into electrocuting a stranger is a smartly pressed lab coat and a few vacuous words of encouragement. Just imagine what can happen when authority figures ratchet up the pressure, when leaders really put their minds to capitalizing on the pull of conformity and the potential mindlessness of social influence.

FIGHTING THE URGE

I don't do the wave.

That's right, I refuse to follow my fellow sheep down the well-worn path of spectator conformity, much to the dismay of many a vocal fan seated in my section of the bleachers. The whole scene is just a little too Leni Riefenstahl for me. Having learned about the ubiquitous role conformity plays in life, it's one opportunity I take to reassert some semblance of self-determination. I'll resist even when those who take offense to my conscientious objection are loud, inebriated, and shirtless—and let's face it, the bleacher wave dude is almost always loud, inebriated, and shirtless.

Plus, if I may be blunt, the wave is stupid. It might've been clever the first few times it materialized spontaneously, but the whole act has grown a bit stale by now. Yeah, I know . . . some arenas put a creative twist on the routine, varying wave speed, number, and direction. Oooh, I'm *really* impressed. Short of genome projects and Big Bang simulators, my faith in human ingenuity has rarely been so bolstered.

Just call this my one-man rebellion against the mindless capitulation that otherwise pervades life. I'll admit that it's hardly a stirring example of civil disobedience—a latter-day Gandhi or Thoreau I am not. But knowing how often and how thoughtlessly we conform in so many daily situations, I consider staying glued to my seat while the wave circles around me to be a worthwhile if symbolic gluteal gesture toward recapturing my independence.

Not that there's anything wrong with conformity per se. As discussed above, going with the flow serves productive purposes, and it's hard to imagine society operating smoothly without it. It's a social lubricant that helps make a positive impression and strengthens ties within groups: the secret handshake, regular hangout spot, repeated movie quote, and inside joke all initiate and reinforce bonds between group members. We like being with people who act like us.

Conformity conveys practical advantages, too. Merging in traffic is less arduous when drivers stick to the established rule of alternating lanes. Without norms, all of Manhattan would grind to a halt, what with a million and a half people crammed into twenty-three square miles. And conformity is essential to efficiency in smaller-scale settings as well, like the busy lunch counter. My favorite burger place in graduate school had a precise ordering procedure so well established that it was printed on the menu: tell them your fried sides first, then burger size, bun type, veggies, cheese, and, finally, condiments. Adhere to precedent, and lunch was quick and delicious. Deviate, and—as posted signage warned— you "risk the scorn and derision of the cooks."[20]

So I admit that conformity contributes to the efficient functioning of society. But we conform so often that doing so can become a mindless default to which we defer in the effort to make life easier as opposed to better. Thus, my perceived need for periodic rebellion. Because as unimpressive as my token boycott of the wave may be, I can't help but wonder how different the outcomes at Heaven's Gate or Abu Ghraib might have been had just one individual—or better yet, several people—more forcefully questioned the direction in which their group was headed.

You may find it easy to rationalize those examples—mass suicide and prison abuse—as extreme episodes involving aberrational individuals. But the dangers of conformity are apparent elsewhere as well. For instance, less than two years before President Kennedy's successful navigation of the Cuban Missile Crisis, the same administration fared far less impressively in another international affair centered on the island nation. In April 1961, a U.S.-led attempt to overthrow Fidel Castro failed spectacularly. The end result of what was intended as a covert invasion at the Bay of Pigs included more than one hundred casualties among U.S. and exile forces, over one thousand men captured, and the dismissal of the director of the CIA.

Many a postmortem has suggested that the failed operation resulted from a lousy plan based on unrealistic assumptions. And conformity greased the skids for the flawed decision making behind it all.[21] Though several in Kennedy's inner circle harbored private doubts about the invasion's feasibility, few voiced concerns during group meetings. According to Yale psychologist Irving Janis, the advisers didn't want to disrupt the presumed consensus of the team or the momentum behind a plan that had existed in some form since the Eisenhower administration. Each man assumed that the silence of the others indicated agreement; group cohesion was prioritized over sound decision making. As Arthur Schlesinger would later rue, "I can only explain my failure to do more than raise a few timid questions by reporting that one's impulse to blow the whistle on this nonsense was simply undone by the circumstances of the discussion."[22]

Kennedy's advisers emerged from the Bay of Pigs fiasco looking a lot like the participants who evaluated Asch's lines. This emphasis of team unity over rigorous debate—this phenomenon of groupthink—has also been implicated in other high-stakes group decisions gone awry. Like NASA's inattention to mechanical concerns during two ill-fated space shuttle missions. Or the failure of the financial sector to fully appreciate the risks posed by the housing bubble and subprime mortgages. And, perhaps only slightly less famously, Van Halen's repeated inability to successfully replace a departed lead singer.

WHAT, THEN, are this chapter's concrete lessons? First, if you're out to change the behavior of others, keep in mind how invaluable a tool conformity can be. Much like the crowd whisperer, you can create new norms by modeling the very actions you hope to see in others. Stuff a few dollar bills in your own tip jar to raise the expectations of future customers. Recruit friends to populate a long line outside your restaurant, club, or gallery opening. Make use of reciprocity and public commitment when trying to win over new clients. Give your spouse the type of gift that you hope to receive in return.

And when your goal is the opposite one—to curtail conformity among those around you—look to the case studies of riled-up sports crowds and cults. Then reverse engineer these situations in the direction of independence. Anything you can do to emphasize individual identity has the potential to reduce conformity.

For example, in a clever Halloween study, researchers instructed visiting trick-or-treaters to take one and only one item from a candy bowl placed inside a house. But free candy is hard to resist, and the kids were all too eager to follow the lead of the costumed gluttons preceding them: 83 percent took extra candy when the first kid in their group did likewise.[23] However, when the adult at the door had previously asked the children their names and what street they lived on—stripping them of their anonymity and reminding them of their individuality—candy-stealing conformity dropped to 67 percent. Those little ghouls and goblins with the confectionary misfortune of being asked their name *and* arriving at the house solo, without anyone to set a bad example? A paltry 8 percent left with extra candy.

Learning the names of all the neighborhood kids isn't the only way to combat conformity around you. When it comes to group decisions, create a new set of expectations in which disagreement, not unanimity, is the norm. We may enjoy being around similar others, but there's a big difference between harmonious decisions and wise ones. From Abraham Lincoln's famed "Team of Rivals" cabinet[24] to the sniping of judges on reality TV competitions, diverse perspectives and debate are hallmarks of rigorous decision making. So if your committee meetings are peaceful or even pleasant affairs, start asking whether the group is getting as much out of its members as it should be. Instead, fill out your board or panel with people of varied backgrounds and perspectives. Keep changing up your work groups before a norm of complacency sets in. Force yourself to compare notes with those who are likely to disagree with you.

And if you want to initiate debate within an already established organizational structure, research offers specific suggestions for tipping the situation to your advantage.[25] Find an ally in dissent: breaking with the group is hard work, but it's not as big a burden when someone shoulders it with you. Be consistent and stick to your guns: hesitation and vacillation are luxuries that minority factions can't afford.

Don't forget about reputation, either. Having been a loyal citizen in the past—one who has consistently toed the party line—you'll have more banked capital to spend in later disagreements than will the chronic nonconformist. It carries more currency when the dyed-in-the-red-wool Republican suggests that the GOP should reconsider a position than when the same call comes from the moderate with a long history of breaking rank. So choose your battles carefully, building up and saving the credibility you may need to later challenge your group's momentum.

Moreover, just as I argued that becoming acquainted with the obstacles to helping behavior can change how you look at subsequent emergencies, simply understanding the basic tendency to go with the flow can short-circuit your automatic deference to conformity. Knowing now about Asch's findings, you probably wouldn't abandon your personal line-judging instincts in a comparable situation. I'm sure you'd take a similarly principled stand against a nattily attired researcher asking you to administer electric shocks.

Such lessons also translate to novel, unfamiliar settings. Maybe in the form of efforts to resist your supervisor's ethically problematic directives. Or the resolve to break from your pack to pursue objectives that will make you happy rather than popular. Just recognizing that going with the flow is a double-edged sword can be enough to jar you out of mindless action, prompting you to question whether you're engaged in harmless conformity in the name of smoothing over social relations or perhaps caught up in a more problematically short-sided form of groupthink with graver potential consequence.

So stop resting easy on the assumption that you're a freethinker who isn't swayed by those around you. If you want to avoid undue conformity, you have to stay vigilant—against both the intentional efforts of others as well as your own mindless tendency to go along with the crowd. The subtlest strategies of social influence usually only work when the target isn't aware of them; realizing that someone is pulling your strings is enough to get you to yank right back.

Who knows, after all this new reflection on conformity, you just might stumble upon your own symbolic form of protest— your own variation on boycotting the wave. Maybe it'll be an unwillingness to capitulate to a standing ovation for merely average performances. Perhaps a conscious effort to avoid the grating catchphrase of the month, be it "Don't go there," "It is what it is," or the use of "literally" when speaking figuratively. Or a refusal to follow blindly the waitstaff's admonition that the plate is hot and cannot, under any circumstances, be touched. That's right, the vicarious pleasures offered by sitcom norm violators are also available to you personally if you're willing to risk public excoriation in the bleachers and minor burns when dining out.

Such deviations from expectation once in a while are liberating. They allow you to feel "more like yourself" even in a mass of people. These dollops of disobedience can make our obligatory forms of societal conformity that much easier to stomach.

Still, I'll admit, as with all norm violations, they also come with strings attached: I asked Cameron Hughes what he'd do with a guy like me, someone who deemed himself too refined for an exercise as proletarian as the wave. He quickly disabused me of the notion that I'm any sort of nonconformist, informing me that he runs into stubbornly sedentary spectators everywhere he goes. Then he warned me that "the guy you're talking about . . . is just great fodder for the crowd. It makes it too easy."

So you wouldn't just leave me alone and let me sit in peace? I asked him. "No way," he replied with a laugh.

You mean, staying in my seat actually just puts a bigger target on my back? "Absolutely," he said.

Dammit. The costs of going against the flow just keep piling up.

Fine, Cameron, I'll do the freakin' wave once in a while. But no one's going to force me to have a good time doing it.

4.

YOU'RE NOT THE PERSON YOU THOUGHT YOU WERE

Just who do you think you are anyway?

We humans make it a habit wrestling with questions about the self. Existential musing lies at the heart of our most beloved forms of art. Music. Poetry. John Hughes films. It dominates our internal commentary as we stare in the mirror each morning; it's the recurring story line of our diaries. The question of who we really are sends us off on inspiring journeys of self-exploration but also toward sobering epiphanies of personal shortcomings. Not to mention interviews with Barbara Walters and Larry King.

As with much of daily life, this process of self-perception is subject to the power of context. That is, the conclusion that situations matter isn't limited to public behavior or how we think about others. Even the most private of perceptions—our very sense of self—is shaped by where we are and who we're with, though we may resist this notion.

How do I know this? How can I be so sure that situations shape self-perception? For that matter, how do you even begin to gauge someone else's private thoughts about the self? Well, for starters, you can use simple fill-in-the-blanks.

Below you'll find the same phrase repeated five times. You should complete each statement with the first word or words that pop into your head, making sure to provide five different responses in the end. Go ahead and do it now, preferably in ink so that the next reader has to pony up for a new, clean copy of the book. If you're reading an electronic version—or if you just insist on being a stick-in-the-mud—you can do the exercise in your head.

Remember, don't agonize over what to include or what not to—just complete each statement with the first words that come to mind:

1. I am _____.
2. I am _____.
3. I am _____.
4. I am _____.
5. I am _____.

Researchers refer to this as the "Twenty Statements Test."[1] Clearly, you took the abridged version.

You have tremendous flexibility when taking the Twenty Statements Test. There are dozens and dozens of ways in which you can plausibly describe yourself. You could start with physical descriptors, like "tall" or "left-handed." You could go with different roles you play in life, including occupation or family status. You could draw upon categories including gender, race, and religion. Of course, you could also rely on WYSIWYG by using personality traits like generous, curious, shy, and others.

Bottom line? You have almost unlimited possibility here because identity is a multiheaded beast. In fact, you have so many choices available to you that it's reasonable to ask whether your responses would have been the same had you filled in the same five blanks yesterday. Or last week. Or had you been situated in a different room or in a different mood.

Actually, I'm confident that the answer is no—you wouldn't provide the same answers if I gave you the same test in another setting. Without question, your responses would have been different ten years ago, right? But even smaller changes in context have big effects on how you see yourself, with one of the critical factors influencing your identity—whether or not you realize it—being who's around you.

Because there are so many aspects to identity, different dimensions of the self-concept become salient in different situations. As just one example, research suggests that we tend to think of ourselves in terms of that which makes us distinctive.[2] So when I give my students the Twenty Statements Test in class, they rarely respond "college student." But given the same test at the train station or doctor's office, their status as students is more distinctive and therefore more accessible as they flip through their identity Rolodex.

This principle explains why in most of America, whites are less likely than people of color to mention race on the Twenty Statements Test. Drop a white student on a Historically Black College campus, though, or a white pedestrian in the heart of Chinatown, and whiteness quickly becomes salient. For the same reasons, exchange students more often describe themselves using nationality when abroad than at home, men are more conscious of gender at a baby shower than a baseball game, and blondes give more thought to hair color in Seoul than Stockholm.

In short, just as context influences how we perceive and interact with others, it also colors the way we see and think about the self.

PAGING DR. PHIL

In pondering self-perception, the first step is to pose a question we rarely ask: Where do beliefs about the self actually come from? We infrequently consider the origins of self-knowledge because we usually take this information for granted.

How do you know your strengths and limitations? Your likes and dislikes? Your brightest dreams for the future and deepest regrets about the past?

You just do, that's how.

But there's a more profound answer to such questions. In fact, there are several, though you wouldn't know it from listening to the presumed experts, the gurus of self-help who populate the bestseller lists and the couches of daytime talk shows. The cottage industries of self-help, self-insight, and self-actualization suggest that you come to know yourself by exploring your own thoughts and feelings—by turning the lens of social vision inward. A core treatise of these books is that you need to locate your true, "authentic" self. You have to get in touch with who you really are, they keep telling us. Thou can't be true to thine own self if that self remains a mystery, the thinking goeth.

How, exactly, do we get acquainted with this core self? A trip to the local bookstore suggests that the answer has something to do with chicken soup. That, plus we're supposed to ask ourselves questions like these suggested by Dr. Phil:[3] "What are the 10 most defining moments of your life?" "What are the 7 most critical choices you have made to put you on your current path?" "Who are the 5 most pivotal people in your world and how have they shaped you?"

Dr. Phil's questions share a common link. And I don't just mean the use of arbitrary digits that I can only assume were once his fortune cookie lucky numbers. Their more important shared characteristic is the assumption that introspection produces reliable self-insight. These questions imply that looking inward provides some sort of direct channel to your internal preferences, deepest thoughts, and true motivations.

It's a nice idea, that you have an authentic self lurking within, waiting to be unveiled. But your answers to Dr. Phil's questions—like your responses to the Twenty Statements Test—change across time and location. So which are the authentic ones?

In trying to name my 5 most pivotal people, my biggest challenge is whom to rank higher: Jennifer Aniston or Eva Longoria. Yet, somehow, when my wife's in the room, they both drop off the list entirely. But even when you strive for honesty, looking inward only gets you so far in the effort to learn about the self. While Dr. Phil's assumption seems reasonable enough—the idea that we can accurately articulate the influences on our own behavior or how happy we are with various aspects of our life—it just isn't how self-perception really works. Introspection turns out to be far more difficult and limited than we give it credit for.

For starters, take the presumption that we can reliably explain why we make the decisions we do, one that underlies Dr. Phil's questions about "choices that put you on your current path" or "how others have shaped you." This is the same assumption that drives political pollsters trying to forecast voting behavior or marketing departments conducting focus groups. However, research demonstrates that we're not nearly as good at explaining the factors that shape our preferences and actions as we think we are.

Consider a series of experiments conducted at the University of Michigan by Dick Nisbett and Tim Wilson.[4] In one, they investigated consumer behavior, with hundreds of male and female respondents asked to evaluate various household items. One set of participants examined four pairs of nylon stockings in an effort to determine which was the best product. In addition to visual inspection, they were allowed to handle each sample to assess its feel, durability, disguise potential for convenience-store robbery, and whatever other characteristics one looks for in evaluating this product. Their ultimate preferences increased in a clear left-to-right progression: the far right pair of stockings was, on average, rated the highest, followed by the pair to its immediate left, and so on. In fact, the right-most stockings were selected almost four times as often as those on the far left of the nylon stocking array.

Fascinating data for those hosiery aficionados out there, sure, but what do the rest of us learn from the study? First, on a personal note, I learned that when using your visible-from-the-hallway work computer, it's probably best to close your office door *before* Googling "nylon stockings."

Second, this study captures the limitations of introspection in action. Because it just so happens that all four pairs of stockings used in the array were identical. Same brand, same style, same color. One would have predicted, therefore, that ratings for pairs A, B, C, and D would have been comparable. That they weren't— that they varied systematically as a function of position in the array—suggests that consumers often hold off on selecting a product until they've been able to "shop around" and view multiple possibilities (since respondents typically inspected the stockings in left-to-right fashion).

But the researchers never would have realized this had they relied on participants' introspective explanations. When asked to account for their choice, not a single person cited stocking order. Instead, they talked about knit and sheen and weave and other product characteristics that transcend the imagination of a mere nylon neophyte such as myself. These individuals had no idea what had actually shaped their behavior, but they had little trouble generating explanations. And confident ones at that. When the researchers asked respondents—point-blank—about how the order of the stocking array might have impacted their evaluation, "virtually all subjects denied it, usually with a worried glance at the interviewer suggesting that they felt either that they had misunderstood the question or were dealing with a madman."[5]

Just as we sometimes fail to note the true influences on our behavior, in other instances we show the opposite tendency: thinking that factors have influenced us when they actually haven't. In another study, Nisbett and Wilson asked a different set of participants to watch a documentary about urban poverty. One group viewed the film under normal conditions. Another watched the movie while suffering through construction-related noise from a power saw in the hallway outside.

When asked how they liked the film, no meaningful differences emerged between the responses of the two groups. If anything, the film ratings of those viewers subjected to the construction noises were trivially more positive. But when the person supervising the screening apologized to audience members in the loud room and asked whether their ratings of the film had been adversely affected by all the noise, more than half—55 percent—said yes. Once again, these people were confidently answering questions regarding what shaped their judgments, but they were flat-out wrong.

Voters claim to ignore negative political ads, jurors tell you they're not swayed by inadmissible evidence, and my younger daughter simply can't eat another bite of dinner because there's no room left in her tummy. But the data are in: negative campaigning works,[6] inadmissible evidence isn't disregarded,[7] and, miraculously, just minutes later, there's enough space in that belly for a whole ice cream cone plus some of *my* dessert.

So think twice the next time you're tempted to make major changes to your physical appearance, wardrobe, or first-date strategy based on some magazine's "What Men/Women Really Want" poll—the respondents may be answering confidently but still misleadingly. It's easy to think of potential reasons for our decisions or influences on our preferences. Being accurate about it all is the hard part.

———

THESE CONCLUSIONS aren't limited to trivialities like stocking preferences and film ratings. Consider a recent study in the *Journal of Arthroplasty*, in which researchers interviewed 101 adults preparing for hip replacement.[8] Patients were given a checklist of twenty-five possible reasons why they might be planning to undergo the procedure; one year later, they were given the same checklist and asked to offer retrospective explanations for why they had opted for surgery. For the majority of patients, these pre- and post-surgery responses differed. That is, the explanations they gave before the procedure were markedly different from those they gave afterward, particularly among patients who felt that the surgery didn't live up to their expectations.

For example, before the procedure, 36 percent of patients had said that difficulty putting on their shoes (and taking them off) was an important basis for having the surgery. One year later, only half of this 36 percent identified such problems as one of their original concerns. Before the surgery, 29 percent said that difficulty navigating stairs was a major factor; a year later, fewer than one-third of this 29 percent cited issues with stairs as having been an important consideration in their decision.

These patients aren't alone—we can all think of examples when our own explanations for a decision changed over time. How did you decide on your profession? Why did you choose your college major? What made you realize you wanted to marry this person? These are tough questions, and depending on what stage of life you're in, your mood, and who asks you, introspection produces different insights. When your answers to personal questions evolve in this manner—whether over time, context, or company—it becomes difficult to put much stock in the ability of introspection to provide direct access to authentic attitudes and an indisputably true self.

Over the years I've given many different answers to the question of how I chose a college. At the time, I would have said that coming from a small high school, I wanted a small college with a similar feel. After graduating and beginning work toward my Ph.D. elsewhere, I would have emphasized the research opportunities available at a liberal arts college. Today I look back at my seventeen-year-old self with the jaded perspective of presumed wisdom and insight. I'd tell you that my parents took me on a seven-day, eight-school college visit marathon, in which one campus walking tour started to look a lot like another campus walking tour, until I became no different than the average nylon stocking shopper and decided that the last school I visited was the best one.

You might propose that introspection should be more reliable when it comes to other forms of self-insight beyond explaining past decisions. Even if it is more difficult than expected to articulate why we've made the choices we have, surely we're able to give an accurate reading of highly personal ideas such as our likes and dislikes, or what we need to be happy in life. Right?

But behavioral researchers have consistently found that even the assessment of our own life satisfaction is, in a word, malleable.[9] How happy are you with your life? It depends. More so right after your favorite sports team has won or when you're seated in a pleasantly decorated, comfortable room. You're more satisfied with the entirety of your life when it's sunny outside. Hell, all it takes to boost overall life satisfaction is the pleasant surprise of finding a dime before you're interviewed.

As Harvard psychologist Dan Gilbert explains throughout *Stumbling on Happiness,* we're not so good at anticipating what will make us happy in the future.[10] It's no wonder—we have trouble making up our minds about how happy we are in the here and now!

So it goes for a wide range of personal beliefs. Including politics: Americans' evaluations of Republicans become markedly more positive when they're first asked about a particularly popular member of the party (think mid-1990s Colin Powell).[11] Perceptions of physical attractiveness, too: Men asked to rate photos of unfamiliar women see the strangers as less attractive after watching the provocatively clad detectives on display in *Charlie's Angels.*[12] Which are the "true" perceptions about Republicans? Or the "authentic" assessments of attraction? There's no way to know.

Sure, there's *something* to be learned when we look inward to explore our attitudes, preferences, and decisions. But much of the information that introspection generates is fleeting, on-the-fly construction at a particular point in time: how we *think* we feel; why we *guess* we've made the choices we have. By looking inward, we don't gain access to a stable set of impressions regarding an unwavering, authentic self. We produce a temporary status report.

In other words, the gurus of self-help got it wrong. Our sense of who we are is no less context-dependent than the behaviors of everyone else around us. Book sales, Nielsen ratings, and *Oprah* appearances notwithstanding, introspection just isn't all that it's cracked up to be.

COMPARED TO WHAT?

If introspection isn't enough, how else do we come to learn about ourselves? For that matter, how can we account for the surprising context dependence of our sense of self? To answer these questions, I refer you to one of the great unheralded commentators on the mysteries of human nature. I speak, of course, of none other than my wife's late grandfather, Grandpa Syd.

Grandpa had no formal training in disciplines such as psychology or sociology. He was not well versed in the intricacies of the scientific method. Grandpa Syd was a pants salesman from Cleveland, not a behavioral researcher from the Ivy League. Yet he was, in his own inimitable way, a very keen observer of human behavior.

He was also hilarious. Throughout years of interactions, my favorite Grandpa Syd line was, by far, one that he enjoyed unveiling at dinner—and the more formal the occasion, the better. He'd pick up an item under the guise of passing it down the table, then announce in a loud, clear voice, "Sam, you want this butter up your end?"

Unfortunately, this joke has no relevance whatsoever to understanding self-perception.

But my second-favorite Grandpa Syd line is germane to the present analysis. Whenever we'd call to talk to him, inevitably the first question we'd ask was, "How are you doing?" Occasionally, his response would be "H and D," shorthand, naturally, for "Hot and Dull," his description of retirement life in Sun City, Arizona. But more frequently, it was simply, "Compared to what?" As in:

Q: "Grandpa, how are you and Grandma doing?"

A: "Compared to what?"

Now, a few of you might quibble with my attribution of this quotation, asking, hey, isn't that a Henny Youngman line? To which I'd reply, hey, isn't everything? As far as I'm concerned, this was and always will be Grandpa Syd's joke. And with these three simple yet astute words, my wife's grandfather managed to capture an important essence of how we think about the self.

The Colin Powell and *Charlie's Angels* examples on the previous pages illustrate that much of how we see the world relies on comparisons: the Republican brand looks better with Powell in the mix; women you've never seen before look less attractive compared to Farrah Fawcett (or, for you cineasts out there, Cameron Diaz). As Grandpa Syd's canned response implies, how we feel, what our preferences are, and, indeed, how we see ourselves also depend on the specific basis for comparison.

You compare your present self to your self of the past. You compare reality to the way you wish your life was. But not all of the comparisons guiding your self-perception are strictly internal— many are made with other people. In fact, quite often we have great difficulty answering questions about ourselves unless we're able to draw upon comparisons with others.[13]

Think about the last time you were handed back a paper or exam in class, whether it was days or decades ago. If you're like most of the students I teach (or, for that matter, like me when I was a student), your first reaction was to wonder what the average was, to ask your friend how she did, or to sneak a peek at the score of the guy down the row. Even absent a rigid grading curve, students need some context to figure out how best to translate the number they see into an assessment of personal competence. Outside the classroom we also rely on social comparisons like these to gauge our own abilities and situate our opinions, accomplishments, and personal characteristics.

Simply put, one critical source of information about ourselves is other people.

Our need for such social comparison is more pressing in some contexts than others. For instance, the presence of objective indicators can render such comparisons unnecessary. Wishing to know how much I weigh, how fast I swim, or how high I jump, all I need is a scale, a stopwatch, or, in my case, a very small ruler. But often, there are no objective criteria for the self-evaluations we care about most: Am I a good parent? How attractive am I? Has my life been a success?

Questions like these beg for the Grandpa Syd response— compared to what? To answer them, we rely on comparisons to similar others in our immediate environment. What this means is that our choice of company colors how we see the self. Who we're with has a profound impact on who we believe ourselves to be.

As a middle school student in a tiny class of six at a Jewish day school, I fancied myself a basketball prodigy. A regular LeChaim James, if you will. Upon moving to a secular high school with double-digit class sizes, I discovered that it was a tad more difficult defending a point guard who didn't hold his yarmulke on with his left hand while dribbling with his right. One crossover move later, I had readjusted downward my odds of a future athletic scholarship. And so it goes for even more important judgments about the self, including those alluded to earlier: parenting prowess, physical attractiveness, personal success. There's no self-evaluation too intimate to be guided by those around us.

BEAR IN MIND, I'm not arguing simply that other people inform our sense of self. That would be an obvious, unremarkable conclusion. Most of us readily acknowledge that we've been shaped by a variety of role models—particularly parents. And even if we don't, those parents would eagerly remind us at the next family get-together.

The more surprising conclusion, though, is that it's not just our friends, teachers, and loved ones who mold our sense of self. So does the stranger on the bus, the woman pictured in the magazine, and that guy down the row in chemistry class. Without their knowing it, we often look to these people to evaluate our own abilities and attitudes. The company we keep shapes our identity, our self-esteem, and even our emotional state.

That's right, even the way you read your own emotions can be dictated by the strangers in your midst. We learned this from an experiment by Stanley Schachter and Jerome Singer at Columbia University that bisected the fields of psychology and physiology.[14] In the study, 184 men were injected with a small amount of either adrenaline or saline solution. Even a small dose of adrenaline—or epinephrine—has clear physiological impact: increases in heart rate, respiration rate, and blood flow to the muscles. A similar amount of saline solution—or salt water—does not. So the study's major comparison was between two groups of men, one feeling the arousing effects of adrenaline, and one experiencing no such arousal.

But the participants didn't know what was in these injections. They all thought they were receiving a vitamin called "Suproxin" and believed that the objective of the research was to test the vitamin's effects on their vision. Therefore, the uninformed participants injected with adrenaline had no idea of the true source of their arousal.

After the injection, the men were led to a different room and asked to answer some questions before their final vision test. Taking a seat next to another respondent, they began the questionnaire. But this was no ordinary research participant they were next to, and this was no ordinary questionnaire. The other person in the room was actually an actor in cahoots with researchers, and within minutes he began his best imitation of John McEnroe protesting a line call: He scoffed angrily at the questionnaire. He cursed the researchers who devised it. Finally, he ripped the packet into pieces, threw them on the ground, and stomped out of the room exasperated. In a matter of seconds, things had deteriorated from vision study to health-care reform town hall meeting.

What was the basis for this tantrum? Well, the questionnaire was a touch personal. Not to mention insulting. One question required respondents to list their relative most in need of psychiatric care. Another asked about the family member best described by the phrase "does not bathe or wash regularly." My favorite was this last question:

With how many men (other than your father) has your mother had extramarital relationships?

_____ 10 or more

_____ 5–9

_____ 4 or less

Of course, the researchers weren't interested in the sex life of participants' mothers. They wanted to see the emotional impact of the actor's outburst. The respondents who had been given a saline injection exhibited little if any angry behavior of their own. Mostly they just looked on at the irate actor with a mix of befuddled curiosity and annoyed resignation—a bit like the face that White House officials make when they watch Joe Biden ad-lib near a microphone.

But those participants who—unbeknownst to them—had been given adrenaline reported feeling angry themselves. Unaware of the source of their arousal, they followed the actor's cues, deciding that they must be agitated by the questions as well. In another variation of the study, participants were instead paired with an oddly euphoric actor who passed his time building a tower out of folders, flying paper airplanes, and twirling hula hoops he had found in the corner. Here, participants surreptitiously injected with adrenaline not only joined in the fun, but also reported comparable feelings of elation.

These results demonstrate that even our own emotional states are not as cut-and-dried as we think. Both anger and euphoria are accompanied by physiological symptoms similar to the effects of adrenaline: racing heart, dilated pupils, elevated blood sugar. When we experience these sensations, our body doesn't automatically translate them into the corresponding emotion. Rather, we look to those around us to figure out what it all means, to determine which of the many emotional labels available fits the situation: *This guy sure is angry and this questionnaire sure is offensive . . . hey, I must be angry, too!*

Your emotions, your identity, your sense of how you're getting along in life—none of this self-knowledge emerges in the privacy of strictly internal processes. All of it is influenced by and even dependent on information gleaned from those around you.

CULTURAL SELVES

Sometimes people in our lives tell us directly who we are or should be. In other instances we use the performance of others as a point of mental comparison. But the influence of others on how we think of the self can be seen on a more societal level as well— broader social contexts also shape our sense of self in meaningful ways. The culture in which you grow up teaches you how to think about yourself through both explicit instruction and more subtle reminders.

In the United States, there's a saying that "the squeaky wheel gets the grease." In Japan, the prevailing fix-it-related axiom is "the nail that sticks out gets hammered down." This divergence in popular wisdom reflects differences in how people in these cultures typically think about the self.[15]

As I've alluded to previously, researchers have noted that Americans—and, more generally, those fitting the broader category of "Westerners"—tend to value in the self an independent streak. In Western culture, we emphasize what it is that makes us unique; we talk about each individual living up to his or her own potential. So educational TV shows tell us that "everyone is special." Preschools include self-esteem building as part of the curriculum. Squeaky wheels get grease and identity is conceived of in Dr. Philian terms of well-defined, internal selves.

When Americans or Canadians or Western Europeans complete the Twenty Statements Test, they use many a personality characteristic and other stable attribute:[16] "I am friendly." "I am funny." "I am an outgoing person." It's not too far removed from how Westerners perceive the behaviors of others. Indeed, the idea of a "core self" and the more general WYSIWYG mentality have much in common, epitomizing as they do a mind-set focused on character, on the distinctness of individuals, on the self as an entity independent from its surroundings.

These ideas stand in sharp contrast to the more interdependent view of the self prevalent in Japan, other Asian countries, and many African and Latin American cultures. In these societies, identity is typically a more collectivist concept that emphasizes the connectedness between the individual and those around her. That is, the self is most meaningfully thought of in terms of relationships with others and how one fits into the fabric of the larger society.[17]

What happens when Japanese complete the Twenty Statements Test? They tend to give responses less indicative of stable personality and more context-dependent: "I am a hard worker when at school." "I am patient with my children." "I am currently in my psychology class." In general, taking the test can be awkward, as self-assessment absent information regarding context is a relatively unfamiliar request in many such cultures.

Of course, as with any generalization, this divergence in cultural mentality is a tendency and not a rule. Individual excellence and personal achievement are not ignored in Asian societies; interpersonal cohesion is not a foreign concept to North Americans. But it's clear that self-perception differs by culture, and one doesn't even have to leave North American airspace to observe this. To illustrate, I ask you to visualize the following scenario: You're walking down a narrow corridor. A man walks toward you and, as he passes, refuses to yield, bumping into your shoulder. He then punctuates the exchange by bestowing upon you a new, vulgar nickname. How would you respond?

I know how I would, having experienced a variation on just such an interaction as a thirteen-year-old while hanging out with friends at the local suburban mall. My reaction? I came up with two years' worth of creative excuses not to go back to that mall. "Courageous" rarely makes an appearance when I take the Twenty Statements Test.

Your response would likely depend on where you were raised. When behavioral researchers exposed young American men to this experience—for shorthand, let's call it the "asshole" scenario[18]—those individuals who had grown up in the southern United States reacted very differently than did residents of the North. Compared to Northerners who suffered the same indignity, Southerners who were bumped into and insulted were more visibly agitated, more likely to think that their masculinity had been assailed, and even more primed for retaliation according to elevated testosterone levels.

To explain these findings, the researchers cited a "culture of honor" that exists in much of the southern United States. Drawing on the work of anthropologists and historians, they suggested that the herding-based economy of the frontier South, combined with an absence of adequate law enforcement, has led Southern males to develop and project an identity emphasizing toughness. In such a society, even trivial insults require overt responses, because to do otherwise would invite future exploitation—much like the importance of reputation in some contemporary urban neighborhoods or even prison yards. Raised in such an environment, the researchers argue, one learns to value a tough suffer-no-shit sense of self, perhaps explaining why argument-related homicides are more prevalent in the southern U.S., while other forms of homicide are not.[19]

The data are clear: I'd make a lousy herder, and I'm the last guy you want backing you up in a street fight. But more important, both the cross-cultural and "asshole" studies illustrate how profoundly context shapes our sense of self, and how such influence grows out of both mundane situation and cultural mind-set. The person standing next to me as I take the Twenty Statements Test impacts my responses, but so does the broader environment in which I was raised. We are social beings through and through, shaped by our surroundings even for the most personal of thought processes.

THE MIRROR ~~NEVER~~ LIES

Why is your sense of self so variable across situations? Because it depends, in large part, on who's around you and the culture in which you grew up. Because the process of introspection produces but a temporary snapshot of how you feel in this fleeting time and place. But there's another explanation, too.

To illustrate, consider the following: How good a driver are you? Admittedly, as an open-ended question, it's difficult to answer.

So use a scale of 0–100, where 0 is the absolute worst in the world, 50 is completely ordinary and average, and 100 is the absolute best in the world. Choose any number between 0 and 100—how does your driving stack up? Settle on your response before reading further.

Now, another question: How strong are your leadership skills? Again, compare yourself to the average person on the same scale of 0–100.

You should now have two numbers in mind—two numbers that quantify specific aspects of your self-concept.

Five bucks says both of them are greater than 50.

That's right, I'd put up my own money to bet you—and everyone else who reads this book—that you rated yourself an above-average driver and an above-average leader. From a purely rational perspective, the odds aren't in my favor. As far as I know, driving and leadership skills aren't usually related. In fact, I'd suggest that the mere existence of the occupation of chauffeur implies that the more successful leaders become, the less likely they are to drive themselves anywhere. So when calculating the probabilities underlying my wager, there's a fifty-fifty chance that you're an above-average driver and a separate fifty-fifty chance that you're an above-average leader. Multiply those, and there's only a 25 percent likelihood that you're above average in both domains.

Why, then, would I make such a wager, other than the fact that you and I don't have firm plans to see each other in the near future, making it difficult for you to collect if I lose? Because I didn't bet that you *are* above average in both. No, my bet was that you'd *think* you're an above-average driver and an above-average leader. And by my calculations, I'll win this bet twice as often as I'll lose it.

Put one hundred people in a room and with enough creativity and stamina you can collect the data to rank them by ability in any domain. By mathematical necessity, half will be below average and half above average. But put the same one hundred people in a room and *ask* them about their abilities? I do this every semester, asking students in my class the same driving question I posed to you. I explain the scale of 0–100. I tell them to compare themselves to "the average college student" and not just any average person (a preemptive strike against the potential argument that the class truly is full of above-average drivers when compared to the performance of, say, their grandparents). Before determining by a show of hands how many rated themselves above 50, I even have them close their eyes so as to prevent peer pressure or embarrassment.

What happens when the one hundred students open their eyes? They see eighty-five classmates with hands up.

Semester after semester, more than eight out of ten of my students report being above-average drivers. In Boston, mind you. In the capital of a state whose residents ranked number forty-eight out of fifty in an insurance company's recent "how well do you know the rules of the road" survey. A state with a department of motor vehicles that has deemed necessary the creation of something called "Driver Attitudinal Retraining" courses. A state so renowned for the aggressive driving habits of its residents that its name has inspired a vulgar portmanteau popular on T-shirts in the rest of New England—that's "Masshole" for those of you sartorially deprived by the options available at your local boutique.

(As an aside, to be fair to my fellow citizens of Boston, *you* try driving for a few months in a city whose allergy to grids and other right angles, allegiance to rotaries and one-way streets, and total indifference to road signs renders even Google Maps a shot in the dark. If your corresponding decline in driving performance and rise in arterial blood pressure don't convince you of the power of situations, few other experiences will.)

The notion that 85 percent of any audience is above average is, of course, a mathematical absurdity. Yet research suggests that this "better-than-average effect" is reliable enough to bet on:[20] If you ask them, most high school students have above-average organizational skills, most college students are better than average at getting along with others, most college professors conduct superior scholarship, and most married adults are in relationships that are happier than the norm. Oh, and most of us are better looking than the average person to boot.

Problematically and perhaps amusingly, this tendency is most exaggerated among those of us least competent to begin with. The worse we are at something, the better we often think we are, as any fan of *American Idol* can tell you. Knowing so little to begin with about a domain as basic as grammar, I'm left in no position to evaluate just how bad my own grammar be. Or how bad it is, for that matter. So while voice lessons will improve my singing and English courses my syntax, this increased competence may, ironically, also leave me better able to appreciate how far I have left to go.

IN SHORT, even if self-perception was not so dependent on context and other people, an "authentic" self would still be elusive because we so often fail to see ourselves for who we really are. Our processes of self-perception are usually less focused on accuracy than on self-enhancement and ego stroking. Like the dieter who goes out of his way to assess progress via "friendly" scale or mirror, we frequently feel the need to take stock of who we are and how we're doing—we just don't want the whole, unblemished truth.

How deeply ingrained is this tendency? Try the following experiment on a friend. First, jot down two columns of colors so that you wind up with a list of several pairs. Something like:

blue	yellow
green	purple
white	pink
black	gold
orange	blue
yellow	silver
purple	black
red	green

It doesn't matter if you repeat colors. In fact, it doesn't much matter if you use colors, ice cream flavors, or names of Pitt-Jolie children; this is just a warm-up act to throw her offtrack. When you show your friend the list, tell her to move down it as quickly as possible, circling in each pair which of the two items she likes most.

The second list you need to prepare should be in the same format, but containing letters of the alphabet. This one you can't throw together quite as haphazardly. Each pair should include one letter from your friend's first name and one letter not in her name.

So if you and I were friends (just humor me—the hypothetical enhances my own ego), you might make the following list, with target letters in bold just to illustrate:

S	P
K	**M**
Z	**A**
P	**M**
S	O
W	**A**
W	**M**
S	K

Now have your friend do the same thing as before, circling which letter she likes better in each pair as quickly as possible and without too much thought. It's a strange request, to be sure, but less so following the color-choosing warm-up.

Most people choose the letters from their own name at a rate far greater than the 50 percent that chance dictates.[21] We like ourselves a lot, even unconsciously. And this association of positive sentiment with the self rears its head in far more meaningful decisions as well (again, often unconsciously). Believe it or not, statistical analysis reveals a disproportionately high number of women named "Florence" living in Florida, as well as "Georgia" in Georgia, "Louise" in Louisiana, and "Virginia" in Virginia. For that matter, Dennis and Denise are more likely than others to go into dentistry, Larry and Laura to become lawyers, and George and Geoffrey to become geoscientists. One shudders to think of who's drawn to practicing gastroenterology in Saskatchewan.

Like the better-than-average effect, these surprising name-related findings reflect a propensity for seeing the world in an ego-enhancing light. Such self-serving tendencies are particularly likely when we're confronted with our own shortcomings and failures. Indeed, we have an entire toolbox of strategies that we use to maintain positive self-regard in the face of the humbling and threatening experiences that constitute daily life:

- We bask in the glory of others, even when we've had little to do with their success.[22] Whether touting our tenuous connections to the childhood-acquaintance-turned-celebrity or getting decked out in our alma mater's insignia after a football victory, it feels good to run with the winners. There's a reason those giant foam fingers sold at sports stadiums don't say "*They're #1.*"

- But when it comes to learning about ourselves through comparisons with others, it's the unsuccessful, unaccomplished individual who's the ideal target for our mental maneuvering.[23] Why do we look down the row to see how other people scored on the exam? In part because we seek context in which to place our own performance. But after a failure or other setback, we often just want to console ourselves with the conclusion that *at least I'm better off than that guy.*

- Even our deference to WYSIWYG falls by the wayside when ego is on the line.[24] We see others' missteps as indicating deficient personality, but we chalk up our own failings to external causes. When the customer in front of you in line pockets the extra change the cashier mistakenly gives him, you view him as dishonest; when you do the same thing, it's because the cashier was rude, you're in a hurry, and you're pretty sure the store is marking up prices to begin with.

We see the world around us in ways that are easy on the ego. Sure, these strategies amount to self-deception, but they help us through the rough patches in life. Injecting ourselves into the success stories of others . . . deflecting blame when things go wrong . . . tactics like these have restorative effects in the face of unfulfilled expectation; they buffer us from the threat of negative feedback. And these rose-colored lenses through which we see ourselves constitute just one more reason why getting to know "who you really are" isn't as easy as some would lead you to believe.

SELF-HELP REVISITED

What, then, *should* the gurus of self-help be telling you? Should they call you out on the habit of bending the truth when you look in the mirror? Might a forced dose of reality allow you to cut through the distortion and finally get to know your authentic self?

Nah.

Reality isn't all that it's cracked up to be, either. Sure, refusing to accept truths about the self poses problems. Consider the social drinker who's sure that he's OK to drive home because, unlike his friends, *he* can hold his liquor—not to mention that like Rain Man and 85 percent of the rest of us, he thinks he's an excellent driver. And if you always seek out less accomplished individuals for social comparison, how will you ever improve yourself? If you never take responsibility for anything that goes wrong, don't you become an intolerable blowhard?

Still, despite all this, stretching the truth a bit for ego's sake is arguably an important ingredient of, quote-unquote, normal daily functioning. Many of the unrealistic self-views we cling to are illusions, but they're positive illusions without which we'd spend much of our time miserable or wallowing in self-doubt.[25] Compared to those who are less satisfied, people content with life tend to exhibit more self-serving tendencies: from an unrealistically high opinion of themselves to an overly optimistic view of the future to an exaggerated sense of control over events around them.

Findings like these turn on its head conventional wisdom concerning what it means to be "normal." Ask most people about the thought processes associated with depression, and they'll describe an unrealistically pessimistic take on life, an Eeyore-like tendency to see things as gloomier than they really are. But the pervasiveness of self-serving distortions suggests that the ostensibly normal or happy among us are actually the ones out of touch with reality. Some research goes so far as to suggest that unfailingly accurate and unfiltered self-perception is linked to depression.

In a series of studies conducted by Lauren Alloy and Lyn Abramson at the University of Pennsylvania, male and female participants completed a written assessment of their depression level.[26] Immediately afterward, they were each led to a different location and seated in front of a green light with a button next to it. They were told that upon a signal from the researcher, they could push the button or choose to leave it alone. Sometimes when they pressed the button, the green light went on. Other times it didn't.

In reality, in most versions of the research, the button had no impact on the green light at all; it went on or stayed off a predetermined percentage of the time, regardless of what respondents did.

At the end of each session, participants were asked how much control they had over the light. Those individuals whose earlier questionnaire scores indicated that they were depressed accurately reported that they had little to no control. They recognized that there was no relationship between their button and the light. But nondepressed respondents saw things differently. These "normal" people exaggerated their control over the green light—a similar illusion to the one harbored by the overconfident patient who's sure that he'll be the one to buck the odds and avoid the treatment's side effects, or the superstitious sports fan who thinks that where she sits and what she wears might just change the outcome on the field. Beliefs like these are a familiar part of daily life.

And so it would seem that much like red wine, chocolate, and Jim Carrey movies, self-serving distortions have positive effects when enjoyed in moderation, but too much becomes hard to stomach. In the short term, a touch of self-enhancement allows you to salve the wounds of negative feedback and distressing outcome, buffering the ego until self-regard rebounds enough to resume the pursuit of long-term goals. Often, it's not accurate knowledge about the self that allows peace of mind; it's the bit of self-deception that helps us bounce back from setback and trudge on through failure.

ARE YOU LOOKING to be a happier, more productive, more successful person? Are you in the market for self-help? Then stop worrying about how to see yourself for who you really, truly are. Forget about this "authentic" self business. Instead, learn to embrace the notion of the self as flexible.

Yes, your processes of self-perception are context-dependent. And introspection yields different information at different times. Your sense of self varies depending on who you're with. Identity is malleable and personal preferences are constructed on the spot. But none of this is bad or distressing news.

So you're not the person you thought you were, at least not all the time? Big deal. Let that conclusion empower not alarm you.

It's refreshing to realize that you're not a finished product—that who you are in the here and now may not be the same person you'll be in the then and there. In fact, it's that opposite view of the self as a fixed entity that causes problems. When you assume that there's a true core self waiting to be discovered, that's when your potential seems limited and the world around you is full of threats to be rationalized away.

Consider one study of college freshmen in Hong Kong.[27] Researchers presented them with a series of statements regarding the stability of intelligence, including "you have a certain amount of intelligence and you really can't do much to change it" and "you can learn new things, but you can't really change your basic intelligence." Based on students' agreement or disagreement with these ideas, the researchers created two groups: those who saw their own intelligence as a predetermined, stable entity and those who thought of their own intellect in more malleable terms.

The freshmen were then asked whether they intended to enroll in a remedial English course in the years to come. Not surprisingly, those who had aced their high school English certification exam were less likely to plan on taking such a course than students who had scored in the C range or worse. But even among low-performing students, those who viewed intelligence level as etched in stone saw no need for remedial work. They were already as good as they were going to get at English, they figured. So why bother? Only the low performers with a less fixed view of their own intellect were willing to sign up for the additional English work that they really needed.

In other words, seeing the self as a static and stable entity is what puts us on the defensive and mandates chronic self-deception. Think of a characteristic like intelligence in terms of fixed capacity and the poor exam grade or subpar performance review becomes intolerably threatening. Instead, you should train yourself to view intellect—and any other aspect of your personal skill set—as a muscle that grows with effort and atrophies with neglect. When you accept that the answer to "Who am I?" should be written in pencil and not pen, threats become opportunities and failures transform into life lessons. Even if this isn't how you usually see things, it's not too late to start now.

Because in a follow-up study, the same researchers in Hong Kong demonstrated how easy it is to change how you think about yourself. They gave a new group of students one of two different, ostensibly scientific articles—articles that depicted intelligence in either static or flexible terms. Those led to think about intelligence as a fixed quantity took the easy way out: they showed little persistence on tasks in the wake of poor performance and they avoided taking on new challenges later. Only students told that intelligence was malleable showed the stick-to-itiveness necessary for self-improvement.

Or consider another study, this one with American students at Stanford asked to serve as pen pals with "at-risk" middleschoolers.[28] The college students were instructed to offer encouragement to the younger kids by explaining in their letters that they, too, had struggled at times in school but eventually persevered and found academic success. They were told to emphasize the idea that natural ability is overrated—that intelligence "is not a finite endowment but rather an expandable capacity."

Did these letters help the middle school students bounce back from adversity? It's impossible to say—the letters were never delivered. But the mere experience of writing them had a lasting impact on the college students themselves. Months later, the letter writers were still reporting greater enjoyment of school than were other Stanford undergrads. Their grade point averages were higher, too, by a full third of a point on a four-point scale. The effect of writing the letters was particularly strong among African American participants, a promising finding for diverse universities seeking to remedy the underperformance too often observed among students of color.

So what *should* the gurus of self-help be telling you?

That the aftermath of failure and setback is precisely when you need to remember that the self is flexible.

That you're better off focusing on effort and other controllable factors rather than fixed aptitude.

That you can forget about "not being a _____ kind of person," whatever the presumed deficit in your supposedly authentic self may be.

Bad grade on your paper? Lousy earnings projections for the quarter? First one voted off the celebrity dancing show? Now that you recognize how self-perception really works, you know the dangers of chalking up setback to a hopeless lack of ability. But you also know better than to automatically shrug it off as bad luck or someone else's fault. Instead, force yourself to ponder or even make a list of the changeable factors—internal and external—that can bring about better outcomes the next time around.

Because whether you're a Hong Kong student struggling with English or a pen pal at Stanford, good things happen when you embrace the self as malleable. Regardless of what you read in the self-help aisle, you don't have to lose sleep hunting for your core identity or reconnecting with your inner you. Chicken soup and numbered lists are overrated.

Instead, it's time to start appreciating that you're a different person in different settings.

To recognize that who you are today need not dictate who you'll be tomorrow.

And to accept that the "authentic" self isn't some sort of Holy Grail, unless by the analogy you mean that you aren't sure whether or not it even exists in the first place.

5.

MARS AND VENUS
HERE ON EARTH

ACCORDING TO LITERALLY HUNDREDS OF RESEARCH studies, the human male is more physically aggressive than his female counterpart, regardless of age group, culture, or geographical region.[1]

According to statistical analysis of newspaper personal ads, women tend to seek older partners with stable incomes, whereas men place greater emphasis on a potential mate's youth and physical appearance.[2]

According to my brazenly loud, then two-year-old daughter during the course of a formal dinner reception, girls have a butt that only goes potty sitting down, while a boy's butt works standing up.

There are myriad differences between men and women, as we learn at a young age. Life expectancy. Earning potential. Crying during weddings. Propensity for bringing reading material to the toilet. This litany of apparent sex differences runs the gamut from fodder for stand-up comics to more important discrepancies with sobering societal implications.

Though "gender gaps"* are visible across a range of domains, they share something in common: how we think about them. Like the personalities of others and our own identities, we usually see sex differences as fixed—as stable and even inevitable disparities arising from internal causes. When we hear that boys are more likely to X, or women are better at Y, our first instinct is to turn to innate explanations based on physiology, hormones, or predisposition. In other words, as someone once famously and lucratively suggested, men are from Mars and women are from Venus.

Why, then, are males more aggressive? Because of testosterone, we assume—it's just boys being boys. Why do women often prefer older, career-minded men? Because in the more dangerous societies of our genetic ancestors, natural selection must have bestowed advantages unto those females who landed a high-status mate. And so on.

This notion of immutable, inborn gender gaps overlooks the critical role of context. Just as situations help dictate our sense of self and whether we remain passive or take action, so, too, are many gender differences surprisingly context-dependent. While

---

*Technically speaking, "sex" is a biological descriptor and "gender" is a social construction related to roles, perceptions, and identity. Colloquially, however, we tend to use these two terms more or less interchangeably, as many a demographic questionnaire illustrates. So in this chapter, you'll see phrases like "sex difference" and "gender gap" used more or less interchangeably as well.

the analogy of men and women as life-forms from different planets is amusingly and appealingly straightforward, in the end, it's just extraterrestrial WYSIWYG. My daughter's anatomical observations aside, we male and female earthlings are far more similar than different—at least in terms of how we see and react to the social universe.

THE PREVIOUS CHAPTERS shed light on the ways in which other people shape our thoughts and actions. But the power of situations doesn't always come in the form of specific others in our immediate surroundings. The effects of context can be more ethereal. With gender, it's not typically that particular individuals around us tell men to behave one way and women another. Instead, subtler forces of unspoken expectation and societal norms drive the emergence of gender difference. And nothing I've studied academically has taught me this lesson as well as my fledgling parenting career has.

Having grown up as one of three brothers, my new status as the father of two girls has been the source of repeated revelation over the past half decade. These days, I'm well versed in sartorial concepts such as the halter top and pinafore. I can pontificate on the relative merits of hair bands versus clips. I find myself able to explain the difference between passé and plié, and depending on how my back feels, I can even demonstrate.

But perhaps the greatest change I've experienced in the past few years is my newfound sensitivity to the gendered messages we convey to kids on a regular basis. As just one example, to celebrate the birth of each of our daughters, some family members gave us embroidered alphabet quilts. Not wanting to get two of the exact same gift, they opted for a different color scheme the second time around. So we now have one blanket that's pink and green and one that's blue and red. According to the experts at Pottery Barn Kids, the difference transcends color scheme—per official catalogue nomenclature, we own one "girls' quilt" and one "boys' quilt."

What does this actually mean? Well, most of the images on the two quilts are the same. Both have a picture of apple for *A* and blocks for *B*, for example. For other letters, there are slight variations: the boys' quilt depicts an empty wagon for *W*, while the girls' quilt shows a wagon with a doll in it.

Boys' Quilt   Girls' Quilt

But there are some not-so-subtle differences as well. Boys get a pencil for *P*. And why not? Boys grow up to be authors, architects, draftsmen.

What about girls? Their quilt has a purse. Girls like to shop.

Now, look at the *R* and *S* panels on the previous page. On the left is the "boy" version, with a radio for *R* and a shooting star for *S*. On the right is the "girl" quilt: *R* is for ring and *S* is for shoes.

Naturally. Because girls aren't interested in music or astronomy or science. Only jewelry. Oh, and fashionable footwear.

These quilts are but the tip of the iceberg when it comes to the different contexts in which boys and girls grow up. They capture the well-entrenched gender norms we convey to children as soon as they're born (and sometimes even earlier). Mere minutes after becoming parents, new mothers and fathers are already more likely to see their daughters as "fine-featured" or "delicate" and their sons as "strong."[3] This despite the fact that newborn humans are a lot like snails—the male and female varieties are nearly indistinguishable unless you flip them over and blow on them.

Indeed, when my older daughter tells me she wants to be either Peter Pan or a knight for Halloween because the female protagonists from the movies she watches "don't do anything interesting," it's hard to argue. These female characters mostly tend to domestic concerns while patiently and prettily awaiting the rescue of a prince or other male lead. Fighting for the right to choose their own husband is what passes for strength of character and independence of spirit. And this is just eighty minutes' worth of gendered messages in the course of one day. In some cultures, different opportunities for men and for women are still codified by law or religious decree, rendering the impact of gender-based expectations far more problematic. But even subtler societal cues about gender have a dramatic impact on how we think and act.

This chapter explores gender through the lens of context. It considers situational influences ranging from the mundane world of baby quilts, Disney princesses, and fast-food drive-thrus to more institutionalized expectations conveyed in the classroom and workplace. It challenges the notion of entrenched gender gaps, asking instead under which circumstances such differences emerge and when they disappear. Because situations matter, even for a distinction as basic as male and female, and that's a conclusion that matters as well, whether you're a parent or principal, manager or marketer.

Far too infrequently do we ponder how ordinary situations shape our thoughts about gender. Or to what extent the apparent differences between men and women are context-dependent rather than inevitable. All too often even the most well-educated and powerful among us look right past the situation in thinking about gender.

Just ask Larry Summers.

MATH IS HARD

It's inescapable: women are vastly underrepresented in the fields of science, engineering, and mathematics. In January 2005 the National Bureau of Economic Research held a conference in Cambridge, Massachusetts, devoted to exploring this disparity. One of the headlining speakers was Larry Summers, then president of Harvard University.

In a lunchtime talk, Summers focused on the gender gap in science and engineering positions at elite universities, evaluating three possible explanations.[4] The first, as he referred to it, was the "high-powered job" hypothesis, the idea that women are less likely to consent to the schedule and family sacrifices necessary to attain such a position. Second, he discussed the possibility of gender differences in innate math and science ability. Third, he addressed societal considerations, such as socialization pressures that steer boys and girls toward different disciplines, and the potential for discrimination in hiring and promotion decisions.

Within two months, prompted in large part by this very talk, the Harvard faculty passed a motion of "no confidence" in the leadership of their president. By the following winter, Summers had resigned.

What was so incendiary about his remarks? After all, Summers just articulated, in his own words, "three broad hypotheses about the sources of the very substantial disparities that this conference's papers document." And he was anything but dismissive of the problem—to the contrary, he ended his talk by stating that "I think we all need to be thinking very hard about how to do better on these issues." So why the controversy?

Summers ran into trouble because he did more than present three hypotheses worthy of exploration. He also ranked these explanations in terms of how he saw their relative importance. There would have been no controversy had he stopped after the suggestion that the relative dearth of female scientists and mathematicians could be attributable to 1) family-related pressures *or* 2) inborn differences in aptitude *or* 3) societal expectations. But he continued as follows: "In my own view, their importance probably ranks in exactly the order that I just described."

It's easy to see why so many at Harvard were distressed by their president's belief that innate ability plays a greater role in the underrepresentation of females than societal or institutional factors. After all, he's the guy who signed off on faculty performance reviews and pay raises, and here he was endorsing a view of the gender gap as largely biological and inevitable. Even before he gave this talk, many faculty members already had questions about Summers's commitment to gender equity: during his administration, tenured job offers to women at Harvard had dropped dramatically, to the point where only four out of thirty-two new hires the previous year were female.[5] So while some outsiders and media pundits decried Summers's ouster and celebrated him as a victim of the overzealous speech police, it's easy to appreciate the concerns held by those who were working under his immediate supervision.

But even from across town and outside his jurisdiction, I found Summers's comments disquieting. Living in Boston in the aftermath of the controversy, I felt the need to bestow upon him a parenthetical middle name anytime casual conversation veered in his direction—as in, Larry (No Relation) Summers. This desire to distance myself from his comments reflected not political considerations but rather more scientific concerns. You see, beyond being controversial, Summers's conclusions were also flat-out wrong. And twice over, at that.

Take a closer look at one brief passage from Summers's remarks: In arguing his position, he claimed that "the human mind has a tendency to grab [on] to the socialization hypothesis when you can see it. And it often turns out not to be true."

Really?

Let's take these assertions one at a time. First, the argument that the human mind tends to grab on to socialization hypotheses. This was an off-the-cuff remark for which Summers offered no real supporting evidence. And it flies in the face of everything you've now learned regarding the WYSIWYG mentality.

Just think about it: When the mom at the playground tries to excuse her son's rambunctiousness, does she latch on to the socialization hypothesis, suggesting that he's only acting this way because this is what society expects of boys? Of course not—she shrugs her shoulders and says something along the lines of "Well, you know how it is with boys."

In analyzing the actions of the cheating husband—be he politician, athlete, or next-door neighbor—do we veer toward the socialization account, arguing that society is simply more tolerant of such bad behavior from men versus women, thereby reinforcing the male tendency for infidelity? No, our first move is in the opposite direction, toward debate about whether monogamy runs contrary to the way that men are naturally wired.

And when the best-selling author pitches his manifesto on the psychology of gender differences, does he title it "Men Are Taught to Act Like Martians, Women Learn to be Venusian"? Clearly, no. He opts for the quintessential WYSIWYG thesis, that men and women might as well be beings from different planets.

Despite Summers's claim, we don't gravitate toward the socialization hypothesis—quite the contrary. Our knee-jerk reaction to gender disparity is to offer internal, innate, and immutable explanations. Often, it's only the concern of appearing sexist—our deference to political correctness—that leads us to claim otherwise in public. Larry Summers had it backward.

Admittedly, though, it's the second half of Summers's quoted statement that's the more important part. So what to make of this claim, the idea that the socialization hypothesis "often turns out not to be true"? If Summers was right, it would lend empirical heft to the argument that he was unfairly pilloried for his remarks. To the extent that gender differences in domains such as science and math are consistent across situations—that is, resistant to variations in context and expectation—his conference comments, while still controversial, would at least carry the stamp of research support.

Unfortunately for Summers, the data aren't kind to him on this count, either. But don't feel too bad for Not-My-Uncle Larry—I'm sure he'll land on his feet somewhere. You know, like director of economic policy at the Obama White House, for starters.

ALMOST A DECADE BEFORE Summers's talk, three researchers at the University of Michigan—Steve Spencer, Claude Steele, and Diane Quinn—set out to test just how entrenched the gender difference in math is.[6] Their first study was straightforward: they recruited twenty-eight male and twenty-eight female college students to take a difficult standardized test. These students were all high achievers—to be eligible for the study, they had to have scored in the eighty-fifth percentile or better on their math SAT.

The study's results were also straightforward: the men did much better than the women. In fact, the average score for male test takers was more than twice as high as the average for females, a gender difference practically begging for a simple Mars/Venus/Larry Summers explanation.

But the researchers refrained from jumping to conclusions about sex-based differences in math aptitude. Instead, they kept digging. They wondered why such a gender gap would emerge when all these men and women had enjoyed previous success in math. The women in the study spent just as long working on each problem as did the men—why were their scores so much lower? To answer these lingering questions the researchers ran another study that included more than a simple gender comparison. This time, they also varied the context in which the test was taken.

Specifically, half of this new group of men and women again took a math test under normal circumstances. The other half received a different set of instructions that changed the entire context of their experience. Before the test, this second group was told that while some previous research had found evidence of gender differences in math ability, other studies hadn't. These students heard that the test they were about to take fell into the latter category—it had been found to avoid any type of gender disparity.

This little change in procedure made a big, big difference.

Students who took the test without additional instructions once again exhibited a gender gap: men's scores were almost three times higher than women's. Students who took the test under the impression that it was gender-balanced? No gender difference at all. The average scores for these men and women were nearly identical.

It's a pretty amazing finding. All the students took *exactly* the same math test. Under normal circumstances, the average man out-performed the average woman, a disparity consistent with the idea of entrenched, even inborn differences in math ability. But tell students that the test was engineered to be "gender-neutral"—you know, no word problems involving football blitzes, testicle care, and the like? Then the sex difference vanished entirely. Just like that.

How a test is described is far from the only situational factor that can eliminate (or exacerbate) the gender gap in math. Asked to solve math problems in mixed company, women don't perform as well as men, but this underperformance goes away when the test is administered in single-sex groups.[7] Shown a series of ads depicting girls as fixated on boys and shopping, women do poorly on a subsequent math test, yet there's no gender difference after they watch commercials about intelligent and articulate women.[8]

And in a study that sounds eerily like a recurring nightmare I had in junior high, researchers even examined the effects of taking a math test while wearing a bathing suit.[9] How, exactly, did they pull this off? Participants were told that the study was about consumer preferences. Led to a private dressing room with a full-length mirror, they were presented with a rack of swimsuits—trunks for men and one-pieces for women—and asked to try on the one closest to their size. Then, much as those who climb Everest must stop every few thousand feet to reacclimate, students were told that they'd have fifteen minutes to get used to the unfamiliar clothes they were now wearing. To pass the time, they could help some researchers in the neighboring department of education by completing an ostensibly unrelated test of mathematical aptitude.

Clad in water-repellent Lycra, men outperformed women on

the math test. For the fortunate participants asked to try on and evaluate a sweater instead, the gender difference was far smaller.

What do we learn from these findings? Namely, that the gender disparity in math isn't entrenched and unavoidable. It depends on context, perspective, and expectation. It's actually surprisingly fragile. You can't put much stock in the notion of inborn, immutable differences in aptitude when minor tweaks to a test's instructions—or, for that matter, a nice cardigan—reduces or even wipes out the gender gap.

These very different studies converge upon a situational conclusion: remind women of the low expectations society holds for them in math and they will, indeed, underperform. Whether in the form of purportedly scientific conclusions regarding the genetic superiority of the male brain[10] or a bathing suit that conjures up thoughts of female objectification, simple reminders of gender-based stereotypes are threatening enough to undermine actual math performance.

Think of how little it takes in this research to lead women to worry that they might confirm the expectation that they aren't cut out for math. Merely having men in the room is enough. In fact, just thinking about math does the trick: even though women do fine when they're told a math test is gender-neutral, their default tendency is to assume otherwise. And this message that girls can't do math is a self-fulfilling one. Recent education research demonstrates that it's reinforced in the classroom itself, as female elementary school teachers' own anxieties about math predict increased anxiety and decreased performance among their female students.[11]

The ease with which women can be prompted to think about

low math expectations reflects a reality in which the onslaught of gendered messages begins early in life and never really lets up. And I'm not just talking about my daughters' quilts. Remember the notorious talking Barbie doll from the early 1990s that cheerfully reminded girls that "Math is hard"? OK, so the exact quote was actually "Math class is tough," but same idea. Thanks to movies, TV shows, toys, and blankets, young girls don't even have to leave the comfort of home to learn what's expected of them when it comes to math. The answer is not very much.

Contrary to Larry Summers's suggestion, you can't explain the gender gap in the sciences and math *without* considering the major role played by social forces. A predominantly biological account doesn't square with the data. Not to mention that it never really made sense in the first place why testosterone would draw men to the Pythagorean theorem like some mathematical version of a monster truck rally. How, exactly, is the Y chromosome supposed to help with long division? Sure, over generations and generations, natural selection can lead men and women to evolve in different ways, but why would any of them involve trigonometry?

As one last example, consider that in 1983 boys outnumbered girls thirteen to one in the ranks of students scoring 700 or better on the math SAT. Almost thirty years later, that ratio is less than three to one. Two and a half decades is a long time: long enough in the United States for five different presidents and a doubling of postage rates. But it's nowhere close to long enough for evolution to have reversed course or for hardwired differences between the male and female brain to have evened out. Those explanations just don't cut it.

Arguing that the gender gap in math performance results primarily from inborn, inescapable differences in aptitude is more than just politically incorrect. It's also wrong.

READY TO RUMBLE?

Perhaps you never really bought into the idea of male math superiority. So maybe the fragility of that gender difference doesn't strike you as particularly surprising or impressive. Well, then, how about the granddaddy of all gender differences? What about the well-documented conclusion that men are more aggressive than women? Could situational forces really have anything to do with that gender gap?

As cited in the opening of this chapter, scores of studies have found males to be more physically aggressive than females, regardless of age or culture. Moreover, much like science and engineering are fields disproportionately dominated by men, so is the act of homicide, both in terms of perpetrators and victims. And there are biological explanations for such gender differences: testosterone has been directly linked to aggression in studies involving people as well as animals.

But the nature of this gender difference depends, first and foremost, on how you define "aggression." When talking in strictly physical terms, males are more aggressive than females. However, dictionary definitions of aggression aren't limited to physical acts: rather, they describe a more general category of hostile behavior intended to cause injury. When you cast this wider net, you find that women are actually as aggressive as men—it's just that their aggression often looks different.

Child development research has found that starting in early elementary school, boys are more likely to engage in direct forms of aggression like physical domination and verbal assault, while girls more often practice indirect efforts to cause harm.[12] This *Mean Girls* route to aggression focuses on the manipulation of social relations. Such as, for example, campaigns to convince the group not to be friends with a particular child. Gossip. Or announcing to Mrs. Robbins's entire fifth-grade class that Sam's shirt wasn't "a real polo shirt" because the guy on the horse was holding a flag instead of a mallet.

Damn you, Knights of the Round Table® and your deceptively haute logo!

In strictly physical terms, aggression is more of a male tendency. But defined more socially or relationally, women assume the lead in this Pyrrhic battle of the sexes. And when you consider "aggression" in more general terms, it becomes difficult to identify a consistent gender difference in either direction.

Even if we stick to the realm of physical aggression, however, the gender gap isn't as entrenched as we think it is. When behavioral scientists study aggressive behavior in a research laboratory— by, for example, giving adults the opportunity to administer electric shocks or blast another person with loud bursts of white noise through headsets—men regularly emerge as more likely to aggress. This gender difference goes away, though, when participants are first provoked.[13] That is, while women are indeed less likely than men to initiate an aggressive interaction, they tend to be just as physically aggressive in response to insult or direct threat.

Moreover, you're already familiar with another contextual factor that can eliminate gender differences in aggression: direct orders from authority. Milgram's famous obedience study was also an examination of aggression, as respondents believed that they were giving painful (and even lethal) shocks to a fellow participant. Though most would have predicted otherwise, Milgram found no evidence of a gender gap in aggressive behavior: women in his study performed no differently than men, administering shocks just as great in number and voltage.

So women are just as physically aggressive as men after provocation or in the face of direct orders. And women aren't lacking in the general drive to aggress—rather, they just tend to channel this impulse in different, less physical ways than men do. These conclusions don't jive with the idea of a gender difference in aggression based on innate or biological factors. Instead, it seems more like women have many of the same aggressive tendencies as men, but they're compelled to keep these feelings at bay most of the time. It's as if something else causes them to hold back, or at least to aggress in ways that are less overt or easily recognized.

It's those quilts again. Or, more precisely, those ubiquitous societal norms regarding gender. Women aren't supposed to be aggressive, but men in a scuffle are just boys being boys. Thus, women often refrain from showing an aggressive side unless they have an obvious excuse for it. Or they try to inflict harm, but in subtler ways.

Is this mere speculation on my part, this indictment of gender norms when it comes to aggression? Well, how else to explain why the *M* panel on my daughters' quilts shows macramé for girls and machete for boys?

OK, not really—*M* is always for moon. But there is clear evidence linking gender norms to the apparent gender difference in aggression. Namely, that when researchers place men and women in a context in which gender is unimportant or even unidentifiable, the Mars/Venus difference in aggression disappears.

In one study at Princeton, researchers randomly selected names from a campus directory and invited eighty-four students to the lab in groups of six.[14] Upon arrival, half of each group was directed to sit in the front of the room. They wrote their names on large name tags and were asked aloud a series of questions about their personal background and experiences. The researcher explained to these three individuals that their performance would be monitored closely for the duration of the study.

The other three students stayed in the back of the room throughout this public inquisition. They didn't answer questions, they didn't put on name tags, and they were told that their performance would remain anonymous so as to create a nameless comparison group for the research. They just sat there and watched quietly.

At this point, all six students were led to a computer room and seated at individual terminals. Their next task was to play a strategy game during which they had to both defend their own territory against a bombing assault and attack their opponent's territory. Each participant played the same game against a computer-controlled opponent, though they thought they were playing against someone else in the room.

How aggressively did students attack their cyber opponents? The front-of-the-room name-tag-wearing half exhibited a familiar gender difference: women used only twenty-seven bombs per game compared to thirty-one for men. The women played less aggressively.

But a funny thing happened among the anonymous participants. Informed that their individual performance wouldn't be assessed, confident that no one would know what they had or hadn't done, everyone was more aggressive. Even more noteworthy, women were no longer outaggressed by their male compatriots. Liberated from concerns about appearance or how they were "supposed" to act, the average female now outbombed the average male, forty-one to thirty-seven.

Sugar and spice and everything nice, sure . . . but not afraid to take the gloves off as long as nobody's looking.

THE SHAPE I'M IN

I am directionally challenged. I have made wrong turns that have taken me over out-of-the-way bridges and inadvertently across state lines. When walking to restaurant bathrooms, only if I memorize and then reverse the sequence of maneuvers en route will I find my table again afterward. I once got so lost driving to my own high school that I just went back home and skipped classes for the day—as a senior in my fourth year at the same school.

Unfortunately, my frequent copilot is of little help. My wife claims to be map-illiterate, and the more urgent my request for navigational assistance in the car, the more flustered she becomes. Before the wonderful world of GPS, the only way we were able to find unfamiliar destinations—not to mention save our marriage—was for her to drive and me to read the map.

I know, I know . . . we're quite the impressive couple. You'd think our gene pools would've been weeded out generations ago, yet here we are.

Our different directional shortcomings have more to do with our limitations as individuals than any sort of universal gender difference. But navigation is yet another walk of life for which there are plenty of expectations regarding gender. Like the stereotype that men (present company excluded) have the better sense of direction. Or the notion that women are still less likely to get lost because, unlike their male counterparts, they're not too stubborn to stop and ask for directions.

The former belief, at least, garners support from the scientific literature on spatial skill. Over the years, many cognitive scientists have compared male and female performance on tasks such as 3-D visualization and mental rotation.[15] In one series of studies, respondents were presented with what is known as the "Mental Cutting Test." Not quite the paranormal experience it sounds like, the test requires the participant to recognize what an object would look like if it were sliced in half. Other research studies have asked men and women to navigate through a virtual reality maze or to determine which of several three-dimensional shapes could be created by folding a particular two-dimensional cutout.

Though the exact difference varies by task, a clear conclusion emerges from hundreds of studies like these conducted over several decades: men perform better than women. Be it mental cutting, folding, or rotating—the spatial skill triathlon, if you will—the average man outperforms the average woman.

While these tasks may seem trivial, this gender disparity is of some societal significance. Just think how important shape rotation is to a wide range of meaningful endeavors. Like engineering. Organic chemistry. Moving furniture. Tetris. No doubt, this is precisely the type of research that Larry Summers might have pointed to in support of the notion of innate differences in how men and women think.

To be fair, there is some persuasive evidence that when it comes to the gender gap in spatial skills, biological and inborn processes play a role. How else to explain that developmental psychologists have reported that five-month-old infant boys are already better than girls at recognizing when they've seen a rotated object before?[16] Or that neuroscientists have found women's spatial skills to fluctuate by hormone level, with better performance during menstruation and poorer performance right after ovulation?[17]

So while I've devoted this book to championing the power of situations, I'd never suggest that there are no biological answers to questions about gender differences. That would be an outrageous claim. Biology does contribute to differences in how men and women think and act.

But these gender gaps in thought and behavior aren't nearly as pervasive or entrenched as we think they are. Quite often, situations trump physiology. For example, the male advantage in spatial skill winds up being just as context-dependent as other gender differences. You can eliminate this gap the same way as for math: convince women that the stereotypes don't apply. In one study, German researchers asked 161 adults to complete what they believed to be a measure of their ability to empathize with others.[18] Half of the respondents read about a family-oriented woman who worked part-time; others read about a self-confident man with a high-powered job. They were then told to imagine themselves in this protagonist's shoes while answering several questions.

Only then were all participants given nine shape-rotation problems. After having envisioned themselves in a female role, women answered only 3.9 spatial questions correctly, while men averaged 5.1. But after empathizing with an alpha male, the spatial skill difference went away: women averaged the same 5.5 questions right as the men.

It's a striking finding for what seems like an entrenched gender disparity. But it's also old news. That is, you've already read about this sort of situational influence on math performance as well as aggression. The new lesson offered by research on spatial skill doesn't have to do with expectations of female underperformance. Rather, it's that the outward appearance of gender can distract us from the even more influential differences at play.

Gender is about more than reproductive anatomy or hormones or—as I was recently informed by a preschooler in the midst of what I foolishly assumed would be a private shower—the fact that Daddy's boobies are smaller yet hairier than Mommy's (a conclusion, I'll note, for which the entire family is grateful, two times over). Gender also predicts different life experiences, and these nonphysical divergences often account for gender gaps in domains such as spatial skill.

To affect the gender difference in spatial performance, you don't have to trick or distract people. It isn't necessary to ask research participants to visualize high-powered men or convince them they'll be anonymous or even goad them into taking tests in swimwear. All you have to do is think about what gender really means in the context of mental rotation and the navigation of unfamiliar places. You just need to ask yourself what are the other important differences related to spatial skill for which anatomical sex is but a superficial proxy.

The answer—or at least, one of them—is almost too mundane and lowbrow to believe. One key to unlocking the mystery behind the gender gap in spatial cognition turns out to be . . . video games.

IN 2007, CANADIAN PSYCHOLOGISTS conducted a run-of-the-mill mental rotation study and found, as usual, that men outperformed women. But these researchers did more than record the gender of their college participants. They also assessed other characteristics that they thought might predict spatial aptitude, like age, academic major, and how often they played video games.[19]

It was an idea brilliant in its simplicity. The more time spent playing video games, the more practice students would have navigating unfamiliar spaces, manipulating visual objects, and evaluating novel images. Male or female, gaming experience should translate into better spatial performance. This is exactly what researchers found: students averaging more than four hours of video games per week outperformed the nongamers on a mental rotation task.

What about gender? Well, anyone who has ever been to an arcade can vouch for the fact that there's nothing inherently masculine about video games. But few would argue with the premise that young men devote far more time to the pursuit than do young women. Just ask the dryer repairman who—in the midst of a recent service call at our house—proudly told me of his decision to tighten his budgetary belt by canceling phone service rather than give up the monthly subscription that allows him to play Xbox games against strangers in Europe. Apparently, his girlfriend was less than enthusiastic about his economic recovery plan.

I confess that I have also spent too much time and money on such endeavors. My youth, like those of many men I know, was littered with tropical vacations spent inside windowless game rooms, school formals skipped in the name of "beating the next level," and college Nintendo football leagues that mandated 2:00 a.m. walks across campus to play scheduled games against computer-controlled opponents. Had I devoted even a fraction of this energy to, say, emotionally meaningful conversation with others—standard operating procedure among the females of the species, I'm told—perhaps more of my long-term memory would be devoted to remembering friends' birthdays or the names of their spouses and kids, with less space filled by secret game codes that get you thirty extra lives.

(That's up-up-down-down-left-right-left-right-B-A-start, by the way.)

Does this difference in men's and women's exposure to video games really help explain the gender gap in spatial skill? The same Canadian research team ran a second study to find out. They recruited students with no gaming experiences over the past four years, and, once again, men scored higher than women on tests of spatial skill.

Then these same students were subjected to four weeks of intensive "video game training." They went into a research suite and played several hours of a first-person military shooting game on multiple occasions. The effects of this monthlong not-so-basic training? Spatial test scores improved across the board, but *especially* for women. And this improvement was long lasting: five months later, the positive effects of the video game sessions were still evident in the students' spatial performance. Just imagine the cumulative effects of an entire childhood devoted to gaming.

The lessons of the video game study are twofold. First, our moms had it all wrong. It wasn't a waste of time spending a beautiful summer afternoon squirreled away in a dark basement or grimy arcade exploring cyber castles and dodging monkey-thrown barrels—we were just working toward careers in engineering.

Second, studying gender is tricky. When researchers want to assess the effects of, say, Drug X, they randomly assign patients to take the drug and others to take nothing (or some sort of placebo). Then they compare final outcomes across the two groups. Having assigned the treatment and control groups at random, the researchers can be confident that any disparities at the end of the study must result from Drug X.

But no matter how hard they try, scientists just can't *assign* gender to research participants. All researchers can do is compare outcomes across the naturally occurring male/female distinction and then try to explain any disparities that emerge. That's the blueprint that most gender studies follow. The complication is that our WYSIWYG tendencies send us straight for the internal explanation:

Men outperform women on spatial skill tests? It must be because of physiology. Or hormones. Or sex-differentiated evolutionary pressures.

Young girls read and write at a more advanced level than boys of the same age? Must be those same internal processes at play, just in reverse.

These are the first answers to which we turn. And we get so carried away that we sometimes even fabricate new inborn physical differences that don't actually exist, like the Garden of Eden–inspired allegory of Eve's extra rib (for the record, men and women actually have the same number of ribs).

Rarely do we stop to consider the different experiences accompanying biological distinctions between the sexes. Such as exposure to gender norms—those messages about what men and women are supposed to do or be good at—or the other, nonsexual differences that go along with growing up male versus female in our society. Like the different ways in which boys and girls pass their idle childhood hours, and the extent to which these activities help refine certain cognitive skills (or, alternatively, interfere with the development of other good habits, like reading).

Biology plays a role in men's and women's spatial skills, as the infant and menstruation studies demonstrate. But too often we infer rather than examine directly the physiological basis for gender disparities. If I told you that my latest study found that sixty-five-year-old women are better than men of similar age at getting a baby to sleep or lending a sympathetic ear to a forlorn friend or calculating a household budget, would you attribute the finding to estrogen level? Sex differences in brain structure? I doubt it. And you'd be wise to avoid such jumps to innate conclusions when it comes to other gender gaps, such as those involving mental aptitude and cognitive skill.

RETHINKING GENDER

It can be a chicken-and-egg question, this matter of gender norms and gender difference. Many argue that the differences come first. That, yes, we have divergent expectations for men and women, but they grow out of real preexisting differences between the sexes. That we expect boys, but not girls, to wrestle with friends, get grass stains within minutes of going outside, and turn paper towel rolls into swords, because these are precisely the activities toward which boys are magnetically drawn.

One goal of this chapter has been to get you to ponder the flip side possibility, even if for a fleeting moment. Believe me, I know what I'm up against: it's hardly a popular or intuitive argument that our expectations precede many of the gender differences we observe. I've heard many a parent who has both a boy and a girl explain that their kids were born as if from different planets   one ready to bash into walls, one prone to cautious yet methodical exploration. And researchers now increasingly focus on physiological explanations as well, such as linking prenatal exposure to hormones like testosterone with children's brain structure and subsequent social tendencies.

We're comfortable with this notion of gender gaps as mandated by biological difference. It makes sense. After all, men are taller and heavier than women. So why not inherently better at directions? Or worse at reining in their temper?

But ask yourself what it means that many seemingly well-entrenched differences are so context-dependent. That you can wipe out gender gaps in math, navigation, and even aggression by convincing women of their anonymity or asserting that the well-known gender norms don't apply in this particular instance.

For that matter, even the link between testosterone and aggression is not as ironclad as scientists once thought. A recent European study found that telling women they've been given an oral dose of testosterone leads them to bargain with a partner in a more aggressive manner—that's what we assume testosterone is *supposed* to do. But when the hormone was actually administered, it had no such effect, instead leaving women more likely to make equitable, generous first offers to their partners, exactly the opposite of what we might expect to happen.[20] The more precise conclusion regarding the effects of testosterone seems to be that it increases motivation to seek and preserve social status. In some situations that means physical aggression, but in other contexts it leads to consensus building or efforts to ward off dissent.

Returning to the idea of parental perceptions, as you've read, I have two kids. They've also come into this world exhibiting very different characteristics—in terms of sleep pattern, hair color, hot dog condiment preference, and baseball team affiliation. Some of these tendencies seem more inborn than others. But because I have two girls, I've been liberated from the assumption that my kids' differences are driven by gender.

Freed from this default expectation, I've also come to notice that my kids' skills and limitations, their likes and dislikes, fluctuate wildly by context. It just so happened that the weekend before my older daughter shared her indifference to the female protagonists of standard kids' movie fare, I had purchased the original *Star Wars* trilogy to bring on a beach vacation with a rainy forecast. So we broke out the first DVD a few days early.

It took less than an hour for her to zero in on Princess Leia as her new costume of choice for October. And as the plastic light saber–inflicted damage to my desk lamp attests, the purported link between testosterone and swordplay is tenuous at best.

EVEN IF YOU AREN'T swayed by the argument that gender norms cause gender differences, there's little doubt that societal expectations about gender exaggerate the disparities that do exist. Whether it's math performance, aggression, or spatial skill, reminding people how men and women are "supposed to" act exacerbates gender gaps.

And such gender-based norms are so ubiquitous that they pop up when you least expect them. Like at the drive-thru window. There are plenty of questions I've come to expect when ordering fast food: "Do you want to Supersize that?" "What drink to go with your combo?" "You do know that eating this shaves a month off your life expectancy, right?" But "Boys or girls?" isn't one of them.

Yet that's what I was asked the last time I forsook nutritional concern for culinary expedience in the midst of a family road trip. I was so caught off guard after ordering two kids' meals that I literally had to ask the drive-thru attendant to repeat his question, and it had nothing to do with the sound quality of his milkshake-shaped intercom.

When I pressed him as to why he needed to know, he explained that he had to figure out which prize to include in their Happy Meals. I'll admit that the actual toys my girls received—action figures of some sort—seemed more or less innocuous. But why do drive-thru attendants need to know whether I have boys or girls? Can't they just ask, "Toy boat or toy pony?" If gender norms run rampant at the drive-thru window, is there *anywhere* we're immune from them? The idea that Grimace and the Hamburglar are so interested in my kids' genitals is a little creepy to me.

Simply put, it's hard for us to see the world without getting hung up on gender. Again, just think about how people react to newborns, even when quilts aren't involved. The first thing anyone wants to know after—or even before—a baby is born is the drive-thru window question: boy or girl? Not weight or hair color. Not whether the youngster was blessed with Mom's eyes or cursed with Dad's ears. It's all about gender.

When my second daughter was born, of all the information on the card they stuck to her bassinet in the hospital nursery, the largest, most easily identifiable font belonged to the "I'M A GIRL" declaration at the bottom (see following page). Not her last name, her parents' room number, or even her physician's contact information. No, her gender, printed in bold on an appropriately pink card.

"I'M A GIRL," the card screams. And don't you forget it!

You might suggest that it's only natural to fixate on gender. What else is there to find out after hearing that the baby is healthy? Hair color, complexion . . . those are secondary considerations to the big question of "boy or girl?" Finding out that the baby is eighteen inches long is a mere curiosity; finding out its sex gives you insight into the future. It allows you to start mapping out this little person's path in life.

And *that* is precisely my point. Upon learning gender, we set into motion the cycle of expectations that will shadow this indi-

Baby SOMMERS # 19771500

Mother _____   Room No. 962
       (First initial and last name only, please)

Date of Birth _____   Time 1:35 AM

Weight 7 — 6   Length 18½"

Head _____   Chest _____

Baby's Doctor HV — BTR

Mother's Doctor B&W OB/Gyn Group

I'M A GIRL

vidual for life. We ask "boy or girl" to determine what color clothes to send as a gift. To figure out which books or toys would be appropriate. To get a sense of the type of person the baby will become—something we have a hard time pondering without knowing gender.

Things don't change that much after leaving the hospital, either. Even with infants, passersby always ask whether it's a little boy or girl in the stroller. Idle curiosity? Perhaps. Or maybe we're just so used to gender shaping interactions that we're not sure how to proceed without the information. As I've learned, hell hath no fury like the septuagenarian who can't deduce gender from your baby's outfit.

"Oh, look at him—he's so alert," I often heard when out with our first daughter, presumably because she had so little hair and we refused to Scotch tape a bow to her scalp.

"Yes, she is," I'd reply.

First would come the automatic apology—as if nothing could be more slanderous than attributing the wrong gender to a six-month-old. But then, inevitably, would follow a testier, more accusatory response, one intended to remind me that the mix-up was my fault all along. Something like, "But wait . . . her outfit has blue airplanes on it?!"

Somewhere, Amelia Earhart just rolled over in her . . . well, wherever she is, she's not amused, that's for sure.

SO WHAT, EXACTLY, is the takeaway message of this chapter? It's not that sex differences are imaginary. It's not that celebrating the unique qualities of men and of women is always problematic. It's not that you should ignore gender or pretend that everything about little boys and girls is exactly the same.

The real moral is that situations affect even a distinction like male/female—one that's endemic to how we see the world and one that seems to have a clear-cut biological basis. The gender differences we learn about early in life aren't nearly as entrenched as they seem to be. In fact, like so much else in our social universe, they're highly context-dependent. Much more so than we realize, they're self-fulfilling, growing out of our own expectations about what men and women are like.

When you think of gender this way, you realize the power you have as a parent, coach, teacher, or manager to shape other people's sense of what is achievable. You can do this proactively, like the teacher who comes right out and tells his class there are no fixed gender differences in math skill, or who goes out of her way to choose reading books on topics that will appeal to boys as well as girls.[21] Or the small-business owner who breaks with precedent, assigning a male employee to organize the office holiday party and a female to research the company's best options for a technological upgrade.

You can do this reactively, like the father at the store who uses his daughter's preference for the blue "boys' bike" as an opportunity to discuss how silly the notion of gender-specific conveyances is in the first place. And you can do this subtly as well, without even saying a word, like the mother who simply refrains from wincing or recoiling when her grade-school-age son cries in public, permitting him to forsake stoicism for a genuinely emotional response to a challenging social encounter.

In sum, what you believe about gender guides not only what your children, charges, and underlings believe, but also how they actually behave. That whole idea Gandhi had about being the change you want to see in the world? It rings particularly true for expectations like those we have for gender.

I'll admit that here I'm offering only a vague prescription for action: believe that gender doesn't invariably dictate or limit human potential and those around you will follow suit. So I'll leave you with three more specific pieces of advice, all particularly relevant to interacting with kids, the most impressionable and malleable of us all:

1) *Keep an eye out for gender norms.* Because, I'm telling you, they're everywhere.

It's not that norms per se are bad—as I said earlier, they're the grease that keeps the machinery of society moving. It's easier to handle new situations when we know what's expected of us and what to expect of those around us. But when it comes to gender, while norms may simplify life, their side effects are far more trouble than they're worth. Almost without fail, gender norms pigeon-hole and they patronize.

Don't fall for the line that some gender expectations are positive. Even the so-called good ones cause problems. For instance, what does it mean to suggest that women are nurturing? It implies that they're inferior when it comes to bottom-line thinking, tough decisions, and other aspects of leadership in realms like politics and business. It feeds the mentality that often pits femininity and professional success against each other.

Newly aware that gendered messages are everywhere, keep looking for them on your quilts and in your Happy Meals, in storybooks and on TV, on store shelves and websites that insist on separate categories of "boys' toys" and "girls' toys." And even in the romantic musings of the sentimental crooner, who, in the midst of advising fathers to be good to their daughters, also asserts that "boys you can break; you find out how much they can take." John Mayer's "Daughters" is a catchy song, but as with a lot of popular music, the lyrics offer surprising lessons. Like the idea that girls are fragile by comparison, or at least lacking in resilience. Not to mention the insight that Mayer, of all people, apparently subscribes to the *Full Metal Jacket* school of raising sons.

You can't shield your kids or anyone else from gender norms. But half the battle is knowing what to look for and preparing yourself for conversations about messages that otherwise go unchallenged. Ask your children what they think the moral of the movie is. Talk to them when you hear them describe any activity, school subject, or profession as the domain of just one gender. Have the challenging conversations that we often shy away from because they're uncomfortable or controversial. If you don't, Hollywood, Madison Avenue, and Corporate America will.

2) *Emphasize similarity as well as difference.* We get so caught up in the real and obvious physical differences between the sexes that we lose sight of the conclusion that when it comes to how we think and act, men and women are more similar than different. Consider the average classroom. Think about how many of our grade-school days began with "Good morning, boys and girls." Or how often we heard "Well, the girls are doing a nice job of cleaning up, but the boys still have some work to do."

Now think about how dumb those comments really were.

As University of Texas psychologist Rebecca Bigler points out, the more teachers emphasize a social category like gender, the more kids come to develop stereotypes about the groups in question.[22] *Girls are good listeners and boys can't sit still. Math is for boys and reading is for girls.* It doesn't really matter what the category is: keep dividing the class into blue-eyed and brown-eyed teams or comparing left-handed versus right-handed students, and soon enough kids will read between the lines and start to think that *these* groups, too, share other defining qualities beyond the strictly physical, like personality type or aptitude. Drawing unnecessary distinctions by gender produces the same sort of outcome.

Am I making mountains out of molehills? Isn't "Good morning, boys and girls" innocuous? Well, at the very least, you must admit it's a pointless turn of phrase. It conveys no more information than "Good morning, children." If it's so harmless and trivial, ask yourself what sort of job action would be faced by the teacher who began class with "Good morning, white kids and black kids."

Or who formed teams for a competition by pitting against each other students living with two parents and those living with one.

Parents talking with their kids about gender and other social distinctions makes sense. So does teachers consciously creating school lesson plans that will appeal to a range of interests and learning styles. But publicly drawing distinctions when they're not necessary or relevant is counterproductive. Treat your children or class or workforce like a unit and they'll respond in kind. Think and speak of them as factions and they'll do the same.

3) Finally, and briefly, *don't find out your baby's sex*. I realize this makes me a contrarian: in the birthing class we took the first time my wife was pregnant, we were the only couple out of fifteen not to know. I've heard the arguments for finding out sex: everyone says that they just want to be prepared when it comes to names, clothes, nursery décor, and the like.

But that's the crux of the matter. What, really, is there to prepare for? What color onesie is your newborn son going to object to? What toy will your three-month-old daughter deem too masculine to jam into her mouth? Once they're born, you can't shield kids from gendered expectations, so at least give them a reprieve in the womb. As soon as they arrive, the floodgates will open: dolls and books for girls; building blocks and action figures for boys. For now, just pick two names and wait it out like in the old days.

I admit, when I've shared this philosophy with others, their reaction tends to be lukewarm at best. *I hate surprises*, I've been told. *We just want to learn as much about our child as we can*, the argument goes. But parenting is all about surprises. All you will learn from the discovery of your fetus's sex is the nature of your own preconceived notions about gender. Our very resistance to not knowing a baby's sex ahead of time just goes to show how attached we are to seeing the world through the lens of gender.

When you don't find out the sex of your unborn child, you buy nine more months of freedom from preconceived notions, old wives' tales, and urban legends. And with every puzzled question you hear from well-meaning friends and relatives—*But how will you know what color to paint the nursery? Then what type of gift should I buy? Is it still OK to give you the soccer ball pajamas I picked out?*—you'll be reassured that you made the right decision. When you don't allow yourself (or those around you) to be guided by expectation, you realize just how much you lean on that crutch in the course of ordinary thought and daily interaction.

6.

LOVE

It's amazing what people are capable of, for better and for worse. In our relatively brief time on this planet, we've exhibited an astounding capacity for the terrific but also the terrible. The constructive but also the destructive. The Taj Majal but also *The Tyra Banks Show*.

In other words, human potential falls along a broad continuum. We're born with a flexible fate, our range of possibilities nearly unlimited. Even as we age, move forward, and choose forks in the road, we retain the potential in our lives for both good and evil, heroism and cowardice, leadership and blind obedience. As you know by now, it's the power of situations that emerges as a critical yet underappreciated determinant of which directions our lives take.

Thus far, this book has examined the many ways in which context shapes social thought and behavior. The final two chapters will explore the extremes of this continuum of human capacity, focusing on a dichotomy familiar to us all: love and hate. More specifically, this chapter examines the factors that shape our attraction to others and our intimate relationships; the next chapter probes a darker aspect of humanity, namely the prejudices and biases that pervade our interactions with one another.

Both chapters cover familiar terrain in unfamiliar ways. And both offer surprising conclusions that are, in turns, reassuring as well as disconcerting.

FACE/BUTT/WIT

What attracts you to somebody?

It's a tough question, even if your significant other isn't hovering over your shoulder as you try to answer it. In fact, it's the very type of question for which introspection is poorly suited. For a moment, though, pretend this is a Dr. Phil book and try your best to answer: Whether you're male or female, gay or straight, what are the three most important factors in determining whom you're attracted to?

I posed the same question to a class of undergraduates. Granted, it can be risky to try to generalize from the anonymous responses of college students—after all, most of the world's population doesn't eat cereal for dinner, wear pajamas in public, and consider 10:30 a.m. an early wake-up call. But my guess is that in general

terms, there's plenty that's similar between their responses and
yours, even if specifics and terminology vary.

My students' answers focused on physical characteristics and
personality traits. Here's a fairly typical set of responses:

> 1. Sense of humor
> 2. Smile
> 3. in good (healthy) shape

Another student—apparently a budding country-and-western
lyricist—went with a comparable yet more apostrophe-friendly
reply:

> 1. fitness /body weight
> 2. confidence
> 3. good lookin' face

Some students were even more specific regarding the precise physical attributes they seek:

1. intelligence
2. brunette
3. legs

I can only assume that response number 3 refers to a certain muscle tone or shapeliness and not simply the mere presence of legs.

All in all, 50 percent of their responses stuck to physical characteristics—including several not suitable for reproduction here if
I hope to avoid an NC-17 rating. I suppose that when asking college students anonymous questions about what attracts them to
others, one should expect wiseass answers (no pun intended) like
"left buttock."

Another 47 percent of their responses focused on personality or
disposition. Among these, "sense of humor" was the most popular,
followed closely by "intelligent" and "warm" or "friendly." And in
a low-standards variation on the same theme, one person simply
requested "not a total jerk," generously leaving the door open for
prospective mates with only partial membership in said group.

In short, ask people what leads them to fall for someone, and
their answers seem ripped right from the personal ads or one of
those matchmaking websites that promises scientific compatibility
analysis. They tell you about their ideal partner: personality traits,
physical appearance, perhaps a certain, indefinable quality of character or depth of soul. In other words, they talk about attraction

in WYSIWYG terms—in some cases, monosyllabically pithy
WYSIWYG terms:

```
1,  FACE

2,  BUTT

3.  WIT
```

Face/butt/wit. This not-so-holy trinity epitomizes 97 percent of
my students' responses about attraction. Just 3 percent of their
answers had anything to do with context, such as whether they had
recently ended a previous relationship or how much their friends
like a prospective mate. I'd bet that your responses were similarly
focused on personality and physicality.

But you should know better by now. Attraction, like so much
of daily experience, is all about the situation. Face/butt/wit gets
you only so far when it comes to matters of the heart, as Lord
Byron famously wrote. Or was that Shakespeare?

LOVE THE ONE YOU'RE WITH

We think of love in mystical terms. We romanticize about soul
mates, ponder the mysteries of animal magnetism, and deem attraction too magical for rational analysis. We prefer our love pack-

aged Hollywood-style, with predestined couples that persevere through near misses before finally finding each other in the end. You know, like those movies I bury at the bottom of our Netflix queue when my wife isn't looking.

Our thoughts rarely turn to the more mundane factors that dictate when, where, and with whom we fall in love. Our blissful naïveté on this count makes an easy mark for satire. Consider this tongue-in-cheek headline from *The Onion*: "18-Year-Old Miraculously Finds Soulmate in Hometown." The indictment of our head-in-the-clouds take on attraction continues:

> "They say God puts one special person on this planet who is your
> one true love," said Munter, who has left Marinette County twice
> in his life, both times for marching band competitions in nearby
> Menominee. "It's incredible, but I somehow found mine right
> here in the town where I've always lived."

Much like this fictitious romantic, we resist the conclusion that had we moved to a different building, gone to a different college, or taken a different job, we likely would have forged our most intimate of connections—romantic as well as platonic—with different people. We're uncomfortable with the idea that a simple twist of context is sometimes all that separates the dear friend or loved one from the casual acquaintance or complete stranger.

But be realistic. If Capulet had settled in Venice rather than fair Verona, there'd be no Romeo and Juliet. And if Cunningham Hardware had been based in Madison rather than less fair Milwaukee, Joanie never would have loved Chachi. Like it or not, perhaps the most critical determinant of attraction is simple geography, which—if you're anything like my students—didn't make your list of three.

AT THE END of World War II, the homecoming of thousands of servicemen led to a surge of enrollment at American universities. MIT was no exception. Combined with a preexisting shortage of affordable housing, the fact that many returning soldiers were married or had children forced university officials to look for creative strategies.

Their solution was Westgate. A new residential community with two separate complexes, its first phase included one hundred prefabricated single-family houses arranged into U-shaped "courts." Next came the not-so-creatively named Westgate West, consisting of more than a dozen two-story apartment buildings, each with ten rental units. Taken together, the entire community housed up to 270 families.

From the perspective of behavioral researchers, Westgate was almost too good to be true. Its location on a university campus and its unique status as an enclosed neighborhood into which all residents had moved during a narrow time frame made it a social science version of Biosphere 2. Westgate provided an ideal opportunity for actually quantifying the impact of physical space on relationship development. And that's precisely what researchers did.[1] Five decades later, they surely would have been beaten to the punch by reality TV producers.

The research was straightforward: residents were asked to name their closest friends in the community. The results were just as clear-cut: the nearer residents lived to each other, the more likely they

were to become friends. Those in the subdivision were most likely
to list others who lived in the same court, and the closer the houses,
the closer the friendship. Same for the apartment complex—
60 percent of the friends listed lived next door to the person who
named them, while less than 4 percent lived as far as four apartments away.

At first blush, this might not seem that enlightening or surprising a finding. You may have assumed that the more often we cross
paths with someone, the more likely we are to become friends. But
did you have any idea just how powerful this impact of proximity
is? Nineteen feet. That's all it takes. For every meager nineteen feet
of apartment floor plan that separated two Westgate neighbors,
their chances of developing a close friendship were cut by nearly
half. That's how profoundly context shapes even our most intimate
and meaningful social connections.

Lessons of Westgate transcend strict distance, implicating physical space as well. People with houses looking out on the pedestrian-
friendly common area were listed as friends far more often than
those on the end of a court facing the street. In apartments, those
residents most likely to take the leap and make friends on other
floors of the building were the renters living next to the stairwell.
Location, location, location, indeed.

Though we infrequently and begrudgingly acknowledge it, our
own relationships have similar, proximity-driven legacies. My
freshman year of college I lived in a hallway that contained three
double rooms. By graduation, my inner circle still included my
original roommate and the two guys who had lived next door.
While we might have fancied the idea that some sort of cosmic
plan had placed us near one another—that we would've been

drawn to one another even had we been assigned to dorms in different corners of campus—the truth is that our friendships owed more to the vagaries of the housing office than inevitable compatibility. Quickly, ours became real relationships sustained by less superficial considerations, but proximity opened the figurative door in the first place.

Of course, living near someone doesn't guarantee liking them. Far from it. Of the other two guys in my freshman hallway—members of the basketball team who shared a suite three times the size of the regular rooms—one never bothered to learn our names, and the second spent the entire year calling everyone on the floor "Sam."

Indeed, the strong feelings made possible by proximity can be negative as well as positive. That is, proximity also predicts who we dislike. From the neighbor who always takes your parking spot to the loudmouth in the cubicle next to yours at work, frequent contact can also rub the wrong way. A more recent study of condos in Southern California found results similar to those at Westgate: the closer residents lived, the more likely they were to be good friends. But when asked to list their *least* favorite people in the neighborhood, again the list was dominated by those living nearby.[2]

Sort of like how basketball guy number one and I felt about each other freshman year. He had a habit of playing loud music with his door open at 2:00 a.m., and when I'd come by to ask him to turn it down, he'd look at me earnestly and pause a beat before replying, "Nah."

Charming.

In response, each morning I'd wait until he closed his locked door to walk, half naked, to the shower before I called his room phone. He'd run back down the hall holding his towel with one hand and keys with the other, only to have me hang up as soon as he got inside. I never tired of the audible string of obscenities that would emanate from his room—you would've thought he was waiting for a call from an organ donor registry. And then, at 2:00 a.m. that night, our ritual dance would begin anew.

So, mundane factors like geography and floor plan have a profound impact on our acquisition of close friends as well as nemeses. But when I asked you about attraction, odds are you pondered it in more romantic or even sexual terms. Well, proximity shapes those relationships, too.

Sociologists have analyzed marriage licenses in a range of U.S. cities. Whether Philadelphia, Duluth, or Columbus, the nearer two people's residences, the more likely they are to marry. In the Ohio study, for example, more than half of engaged couples had lived within sixteen blocks of each other when they started dating.[3] More than one-third lived as close as five blocks. Similar results emerge for casual romantic relationships as well, such as dating patterns by college residence hall or, presumably, marching band section.

In short, when you chart the physical configuration of a neighborhood, apartment building, or dormitory, you get a pretty good map of its social configuration as well. About to move and looking to make friends quickly? Hoping to expand your pool of potential dating partners? Pick the apartment near the mailroom or by the elevators. The increased foot traffic may be detrimental to your sleep schedule and carpet wear, but it can work wonders for your social life.

————

YOU DON'T EVEN HAVE to bump into someone—figuratively or literally—for proximity to spin its magic: such effects on attraction don't always hinge on cinematically dramatic convergences. It's not always two hands simultaneously reaching for a taxi door on a rainy night or the happenchance encounter of grocery shoppers each carrying the obligatory paper bag with a loaf of French bread sticking out. The impact of proximity can be much subtler.

Simply encountering people (or objects) with regularity is enough to render them more appealing. Or, as psychologists would phrase the same idea, "mere exposure facilitates attraction." This is not to be confused, of course, with other types of exposure, which facilitate instead a hefty fine and ankle-monitoring device.

This link between exposure and liking even emerges for something as utterly mundane as language. Show respondents a series of nonsense words like *zabulon* and *ikitaf,* and they end up preferring the ones that they viewed the most times.[4] Same goes for English speakers presented with a series of previously unfamiliar Chinese characters.

As it turns out, familiarity doesn't breed contempt. It breeds liking. By default, we associate good feelings with that which is familiar, like comfort food, longtime political incumbents, certain corporate logos, and the sound of the local play-by-play announcer's voice. Reactions such as "I feel like I've heard this song before" and "Haven't we already met?" leave us more positively inclined toward the stimulus in question.

So it goes with love as well. George Costanza was on to something when he'd "accidentally" leave his keys at his date's apartment to give him an excuse to stop by again. It may have been, as Elaine suggested, a pathetic way to weasel a second date. But it worked.

And in real life, too, familiarity is a powerful if often overlooked ingredient of attraction.

How else to explain why merely sitting passively in the same room as someone else can make you feel more attracted to her? That's all it took in one study, in which a professor at the University of Pittsburgh arranged for several women who weren't actually enrolled in his large lecture course to sit in the audience.[5] One woman sat through the class five times that semester. Another did so ten times. The third woman came to fifteen different lectures, all the while sitting quietly and not interacting at all with the more than one hundred students in the room.

At the end of the term, the professor showed the class a series of slides with photos of different women, including the interlopers. He asked the class to rate each photo in terms of familiarity as well as attractiveness. Ratings of the attractiveness of the three women were predicted by how many classes each had attended: students reported the greatest attraction to the woman who had been in class fifteen times, followed by the one who had attended ten times, followed by the five-timer. The greater the students' exposure to each woman, the more attracted they were to her.

The students were largely unaware of why they felt this way— the number of classes each woman went to had a much smaller impact on ratings of how familiar each face seemed. Just like commercial jingles and George Costanza, these women slipped undetected into the mental category "familiar." That was all it took to make them seem more attractive. Again, when you stop to think about it, this is an amazing demonstration of just how important context is for our most treasured of feelings and relationships. In a world in which people shell out money for mate compatibility reports and profiles of romantic personality style, simply seeing someone repeatedly without exchanging so much as a word turns out to be enough to spark attraction.

Indeed, when it comes to judgments of physical beauty, there is a clear link between familiarity and attractiveness—one that often remains subconscious. Because when you ask people to describe the superficial attributes to which they're drawn, they rarely have trouble describing their "type." Just check out the personals section. Inevitably someone is seeking a "tall, broad-shouldered guy with athletic build." Or a "blonde, preferably slender or petite." And then there are the more idiosyncratic preferences—you know, the really weird fetishes like "nebbish, academic type with poor sense of direction and fragile fingers."

But while most of us have clear ideas regarding what we find beautiful, we fail to recognize the role of familiarity. In spite of society's celebration of trademark features—Elizabeth Taylor's eyes, Johnny Depp's cheekbones, Jennifer Lopez's . . . ahem, other cheeks—we actually prefer *average* features, all else being equal. When asked to choose between a photo of an actual individual and a composite combining the faces of several people, we typically find the composite photo more attractive. The more faces morphed together—the more features thrown into the average—the more familiar and attractive that composite becomes.[6]

In short, familiarity helps account for the impact of proximity on liking, and it provides yet another example of a mundane factor that shapes attraction. Just as you prefer the way your voice sounds in your own head to how it sounds on tape, just as you like how you look in the mirror more than how you look on video, you also find other people more attractive the more familiar they seem.

It's almost enough to convince you that it would be a good idea to leave a life-size cardboard cutout of yourself outside the bedroom window of your latest crush, just to capitalize on the impact of familiarity.

Almost. Don't overlook the potential problems of soggy weather and general creepiness. You'd be better off just joining his or her gym instead.

MORE CONTEXTS OF LOVE

It's not only proximity and familiarity that we look past in the name of all that is face/butt/wit. There are actually a number of situational factors that impact attraction, though you wouldn't know it from looking at my students' lists of three. What follows is but a brief sampling:

1. *Reciprocity.* As mentioned earlier, when a waitress brings candy with the check, we feel obligated—even if subconsciously—to reciprocate. So we leave a bigger tip. Attraction works much the same way. Or, at least, that's the assumption driving anyone who's ever bought a drink for a stranger sitting at the bar. It's not a bad strategy: research indicates that men who buy drinks like this are, on the whole, viewed as more attractive afterward, not to mention more likely to eventually win a date.[7]

When it comes to attraction, though, reciprocity does more than elicit feelings of obligation. When you find out that someone has a thing for you, it changes the way you think about her or him. Suddenly, that person seems just a little bit more attractive. Becoming aware of someone else's feelings opens the door to new relationship possibilities, prompting you to see this admirer in a new light. At the very least, you now know that this is a person of refined taste, right?

To illustrate, in one study sixty strangers were instructed to have a "get to know you" conversation with a stranger.[8] Afterward, they were led to separate rooms and eventually shown a questionnaire that their partner had supposedly completed. Some read that their partner had a lukewarm impression of them; others learned that their partner had enjoyed the conversation. When given the chance to interact again, those participants who believed their partner liked them disclosed more personal information than did the others. They even engaged in the conversation with a more positive, pleasant tone of voice, as determined by observers who listened to a recording of the interaction.

In other words, finding out that someone likes you is often enough to get you to reach out and open up to them. Thus begins an anything-but-vicious cycle that ends with a closer relationship.

2. *Obstacles*. Generally speaking, we value our sense of independence. It's not only two-year-olds and adolescents who rebel against being told what to do or how to think—adults also chafe at hearing that a goal is unattainable or "you have no choice." I, for one, have suffered through multiple unpleasant meals at ethnic restaurants because I was unwilling to defer to a waiter's suggestion that the dish might be spicier than I would like. Insisting that the gringo can handle it may not lead to a satisfying dining experience, but at least I emerge with free will intact. Or so the stubborn thinking goes.

It's not a particularly romantic conclusion, but in this sense, attraction isn't that different from ordering the Szechuan chicken.

The harder people try to steer us away from someone, the more intrigued we often become. Literature—as well as real life—is filled with examples of star-crossed lovers and other couples brought together, ironically, by the obstacles between them. Not to mention parents who have learned the hard way that warning a teenager not to date someone can have the opposite effect.

Beyond not liking it when our options are limited by others, there's also a certain allure to pursuing relationships we're not supposed to. As far back as biblical times, there's always been appeal to the forbidden fruit. Indeed, secrecy makes a relationship just that much more attractive. Psychologist Dan Wegner and colleagues at the University of Virginia once asked more than one thousand people about romantic feelings from their past. For both crushes and actual relationships, those described as having some aura of secrecy remained more memorable years later—and, for that matter, were still more preoccupying.[9]

In fact, Wegner and his fellow researchers re-created this power of forbidden love within the confines of a behavioral laboratory. In an experiment best described as the "footsie study," they recruited foursomes for a card game. Each group was split into two mixed-gender pairs, and while both teams heard the same set of game rules, one team also received separate written instructions: they were supposed to play footsie.

OK, so the instructions were a bit more elaborate than that. The pair was told that the study was about nonverbal communication, and that the researchers wanted to see if they'd be able to send information to each another by touching feet under the table. They might use a certain number of toe taps to indicate a card's value, for example. But the end result was that one pair was playing casino-style footsie while the other was not.

What does this have to do with forbidden love? Well, researchers instructed half the couples to keep the podiatric mingling to themselves, while the other half was told that the opposing team knew what they were up to. After the game, participants were asked a series of questions, including how attracted they were to their partner. Mere physical contact wasn't the biggest influence on their responses. Instead, it was those couples who played *secret* footsie that reported the most attraction to each other.

Quite simply, forbidden relationships entice and shared secrets intoxicate.

3. *Similarity*. It's not only sharing a secret that draws us closer to someone. A wide range of common experiences also makes attraction more likely. Like interacting with a stranger and finding out that this person likes (or dislikes) the same band you do. Or laughs at the same joke. Or just gives the same answer to a sentence completion task in a research study.[10] Sharing a response to even the most trivial of events provides a moment of connection to other people.

Other forms of similarity are powerful as well. James Carville and Mary Matalin aside, more often than not we wind up in relationships with others of similar attitude, life experience, and demographics. In large part, this is explained by our tendency to be most comfortable around people like us—to move to neighborhoods, join organizations, sit at cafeteria tables, and sign up for dating websites composed of similar others. While the unfamiliar can be exotic, opposites don't attract as often as folk wisdom might suggest.

In fact, our tendency to be drawn to those who are similar can even be seen in terms of physical beauty. Attractiveness may be a subjective determination, but you still find reasonable consensus when people rate the appearance of others. There's a reason we do a double take when we see celebrity pairings like Julia Roberts/Lyle Lovett, Christie Brinkley/Billy Joel, Paulina Porizkova/Ric Ocasek: studies indicate that most couples are fairly well matched on attractiveness, whether assessed by outside observers or the individuals themselves.[11] This is a research analysis you can duplicate on your own—just head to your local bar, rate the people you see on a scale of 1–10, and count how many couples match up with similar numbers. All you need to pull off this study is the cover charge, paper and pen, and a ready-made excuse for why you're staring at strangers and scribbling down notes.

Such matching by beauty reflects the market-driven nature of real-life relationships. Sure, all else being equal, we tend to prefer the most attractive partner out there. In the end, though, reality usually trumps fantasy, and we gravitate toward mates who are in our own league—those whom we believe to be less likely to reject outright our advances. Unless you're a 1980s-era recording star, that is.

SO YOU CAN ADD to the list a number of other situational forces that affect relationships: reciprocity, obstacles, and similarity, for starters. And this doesn't even touch on other contextual influences on attraction like power, social status, or earning potential. Even though we defer to thinking of attraction in face/butt/wit terms— as revolving around preferences for internal traits and physical characteristics—external forces dictate how and when we're drawn to others. As magical an experience as falling in love can be, it's still one governed by mundane considerations like geography and tempered by the cold-blooded, free-market realities of supply and demand.

HEARTS AFLUTTER

Our shortsightedness when it comes to how attraction really works goes beyond a WYSIWYG fixation on physical and personality traits. A wide range of assumptions about falling in love just don't stand up to scientific scrutiny. And since this chapter has already started to profane the sacred view of love as inscrutable or too magical for the whims of mundane context, why not go for broke and debunk a few other old myths while we're at it?

Take, for instance, our rudimentary understanding of the physiology of attraction. Clearly, there's a biological component to falling for someone, whether a pounding heart, shallow breathing, or sweaty palms. At least, that's what the song lyrics from a wide range of tracks in my iTunes collection tells me. But is this right? Is it valid to assume that falling in love brings about a specific set of physical changes? Because some evidence—scientific as well as cinematic—suggests otherwise, indicating that attraction can actually result from arousal rather than cause it. You may recall this being one of the recurring precepts of that astute mid-1990s celluloid commentary on the human condition, *Speed.* That's right, the Keanu Reeves bus movie.

In the film, Sandra Bullock finds herself behind the wheel of a bus wired with a bomb. In order to prevent it from detonating, she has to weave in and out of traffic, maintaining a speed above fifty miles an hour (or, as some might suggest, driving like a regular city bus driver). As Bullock's character starts to bond with Keanu's transit cop, she warns him about the dangers of falling in love under such harrowing conditions: "relationships that start under intense circumstances, they never last."

In other words, sometimes it's the arousing situation that causes attraction rather than vice versa. Once the extreme conditions that forged the strong feelings have subsided, so do the feelings. It's a surprisingly trenchant analysis of human nature from an action film, not to mention surprisingly prescient screenwriting that provided a built-in explanation for Keanu's (wise) decision to opt out of appearing in the disappointing sequel.

So what's the true nature of the relationship between arousal and attraction? Is bodily change simply a response to falling for someone, or can it also be a precursor of romantic feelings? Can a racing heart actually bring about feelings of love instead of vice versa? To answer these questions, there's really only one place to go. No, not Paris, Venice, or even Monte Carlo. It's North Vancouver, British Columbia. Naturally.

THE CAPILANO SUSPENSION BRIDGE spans 450 feet and is touted as Vancouver's oldest visitor attraction. The bridge rests 230 feet above the Capilano River. But "rests" is a misnomer.

A more apt description of the bridge would be that it's a five-foot-wide pedestrian pathway constructed of pliable wooden planks attached to flexible wire cables. When people walk across the bridge, it sways. Not to mention bounces, teeters, wobbles, and lurches. Footage of the Capilano during a windstorm would make the slow-motion movie clip hall of fame.

Capilano Suspension Bridge, North Vancouver, British Columbia
[Credit: Photo courtesy of Lisa and Pat Shin]

Despite the rocky canyon and shallow rapids below, the wire handrails on the Capilano are quite low—for most adults, no higher than the nipple neighborhood. This makes walking across it a hair-raising experience, which is why each year three-quarters of a million people agree to cough up the $26.95 CAD for the pleasure. So crossing the bridge leaves visitors with the very same physiological symptoms identified above as potential signs of attraction: shortness of breath, elevated blood pressure, quickened pulse.

In an ingeniously creative series of studies designed to assess the possibility that arousal can be the *cause* rather than *symptom* of attraction, University of British Columbia researchers Donald

Dutton and Art Aron capitalized on the spine-tingling nature of their local Capilano.[12] Essentially, they tested whether the experience of crossing the bridge could trick people into feeling like they were falling in love.

They arranged for a female interviewer to approach men aged eighteen to thirty-five right in the middle of their bridge crossing. The interviewer claimed to be researching how scenic views affect creativity. So she asked respondents to spend a minute looking at an ambiguous picture of a young woman who was covering her face with one hand and reaching out with the other. Then she asked them to write a couple of sentences to describe what they saw in the image.

It wasn't an ordinary request, to be sure—I don't know about you, but I rarely do my best writing while perched precariously over rocky terrain. But the interviewer asked politely, she provided a pen and paper, and the respondents went along with it. After the men wrote their quick work of high-elevation fiction, the interviewer offered polite thanks and said she'd be happy to explain the study in more detail at a later date. She tore off a slip of paper, wrote down her name and phone number, and gave it to the participant before walking off for her next interview.

The same procedure was repeated at another site upriver: a heavy cedar bridge running a mere ten feet above a shallow stream. This bridge was wider and sturdier than the Capilano—think Monet oil painting, not Indiana Jones chase scene. But everything else remained identical, right down to the same female interviewer and the request to write a brief story.

After their outdoor adventure had ended, the researchers examined the brief stories written by each respondent. These composi-

tions were evaluated for sexual content—the thinking being that
when sex is on the mind, it seeps unconsciously into how we see
the world. Basically, the researchers treated the nonsexual image the
men wrote about as a social inkblot test. They wanted to see if
the arousing experience of crossing the bridge could morph into
other, more emotional forms of arousal. They predicted that men
on the Capilano would be more likely to inject sexual content into
their analysis of an otherwise ordinary situation—you know, much
like how I unnecessarily used the phrase "nipple neighborhood"
when describing something as prosaic as handrail height a few paragraphs ago.

So they showed the men's stories, anonymously, to people who
weren't working on the research study but were trained in the practice of scoring narratives for sexual content. The experts knew
what they were looking for, but they didn't know which anonymous stories were written on the Capilano and which were written
on the smaller, sturdier bridge. What did the experts conclude?
That the descriptions penned by the Capilano men contained
75 percent more sexual imagery and language than those written
on the other bridge.

Of course, it's possible that much like moths are drawn to light,
authors with a penchant for erotic composition somehow gravitate
to risk-seeking venues like Capilano. To rule out this possibility,
the researchers conducted a follow-up study comparing men still
on the bridge to those who had cooled down after having crossed
ten minutes earlier. The results were the same: the men's writing
was more sexually charged when they were on the bridge in an
aroused state. It's a finding that leads one to wonder just how
rickety the infrastructure must have been wherever Janet Jackson

and Justin Timberlake drew up the choreography for their Super Bowl halftime show.

The men on the Capilano weren't just thinking about love and sex in general terms, though. They found a specific target for their newfound arousal: the female interviewer. Remember how she had given out her phone number so that the men could call for more information about the study? Well, she always used the same number, but she went with a different false name in the two locations. To the men she encountered on the Capilano, she was Donna. On the other bridge upriver, she was Gloria.

Over the days that followed, "Donna" wound up with more than four times as many phone calls as "Gloria." In fact, half of all the men from the Capilano Bridge eventually called Donna, compared to a paltry 13 percent from the other bridge who phoned poor Gloria. The arousing bridge had kindled a lot more than scientific curiosity.

Now, I'm not suggesting that all feelings of attraction are driven by unrelated bodily arousal. And I don't mean to imply that when our blood pressure rises or the bridge we're on bounces, we inevitably latch on to the next mate we see. We're far from helpless in the face of such transfer of arousal from one source to another. In fact, the whole process works only when you aren't aware that it's happening: had the Capilano interviewer started her conversations with "Wow, this bridge sure has my heart racing," the men would have had a clear reminder of why they were aroused. Awareness of the true causes of our feelings usually prevents us from misattributing them.

Still, the study makes clear once again that contrary to intuition, even your most personal of feelings are shaped by the circumstances around you. Remember, for example, the "Suproxin" study a few chapters ago, in which respondents inferred their own emotions by looking to the behavior of those around them, and then labeled their feelings accordingly? Experiencing unexplained arousal, those participants seated next to someone angry decided that they, too, felt anger; those seated in a room with a guy twirling hula hoops decided that they, too, were happy. While the idea may be anathema to die-hard romantics, feelings of attraction operate in much the same way.

Conventional wisdom says that you see a hot guy on the adjacent elliptical machine and your pulse quickens accordingly. But the Capilano Bridge studies indicate otherwise: arousal often *precedes* attraction. You feel your heart race or temperature rise, and only then do you look around to figure out who's responsible. Chew on that the next time you're trying to decide who to sit next to in spinning class—your choice could have life-altering consequences.

LOVE ON MARS AND VENUS

Still other misconceptions about love revolve around a topic explored by the previous chapter: gender difference. As with a variety of cognitive and social aptitudes, we assume that men and women also diverge when it comes to attraction and intimate relationships. After all, "boys being boys" refers to frequent wrestling and rolling around on the playground but also to frequent rolling in the hay.

Like other intuitions regarding relationships, however, common wisdom about gender often fails to stand up to close analysis: the presumed differences between love on Mars and Venus are not as reliable or biologically dictated as we think they are.

Take, for example, the notion that women are pickier than men when choosing a partner. We think of women as selective— shooting down strangers at happy hour, deflecting direct propositions, even playing hard to get with those suitors they're willing to talk to. Men are the opposite, the thinking goes. Men will have sex with anything that moves. (And a few things that don't.)

This is how we see the marketplace of heterosexual dating, in terms of male pursuit and female response. While we expect the man to initiate the courtship process—to strike up the conversation, to make the approach at the bar, to call to ask for the date—it's the woman who holds all the cards. The woman decides who can sit next to her, whether a date will happen, and how heated things get afterward.

There's good reason for these intuitions. Empirical evidence confirms that when responding to personal ads or face-to-face solicitations, women are more selective than men. Consider research conducted two decades ago at Florida State University.[13] In these studies, male and female experimenters approached fellow students of the opposite sex and said that they had noticed them around campus and found them attractive. The experimenter then followed up with one of three blunt requests:

1) "Would you go out with me tonight?"
2) "Would you come over to my apartment tonight?"
3) "Would you go to bed with me tonight?"

Female students agreed to a date 56 percent of the time, but their consent rate for requests numbers two and three were only 6 percent and 0 percent, respectively. Many a female respondent reacted to these direct solicitations with irritation and even anger.

The men? Only 50 percent of male students said yes to a date, but they were much more agreeable to the more intimate requests. A full 69 percent said they'd make an apartment visit, and 75 percent agreed to go to bed. Men who turned down these latter requests often apologized or gave excuses (e.g., "I'm in a relationship"). And at least one particularly agreeable soul asked why they had to wait until the evening to consummate. Seriously.

Twenty years later, in 2009, different researchers ran a variation on this study and found comparable results among American, German, and Italian college students.[14] So, clearly, gender differences in mate selectivity exist and they don't seem confined by era or culture. Where do they come from? Some would suggest that it's all about evolution. Over time, the thinking goes, natural selection has led men and women to develop wholly distinct relationship tendencies. From a purely Darwinian standpoint, the primary objective of life is to ensure that one's genetic material survives into the next generation, and women and men face different obstacles in pursuit of this goal.

The evolutionary argument is that women *have* to be picky when it comes to mating. In life span terms, their window of fertility is relatively narrow, especially compared to men's. For women, each decision to reproduce also requires at least nine months of time and resources, not to mention the primary child-rearing responsibilities that usually follow. Thus, women can't afford to make mating mistakes.

Men are not similarly restricted. The human male remains reproductively viable for the majority of his life. In what might well be the euphemism of the century, successful male reproduction requires but a minimal, one-time investment.

According to evolutionary theorists, these different reproductive constraints have guided women and men to evolve into very different sexual beings. Consider jealousy, for instance. Evolutionary analysis suggests that men are more upset than women by sexual infidelity. After all, in the days of our genetic ancestors, Maury Povich wasn't around to help confirm a baby's paternity. The only way for a man to ensure that he was the biological father of the children in his home was to remain vigilant over his mate's relations. Similarly, evolutionary forces are used to explain why women appear to be picky and men anything but. Sure, we remain independent entities who exercise free will in deciding with whom we're willing to go on a date or have sex, but our default tendencies are encoded into our DNA and, thus, require concerted effort to override.

Or so the evolutionary theorist would have us believe.

Because if these tendencies are so deeply ingrained—if the male as hunter and female as hunted are roles hardwired into our genetic code—then a minor change in situation here or there shouldn't make much difference. And yet it does, as researchers at Northwestern recently demonstrated by hosting their own speed-dating events.[15]

Participants in this study had brief conversations with a dozen different individuals of the opposite sex. In each speed-dating session, twelve women remained seated while the twelve men in attendance rotated around the room, spending four minutes with each prospective dating partner before moving on to the next person. At the end of the session—after each of the twelve women had been visited by each of the twelve men—all participants completed a questionnaire assessing their attraction to each potential mate. Later, from the comfort of their own computers, they also recorded on the study website whether or not they'd be interested in seeing each person again.

As expected, women were more selective than men. Females reported lower levels of romantic desire than did males. Women also identified fewer prospective mates as people they'd like to see again.

But an interesting thing happened when the researchers made a minor tweak to the context of these interactions. In a second set of speed-dating events, they had the men and women swap roles. So now the men remained seated and the women rotated around the room—a simple modification, but one that stood regular dating protocol on its head. Instead of the women sitting still while male suitors paraded through, now the men remained stationary as women approached them. Of course, the "dates" themselves were still the same: four-minute conversations after which both parties were asked for their impressions. But from a strictly structural standpoint, this was traditional dating in reverse.

And you know what? Men and women also reversed roles when it came to selectivity. In this bizarro dating world, women reported more chemistry with their partners than did men. Compared to men, women now identified more prospective mates that they hoped to see again.

None of this fits with an evolutionary explanation. If you buy into the idea that men are less selective because for generations and generations they have thrived in the role of aggressive love hunters, then a minor alteration to a 2009 speed-dating event in Illinois should be of little consequence. Who sits and who rotates should be but an irrelevant blip on the radar overwhelmed by the force of naturally selected predisposition. Instead, this change to the situation was enough to make men come off as downright picky.

The study suggests the intriguing possibility that the apparent gender difference in mate selectivity owes less to evolution or biology than to the established dating paradigm in most societies. Women's more stringent standards for love don't necessarily result from a briefer reproductive window but also reflect the fact that they're the ones who are typically approached during courtship. Being approached means being in control. It means feeling desirable and in demand. It means having options.

Remember a few years ago, back when banks still loaned money to regular people? There were several websites that advertised an ability to present home buyers with multiple mortgage offers. The idea was that when banks compete for your affection, you win. Well, relationships are a lot like home loans these days, right down to the astronomically high rates of default.

So even some of our most deeply held convictions about love and gender are shaky at best. Yes, women are more selective than men, but those tables can be turned. The reputed gender difference in sexual jealousy doesn't fare much better—upon closer analysis, women are just as upset as men by the idea of sexual infidelity.[16] It's just that when you ask women about their partner sleeping around, they figure it could be a strictly physical fling. Men, on the other hand, assume that their girlfriend's having sex with someone else indicates an emotional attachment as well, and double cheating is worse than single cheating. That's not evolution talking. That's just simple arithmetic.

LESSONS OF LOVE

My wife isn't a big fan of this chapter. In fact, she doesn't like it at all when I frame attraction in terms of mundane context or talk about love in economic terms. It just isn't how we like to think of our most intimate feelings and relationships. "I love how familiar you are" doesn't sell many Valentine's Day cards. And few people are as honest as the friend of mine who once justified staying in a lukewarm relationship by explaining that her boyfriend had installed a photo of himself as her computer start-up screen and it seemed like a big hassle to figure out how to change it.

But by no means is the message of this chapter that love is trivial. Quite the opposite, in fact. The emotional bond provided by close relationships is so important that some psychologists refer to it as a human *need*, just a notch below survival basics like food, water, and shelter. Loneliness isn't some abnormal condition confined to a small number of Miss Havishams and Eleanor Rigbys—it's a common experience that serves as your body's way of sounding the alert that important needs are going unfulfilled. So loneliness keeps us from thinking as clearly as usual. It renders us more likely to get sick (and to stay sick longer). It's even contagious, passing from one member of a social circle to the next like a viral infection or mildly amusing YouTube link.[17]

Indeed, the need to bond with others governs much of our social repertoire, becoming only that much more urgent when circumstances turn stressful. Tell research participants they'll be receiving electric shocks and they'd much rather sit with others anticipating the same fate than wait alone.[18] Learn of an ongoing natural (or unnatural) disaster, and you feel the immediate impulse to call someone to commiserate, even if you both wind up just holding the phone silently as the storm rages or towers fall on TV.

Our connections to others are anything but trivial. It is precisely because they're so important that we spend so much of our time dwelling on relationships—both platonic and romantic. This is also why it's actually a *good* thing that attraction is subject to the whims of circumstance and ordinary situations. If love really depended on a perfect match of personalities—if romantic happiness hinged on discovering the needle of a soul mate hidden in the haystack of society—imagine how miserable most of us would be most of the time.

Our flexibility when it comes to love is actually a blessing. Think about it: time and time again, people find each other—and happiness—in places statistically unlikely to include any sort of preordained soul mate. The rural town, the small college, the arranged marriage, the travel-restricted marching band. That prosaic factors like proximity, familiarity, and reciprocity shape attraction is what allows love to flourish almost anywhere. Context greases the skids for the start of many relationships, but this hardly renders such attachments any less meaningful or exhilarating once they emerge.

In other words, this chapter is actually chock full of good news. Your newfound expertise with the context dependence of love means you can stop worrying about the elusive identity of your Mr. or Mrs. Right. There are potential Rights all around you, circumstances permitting. While I won't go so far as to tell you to forget about face/butt/wit altogether in your hunt for romantic happiness, I would suggest that pursuits of the heart require you to spend at least as much time pondering the situations that produce attraction as you do ruminating on the ideal characteristics of the perfect mate.

This chapter's exploration of how context impacts attraction offers some concrete suggestions regarding the search for love. Like making yourself as visible as possible. Familiarity and mere exposure are keys to attraction: the more people with whom you cross paths, the more likely you are to strike up a relationship. Lazy Sunday morning and you want to relax with coffee and the crossword? Fine, but force yourself to sit on the couch at Starbucks instead of in your living room. Want to learn a new skill or broaden your horizons? Great, but sign up for a cooking class, don't settle for the Food Network and a how-to website.

Remember the importance of physical space as well. The apartment across from the stairs, the dorm room next to the common area, the cubicle near the coffeemaker, the office by the front entrance . . . none of these are ideal selections if your goal is quiet time to yourself. But locations like these can increase your odds of making social connections of all types, if that's what you're in the market for.

When it comes to romantic relationships in particular, keep in mind that some locales are simply more fertile ground for such feelings to develop. Looking to meet someone new? I hear Vancouver is lovely this time of year. But if frequent trips to the Great White North aren't in your budget, try the gym, a sports rec league, or a dance class. Planning a first date? Dinner and a movie is the safe bet, but consider something that involves some sort of physical exertion—or at the very least, choose a good comedy or thriller to capitalize on potential transfer of arousal.

This chapter also offers lessons regarding other misconceptions of love. Women aren't inevitably and intractably pickier than men. It's just that conventional dating norms push them in that direction. If you're a woman whose friends tell you that your standards are too high, force yourself to be the approacher instead of the approachee once in a while. You just might start to see opportunities where you never did before.

If you're a straight man suffering from a higher-than-tolerable rate of rejection, do whatever it takes to get out of the rut of obligatory male approach. Get fixed up by a friend. Place a personal ad instead of responding to one. Bribe your local speed-dating organizer to let you stay in your seat while the women rotate around.

For that matter, you can also cast aside many of the old, gendered excuses for poor relationship behavior: "They just can't help themselves." "That's how guys are wired." "It's just boys being boys." These so-called truisms only hold true if you let them. They're just exaggerations based on WYSIWYG. When it comes to justifying relationship missteps or infidelities, lines like these are only a smidgen more persuasive than "I swear, honey, I wasn't up to anything—I was just out late working on my short game with Tiger."

And so it is that even for questions of the heart, situations matter. But this conclusion is no cause for alarm—no reason for the die-hard romantic to lose faith. Just because love is context-dependent doesn't make it less magical or fulfilling. To the contrary, it's a glass-half-full proposition, this notion that we're able to find romance in even the most mundane of circumstances. The very idea speaks to the profound capacity we have for connecting with our fellow man and woman. That we can find love at the drop of a hat or the sway of a bridge is just one of the many marvels of daily life.

That said, there's another side to this coin—the uglier aspect of human nature. There also exists a darker yin to the yang of love, if you will. As readily as we form new bonds with others, so do we exhibit a proclivity for animus and prejudice. Indeed, the broad continuum of human capacity spans liking as well as dislike, love as well as hate. And as with so many of our daily tendencies, it takes only weak nudges of circumstance to goad us into this us-versus-them mentality, as our final chapter details.

7.

HATE

WAITERS WHO TRY TO MEMORIZE MY ORDER INSTEAD of writing it down. Moviegoers who sit directly in front of me when there are plenty of other open seats. Inappropriate quotation mark usage (that's right, I'm talking to you, *Pet Supplies "Plus"*—that's neither a direct quotation nor a double entendre). Grocery shoppers who insist on paying by personal check. Squirrels.

Each of the above has a spot on my top ten list of pet peeves. But number one, without a doubt, has to be people who charge into elevators or subway cars, head down, without waiting to see if anyone is getting off. In my book, this is a felony. I'm pretty sure that only the technological limitations of fourteenth-century Italy prevented Dante from reserving a special level of hell for such miscreants—somewhere, I can only assume, between the carnal sinners and the gluttons.

My disproportionately strong feelings on this count are what led to such conflicted emotions after a recent elevator altercation. I was going up, on my way to a doctor's appointment. As the doors opened and I began to exit, a middle-aged man in a suit that was too big and a rush that was even bigger charged right in, as if entering a Moscow bread store hours after the fall of the Iron Curtain. I had to turn sideways to avoid a collision. Clearly, this guy had vaulted to Public Enemy Number One status.

But a funny thing happened next. My tormenter did a double take, made a U-turn, and followed me right back out of the elevator, all the while managing to keep perfectly balanced the multiple boxes stacked on the cart he was wheeling behind him. He pointed a chubby finger at my chest and asked, "Did you go there?"

After a pause to figure out that he was referring to the college name on my T-shirt, I answered yes.

"Me, too," he exclaimed. "When did you graduate?"

So began a ten-minute conversation that I wasn't thrilled to be having given my desire to get to my destination on time. However, my fellow alum proved to be a pleasant enough fellow, and it's always enjoyable to reminisce about familiar people and places from your past. When we parted ways with a firm handshake, I continued on my way in relatively good spirits.

And that's when it hit me.

I had let my guard down. I pardoned my newfound acquaintance for his grievous offense simply because of the common link of our alma mater. Without this connection, I never would have left the interaction in a positive mood, much less with a vaguely favorable impression. Our common group affiliation was enough to prompt me to view this man in a different light, sufficient to

get me to overlook behavior that was morally reprehensible if
not borderline criminal.

That's the power of "us."

Sharing group membership dramatically affects how we perceive and interact with others. Whether it's a common school,
hometown, religious affiliation, or favorite sports team, we're far
more generous in how we see fellow members of our own in-
groups. And we're much less forgiving of the out-groups.

TAKE RACE, FOR INSTANCE.

I recognize that this isn't the easiest of discussion topics. In fact,
my own research indicates that many of us bend over backward to
avoid the issue altogether. But the difference in how we see in-
group and out-group members is particularly striking when it
comes to race.

As just one example, consider the sobering data regarding death
penalty administration in the United States. Two decades ago,
University of Iowa law school professor David Baldus analyzed
over two thousand murder trials in the state of Georgia.[1] There's a
tremendous amount of discretion inherent to capital trials. First,
prosecutors must decide whether or not to pursue the death penalty. Then juries render a verdict, which, if guilty, requires a final
determination of whether death is warranted.

Of the cases Baldus examined, 3 percent of those involving
a white defendant accused of killing a black victim ended with a
death sentence. Among black defendants with a black victim, a
similarly low rate—just over 1 percent—were sentenced to death.

The numbers looked very different when the victim was white, however. Among white defendants accused of killing a white victim, 8 percent were sentenced to die. For black defendants with a white victim, the rate climbed all the way to 21 percent. These percentages tell the unambiguous story that defendants convicted of murdering white victims are much more likely to receive the death penalty, especially when they themselves are black.

Such disparities persist even after using statistical controls to account for nonracial differences among cases, like heinousness of the crime and caliber of the defendant's lawyer. And they aren't confined to a particular state or time period, either. Years later, Baldus examined death penalty cases in Philadelphia and came to similar conclusions.[2] In fact, when a separate set of researchers explored the same Philadelphia trials, they found an additional form of racial bias: in cases with white victims, the more "prototypically" African American a defendant was—the darker his skin, the broader his nose, the thicker his lips—the more likely the jury was to have sentenced him to death.[3]

Clearly, race matters, even when it comes to life-and-death decisions. But why? Ask Americans if they discriminate by race and the vast majority will tell you no. They'll tell you this honestly and in good faith, as most of us genuinely believe that we're fair-minded, open-hearted people.

This confidence in ourselves derives in large part from the fact that when we do ponder the idea of bias, we think about it in terms of *Crash*. You know, the 2005 movie in which each character takes a turn suffering and then dishing out blatant racial indignities? So the Persian store owner thinks his Hispanic locksmith is a gangbanger, but then when he goes to the gun shop, *he* gets called an Arab terrorist. The black customer service rep is belittled by the white caller, and then she later yells at an Asian driver to learn English. And on and on.

Crash depicts a world in which racial bias is cut-and-dried. It's all about hate—discrimination is overt, unambiguous, and the result of malicious intent. In other words, *Crash* portrays the WYSI-WYG take on racism: bad people with bad attitudes create racial disparity.

There are problems, though, with *Crash* (and I don't just mean a hard-to-swallow screenplay in which a motorist is abused by a Los Angeles police officer one night and then, the next afternoon, is rescued from a burning car in a different part of the city by . . . the very same officer). My biggest reservation about the film is that its take on racism is, for the most part, too neat, too easy. Sure, overt prejudice still exists. But the movie barely touches on the more subtle and covert forms of bias that are pervasive today.

Do prosecutors push for the death penalty for black defendants because they're virulent bigots? Are jurors more likely to return a sentence of death when the victim is white because of deep-seated, race-based hostility? Perhaps. But these sound an awful lot like the "bad apple" explanations for negative behavior examined a few chapters ago.

Of course, the appeal of these conclusions is that they're less threatening than the alternative possibility that even the most egalitarian among us falls victim to the influence of stereotypes. Or that we tend to feel more comfortable around others of similar background. Or that under certain circumstances, almost all of us are more likely to think in us-versus-them terms.

It's more reassuring to think of discrimination as being all about hate—as the result of bad people with bad attitudes. And this is the very reason I balk when anyone suggests that since I study racism, I should show *Crash* in my classes. I don't. And I won't. I know all too well how the students will respond. They'll be comforted by the idea that *hey, at least I don't do anything as bad as those people.* They'll stop at the conclusion that racism simply means the overt display of hostility or antagonism.

In reality, there's so much more to discrimination than hate. To assume otherwise—to pretend that as long as our hearts are in the right place, we're off the hook—is just another misconception driven by WYSIWYG and the desire to see the self in a positive light. This chapter offers a more nuanced exploration of intergroup bias, exploring this darker side of humanity without relying on the bad apple excuse. Because it turns out that we all engage in a number of seemingly innocuous tendencies that, in the end, contribute to group stereotypes and disparities.

For starters, there's the impact of "us," the generosity of spirit and resources that we offer to members of in-groups but not outgroups. As with me and the elevator barger.

Or the voter able to rationalize away the lack of experience of her nominee but convinced that the opposition candidate's thin résumé is a fatal flaw.

Or the baseball fan willing to give the benefit of the doubt to the hometown player accused of steroid use but ready to pounce on comparable rumors about other teams.

Or the police officer who sees a bit of his younger self in a juvenile offender and decides to give a second chance to a "good kid from a good family" but throws the book at a less fortunate, less familiar teenager from the other side of town.

No, you don't have to believe in some widespread racist conspiracy to explain obvious disparities such as those in death penalty cases. Most prosecutors and jurors are well-intentioned individuals working hard to uphold their oaths. But crime seems just a bit more surprising and reprehensible when it happens to someone on the "right" side of the tracks. Jurors feel just a little more outrage and anger when the victim reminds them of someone in their own family or neighborhood.

Sometimes our affinity for *us* is just as problematic as our dislike of *them*. Even when you're convinced that you don't have a hateful bone in your body, the way we see the world can fuel the fires of conflict and inequity.

SEEING SPOTS

Animosity between some groups is understandable, whether because of historical tension, competition for scarce resources, or incompatible ideologies. Like Democrats and Republicans. Red Sox fans and Yankees fans. Mac users and PC users. Those of us who back into parallel parking spots and the mouth-breathing Neanderthals who barrel in front-first. These are irreconcilable differences.

But something about the simple context of groupness also skews thought and action. That is, even without the particular baggage associated with any of the oppositional pairs above, the mere experience of being split into separate groups in and of itself promotes self-interest and conflict.

How little does it take to nudge someone into an us-versus-them mentality? I'll show you. On page 241 is a cluster of dots.

Take a quick look and, within a second or two, give your best estimate of how many there are. No complex geometrical analyses required—just a hair-trigger, first-glance impression. In the spirit of heading off any potential gender differences, I will assure you ahead of time that men and women do not show performance differences on this dot task. Dalmatian owners, on the other hand, should have a built-in advantage.

Ready? Then turn the page and settle on your estimate before reading further.

There are 407 dots in this cluster. I know because I copied and pasted each one myself, having learned the hard way that finding a non-copyrighted image of dots is not as easy as you'd think. After 407, the carpal tunnel kicked in.

How did your guess stack up? Are you a dot overestimator or underestimator? Or do you claim to have gotten it exactly right, in which case you're more of a dot prevaricator?

Actually, whether your guess was too high or too low isn't important. What is important is what I *tell* you about your performance. Were this a research study of intergroup relations, I would have shown you a series of clusters like this one and then, at random, informed you that you're either a chronic dot overestimator or a chronic dot underestimator. That's all it would take to push you into the realm of us versus them.

In one such study, a team of British and French researchers led by Henri Tajfel used this dot task to place school-age boys into one of two groups.[4] They showed forty different clusters of dots, each for less than half of one second. Again, it didn't matter if the boys actually guessed too high, too low, or haphazardly—given the outside possibility that overstimators and underestimators really do differ on some dimension, the researchers took matters into their own hands. At random, each boy was told that he was either an overestimator or an underestimator and was then grouped with fellow students of the same supposed tendency.

Having completed the dot portion of the program, the students were told that they'd be moving to an unrelated judgment task. Led to individual cubicles, they were given a series of numerical charts to use for allocating financial rewards between two classmates. For example, one chart presented options for divvying up fifteen cents between Student A and Student B. Another forced them to choose an amount of money for one student to receive and a separate amount for the other to lose. Each decision they made translated into real financial gains or losses for specific classmates at the end of the study.

Ostensibly a measure of their ability to make sense of the numerical charts, the task was anonymous: the boys never knew the true identity of their Student A or Student B. But they did know group membership. They did know whether Student A was, for example, a fellow member of their recently created group of dot overestimators or belonged to the other underestimator group.

Even though group assignments had been determined minutes earlier—and at random, no less affiliation had a dramatic impact on the students' allocation decisions. Boys who had been told they were dot overestimators made financial choices that favored fellow overestimators 69 percent of the time. Underestimators showed an even more egregious bias for some reason, clocking in with a 94 percent rate of favoritism.

Such increased generosity toward the in-group transcends the financial. Years later, American researchers used Tajfel's dot task to examine how group affiliation affects college students' social expectation and memory.[5] After estimating dots, participants were given two decks of index cards. Each card listed a behavior that had supposedly been disclosed by a previous respondent. Some were positive, such as "I took two disadvantaged kids on a vacation." Others were negative: "I had two affairs while married."

Both decks included the same number of positive and negative behaviors, and the specific cards in each deck were rotated at random. So the only meaningful difference between them was that participants believed that one deck listed behaviors previously written by dot overestimators, while the other deck supposedly came from underestimators.

After browsing through the cards, participants were given a surprise memory test. When it came to memory for positive behaviors, they did an equally good job with in-group and out-group members, correctly identifying just under 70 percent of the positive cards from each deck. For negative behaviors, however, a telling divergence emerged: Respondents correctly remembered only 57 percent of the negative cards from fellow overestimators or underestimators. But their memory was much more accurate for the peccadilloes of the group they weren't in—82 percent accurate, in fact.

In other words, the bad behaviors of people like us are not only more forgivable, they're also more forgettable. These are benefits we don't extend to outsiders, whom we hold to higher, less attainable standards. This tendency is deep-seated enough that it arises even when insider/outsider status is determined by something as trivial as how we see spots. Just imagine how strong these biases become when the two groups in question have a history of bad blood.

CATEGORICALLY SPEAKING

Why this propensity to see the in-group in a positive light? Some of it owes to our more general generosity in how we view the self. The same rose-colored glasses you use to evaluate your own characteristics and behaviors also filter how you see the groups with which you affiliate. Just as the effort to feel good about the self sometimes points you toward downward comparisons with individuals worse off than you are, so does derogating other groups help restore more collective pride and self-esteem.

The other lesson of the dot studies is just how dependent we are on categories. There are too few hours in the day and too many people in the world to permit careful, thoughtful scrutiny of everyone we meet. We have only so much mental energy at our disposal, and categorization is one way to cut cognitive corners.

For a moment, forget about how we perceive people—just think about objects. Early in life we start constructing categories based on the salient features of things in our environment: Furniture. Vegetables. Birds. Trucks. By using categories like these, we save time and effort. Even if you can't articulate a precise definition of "furniture," much like the Supreme Court and obscenity, you know it when you see it. This ability to relate the new to the familiar makes it that much easier to deal with novel items in your environment, freeing up cognitive resources for more important pursuits.

But our reliance on categories leads to problematic side effects as well. One is an exaggerated sense of how different groups of objects are. Like vegetables. The U.S. Department of Agriculture groups fruits and vegetables on the same level of its food pyramid, suggesting that we eat five to nine daily servings. (This, in addition to six to eleven servings of grain, three of meat, and three of dairy, which begs the question of whether they also recommend that we sit down to eight meals a day.) Still, despite the USDA's willingness to group them together, if I so much as include the words *fruit* and *vegetable* in the same sentence with my younger daughter, she scoffs at my galling naïveté. To her and most of her preschool cronies, fruit is delicious but veggies are the scourge of the earth.

Indeed, I once made the egregious error of trying to reason with her, explaining that tomatoes—which she won't eat—are actually fruits, whereas strawberries—which she will—are more vegetablish. She yelled at me. And then started to cry. She only stopped when I assured her that I was kidding, just like the time I had announced in jest that we'd be skipping our long-awaited trip to the indoor water park to go to Costco instead. Well, we adults also prefer to keep a healthy mental distance between competing object categories, even if suggestions to the contrary don't usually move us to tears.

A second side effect of categorization is that it leads us to gloss over differences that exist *within* groups. Like birds. If asked, most of us have little trouble generating examples: robin, sparrow, crow, blue jay, pigeon. But the category "bird" is actually far more diverse than we give it credit for, including as it does the ostrich, owl, turkey, pelican, and penguin. Just as different categories aren't as different as we assume them to be, objects within a category aren't as similar as we believe.

OK, enough of first-grade science class. The moral here is that when it comes to thinking about people, our reliance on categories is no different. First, we turn to categories almost automatically. Second, categorization leads us to exaggerate small differences between groups and overlook big differences within them.

Researchers at the University of Colorado conducted a neuroscientific analysis of just how automatic social categorization is.[6] Participants were fitted with an elastic cap with sensors that measure through the scalp the electricity associated with brain activity. Respondents were then shown photos of faces that varied by race and gender. So one set of photos included four white men and one black man, another had four white women and one white man, and so on.

The researchers were interested in how the brain reacts to changes in race or gender within a set of faces. For race, it only took 100 milliseconds to see signs of brain response. That's one-tenth of one second. Gender didn't take much longer—just 150 milliseconds. In other words, it takes longer for you to sneeze than it does to place the people you meet into social categories.

And what of the side effects of categorization? They also show up when it comes to thinking about people. We maintain rigid boundaries between social categories the same way my daughter does between fruits and vegetables. Consider the deck of cards research described earlier. Not only did overestimators and underestimators have better memory of the other group's negative actions, but in another study they also *anticipated* more bad behavior from the out-group to begin with. This expecting and exaggerating of differences between categories is what opens the door for social stereotyping.

One of the best demonstrations of our fondness for absolute categories is the way we talk about biracial individuals, shoehorning them into more clear-cut category labels. What do Barack Obama, Halle Berry, and Tiger Woods have in common? The consensus is that all three achieved African American firsts in their respective professions. But all three are also multiracial, even if you wouldn't know it by ubiquitous references to, for instance, "the first African American President." No one talks about Halle Berry as the first biracial woman to win the Best Actress Oscar, or

Tiger Woods as the first Asian golfer to win the Masters, even though both statements are factually sound. As with fruits and vegetables, we eschew ambiguity, preferring to see people in either/or terms.

The other side effect I mentioned—the tendency to overlook differences within categories—also emerges when thinking about people. Look no farther than the popular intuition that members of certain racial groups all look alike. An interesting aspect of the "they all look the same" hypothesis is that it's equal opportunity: while white Americans think this about Asians, in Asia they think the same about white Americans. Another interesting note is that the claim has no objective support: while dozens of studies have confirmed that we're better at recognizing faces of our own race, there's no reliable evidence that certain racial groups actually have reduced variability in facial appearance.[7]

So if these groups don't truly "all look the same," why are we convinced that they do? In large part because of categorization. From a perceptual standpoint, we simply treat faces differently once we've decided that they belong to our own group. We process in-group faces holistically, taking in the face as a unit and noting the relationship between its features in addition to the specifics of those features in isolation. We don't go to those same lengths after determining that a face belongs to the out-group.

Researchers at the University of Texas at El Paso creatively demonstrated this tendency in a study that assessed Hispanic participants' memory of faces.[8] Using a computer program, the researchers created a series of racially ambiguous faces, such that each one could be plausibly categorized as either Hispanic or black. When a "Hispanic-looking" hairdo—medium-length dark hair, often slicked back—was added to a face, respondents' memory for it was reasonably good. But another set of Hispanic participants saw the very same photos with close-cropped, "black-looking" hairdos, and their ability to remember and later identify the faces was substantially impaired. In fact, participants made more than twice as many errors on the subsequent memory test when a face had a "black hairdo" as when the very same face had a hairdo that made it look Hispanic.

In short, categorization drives how we see one another. After putting someone into the category "us," you're more generous with her, you rationalize away her mistakes, you value her as an individual, and you even visually process her facial features more carefully. Upon categorizing someone as "them," however, you lower expectations, harp on his missteps, and see him as epitomizing general truths about "people like that." This asymmetry is most pronounced between rival factions but even emerges when category lines are drawn on the most minimal of criteria.

The repercussions wrought by social categorization are immediate and pervasive. As yet one more example, think of your experiences as a pedestrian. About how easy it is to work up animosity toward the drivers who won't yield to you, who stop in the middle of the crosswalk, who splash you as they speed by. It takes me all of thirty seconds of walking in a congested area to work up a healthy distaste for all things motorist-related—to decide that we walkers are far and away the morally superior breed.

Then I get back behind the wheel of my own car. Before long, I'm muttering under my breath at jaywalkers and those who cross against the light, fully ensconced in the feeling of superiority now bestowed upon me by my newfound category affiliation.

———

THERE'S NO BETTER WAY to illustrate our facility with categorization than a quick reader-participation exercise. So let's go for it. If you were in my research lab, I'd sit you in front of a computer monitor and ask you to use a keypad to categorize a series of words as quickly as possible. That's too high-tech for us right now, so we'll turn to the next most rigorous scientific method for assessing categorization ability: thigh slapping.

Allow me to clarify: In a few paragraphs I'm going to ask you to place both of your hands palm down on your lap. Your right palm will rest on your right thigh and your left palm on your left thigh. You don't have to assume the position yet, as doing so will inevitably impair your ability to hold this book or turn pages. But that'll be the pose I'll ask you to adopt in a moment.

Your task will be to read through a list of words, classifying each one as either pleasant or unpleasant as you go. For pleasant words, you'll slap your right hand on your right leg. For unpleasant words, you'll slap your left hand on your left leg. You should move from the top to the bottom of the word list in order and as quickly as possible—if you make a mistake (and you'll likely realize it if you do), just correct it before continuing. There are twenty-five words in the list, so anyone walking by as you do this should hear twenty-five separate, arrhythmic slaps. They may also start to ponder the appropriateness of a psychiatric consult, so you may prefer to close the door before continuing.

OK, time to assume the position. Give the book a good, firm crease and lay it open on a table in front of you (or do the same with your e-reader, except for the crease part); you'll need to be able to see the word list that follows once you turn the page. Remember, your instructions are to slap your right side for pleasant words and your left side for unpleasant words. If you want, you can even time how long it takes to get through the list, as that will give you a precise numerical outcome to think about later.

Ready, set, turn the page and categorize:

UNPLEASANT WORDS	PLEASANT WORDS
Left Side	*Right Side*

VACATION

HEALTH

EVIL

DEATH

RAINBOW

CANCER

HEAVEN

VOMIT

POLLUTE

CHEER

DIVORCE

FILTH

SUNRISE

LOVE

ABUSE

MIRACLE

ROTTEN

LAUGHTER

SMILE

JAIL

AGONY

TRIUMPH

JEWELRY

PLEASURE

STINK

Not too hard, right? Sure, some people have idiosyncratic responses to particular items in the list. Maybe your birth month gives "Cancer" positive zodiac connotations; maybe you've had bad breakfast experiences with Lucky Charms, creating correspondingly ambivalent associations with "rainbow." For the most part, though, we can agree on whether each of these words is pleasant or unpleasant, and we do so pretty quickly.

Now, let's kick it up a notch. This time you'll be doing two categorization tasks at once. As before, pleasant words will get a right-hand slap and unpleasant words a left-hand slap. But now I want you to simultaneously categorize people as well. Specifically, I want you to sort people's names by apparent ethnicity.

Say what, you ask? Please, just indulge me for a few more paragraphs.

You should also slap your right side anytime you read a stereotypically white name, like Emily or Greg. And when you see a stereotypically black name—let's say, Lakisha or Jamal—you should slap your left side.

I recognize that this may make you uneasy or even upset for several reasons. For starters, maybe your name is Emily or Greg and you aren't white. Beyond that, I know I'm asking you to treat objects and people interchangeably. But I assure you, it's all in the name of science.

So take a moment to remind yourself of the instructions. You should slap your right side for pleasant words or "white-sounding" names. You should slap your left side for unpleasant words or "black-sounding" names. Again, go as quickly as you can, and keep in mind that this exercise is tailored toward those who hail from a country in which you encounter names like these with some regularity. If that's not the case, feel free to substitute another ethnic distinction that makes more sense to you—just go ahead and cross off the names on the following page and replace them with Arab/Israeli names, Korean/Japanese names, or any other dichotomy that's more appropriate.

Ready? Begin:

UNPLEASANT WORDS	PLEASANT WORDS
OR	OR
"BLACK" NAMES	"WHITE" NAMES
Left Side	*Right Side*

GIGGLE

MEREDITH

VACATION

LATONYA

STINK

MADELINE

BETSY

DEVIL

TYRONE

SOPHIE

ASSAULT

JAMAAL

GRIEF

PLEASURE

SHANEKA

AGONY

JAKE

DESPAIR

MIRACLE

EBONY

ROMANTIC

DYLAN

MARQUIS

HEROIC

DARNELL

OK, on to the last task, I promise. Again, you're going to categorize words and people at the same time. But now I want you to switch sides for the "white" and "black" names. That is, this time I want you to use your *right* hand for stereotypically black names and your *left* hand for stereotypically white names. So you should slap your right side for pleasant words or "black" names, and your left side for unpleasant words or "white" names.

This is a big change from the last round, and it may take your brain a second to register it. So go ahead and reread the previous paragraph and maybe even say it aloud before proceeding.

Once you're ready, go to the next page:

UNPLEASANT WORDS OR "WHITE" NAMES	PLEASANT WORDS OR "BLACK" NAMES
Left Side	*Right Side*

GENTLE

POISON

WENDY

DARRYL

DISASTER

KAITLYN

AIESHA

TRAGEDY

INJURY

TREVOR

LAUGHTER

TAMEKA

AMANDA

ANGRY

ABIGAIL

JOYOUS

MOLLY

CHEERFUL

UGLY

SHANICE

PARADISE

JAZMIN

PENALTY

HEAVEN

CONNOR

More than three-quarters of people find this last word list to be the hardest one. Even if you weren't timing it, odds are that you could feel yourself taking longer and maybe even making more mistakes. And if you did time your performance, it wouldn't surprise me if this final set took you more than twice as long as the previous ones.

In other words, I'd predict that most of you found it far more difficult to pair pleasant words with black names than with white names. Or—same idea phrased differently—it was easier for you to link unpleasant words with black people than to do the same with white people.

(What if *you* are black? Would I make the same prediction? Good—and important—question. I'll get to it shortly, I promise.)

You see, not all categories are created equal. Well, maybe they're *created* equal, but we quickly come to think of them in very different ways.

I have a second prediction for you as well. I bet that right now you're feeling a bit skeptical, indignant, and maybe even angry. You're thinking, *now, wait just a minute—any trouble I had with the final list had nothing to do with race*. Instead, you simply got used to categorizing the names one way—with white on the right and black on the left—so the final switch was confusing, right?

A reasonable hypothesis. I thought the same thing the first time I did the task. But that's not what's going on here.

You don't have to take my word for it—just try the three lists again, if you have the stamina for it. This time do the third set of words before the second, but start at the bottom of each list and work up so that you aren't doing the same word order as earlier. Or, if you and your thighs are getting tired, find someone else to serve as your guinea pig, but have them do the third list earlier than the second list. Go ahead, I can wait. . . .

It turns out that order doesn't matter as much as we expect it to. I've led this exercise many times in classes and diversity workshops and I vary the order of the lists. Even when I ask the audience to do list three before list two, the vast majority still has the hardest time combining pleasant words and black names on the same side. And when they go in the opposite order that you did—putting pleasant words on the same side as black names first—do you know what their initial reaction always is? They also maintain that race had nothing to do with their performance. Then they explain that they got better with practice. So it isn't order that's driving the effect, even though it feels like it is.

The bottom line is that categories don't exist in a vacuum. Even when we don't realize it—or won't admit it—different social groups conjure in our minds different sentiments, expectations, and cognitive associations.

EVERYBODY'S GOT SOMETHING TO HIDE, INCLUDING ME AND MY MONKEY

The categorization exercise on the previous pages is a low-tech version of the Implicit Association Test, or IAT.[9] The IAT was devised by psychologists at Harvard, the University of Washington, and the University of Virginia to assess category-based beliefs that people are otherwise unable or unwilling to disclose. You can take online versions on Harvard's Project Implicit website: http:// implicit.harvard.edu/implicit/. The site lists various incarnations of the test based on gender, age, disability, sexual orientation, religion, and other racial groups beyond black and white.

But back to the version you completed. An uncomfortable yet unavoidable conclusion emerges: it's an easier, more natural process for most of us to think about "pleasant" and "white" together than "pleasant" and "black." And the other way around for "unpleasant." I know this is an unpalatable suggestion, but alternative explanations for the changes in your word categorization speed just don't hold up to close analysis.

It's not list order. Order makes little difference when I use this exercise in person. More persuasively, the Project Implicit site reports that 70 percent of Web respondents are quicker to pair pleasant words with white people, regardless of list order.

It's not something particular to the names I chose, either. Of course, not all African Americans have names like Lakisha and Jamal. And, sure, these names may very well trigger an idiosyncratic kind of stereotype not associated with the racial group at large. But using photographs of black and white faces instead of names—as the Project Implicit site does—doesn't change the results much.

It's not merely an us-versus-them effect. Asian Americans are neither an "us" nor a "them" in the black/white comparison. Yet Asians are just as likely as whites to have an easier time pairing pleasant words with white-sounding names. And what of the performance of African Americans? It's *not* a mirror opposite of that of whites, as a strict us-versus-them notion would predict. Instead, about half of black respondents show a bias in favor of the category "black," and half show bias in favor of "white."

The inescapable conclusion is that most of us are quicker to pair pleasant/white and unpleasant/black than the other way around because we've been exposed to these associations countless times before, under circumstances both subtle and not so subtle. Once again, look no farther than the media: In movies, black female characters are five times more likely than white female characters to use profanity or engage in physical violence.[10] On local news broadcasts in the United States, a criminal defendant is four times more likely to have his mug shot put on the screen when he's black as opposed to white.[11] And on prime-time TV, even fictional characters show more distant, less friendly nonverbal behaviors when interacting with black characters, according to research recently conducted in my own department at Tufts University.[12]

We take some of these lessons to heart, even if unconsciously. In the Tufts television research, respondents in one study viewed a series of prime-time clips. After watching excerpts of shows in which white characters exhibited unfriendly nonverbal behavior toward black characters, respondents became even more biased in how they completed the IAT. That is, seeing TV characters interact coldly with black people made it even harder to pair pleasant concepts with African American faces.

So the Beatles got it right—everybody's got something to hide, even if each of us is deluded into thinking that we're the sole exception. Perhaps you're not among the majority who has difficulty pairing pleasant words with black names. Maybe instead you carry around automatic associations about other racial or ethnic groups in the culture in which you live. Or about women. Or men. Or people of a particular religion, age, nationality, weight, skin tone, sexual orientation, social class, or geographical region.

The point is, we don't just group people into categories and leave things at that. Social categories lead to generalizations, expectations, and particular trains of thought, all of which are shaped as well as reflected by the broader cultural messages around us. While we're quick to explain intergroup conflict and disparity in the WYSIWYG terms of hateful people with hateful attitudes, many societal biases owe their emergence and perpetuation to more basic cognitive tendencies possessed by us all.

MOST PEOPLE HAVE HEARD of Kübler-Ross's five stages of grief, the stepwise process that we supposedly go through when coping with loss. You know, Denial → Anger → Bargaining → Book Deal → Oprah. Or something like that.

In my experience, there's also a fairly predictable progression to how people react to completing a test like the IAT. As with the grief model, first comes denial—in this case, the refusal to believe that our change in word categorization speed has anything to do with race. Again, though, other potential explanations for why list three takes most respondents so much longer than list two just don't cut it in the end.

Eventually, then, many of us turn to a response of "so what?" As in, OK, maybe race affects word categorization, but so what? My difficulty pairing "pleasant" with "black" doesn't reflect my personal beliefs about race but simply indicates an awareness of the biases that are out there in society, the argument goes. After all, many of us have grown up in cultures in which the good guys wear white and the bad guys wear black. Where white cake is angel's food and black cake—though far more delicious than its pale counterpart—is the province of the devil. The different mental associations conjured by social categories like white and black don't influence how we actually behave, right?

Ah, but they do. At the very least, you now know that such thoughts impact slapping speed, a conclusion that I don't offer as a trivial or facetious one. You can't dismiss the IAT as a mere cognitive parlor trick: the sentiment captured by the test impacts real behavior. And beyond simple reaction time and word categorization, our expectations about social groups shape more important judgments and behaviors as well.

Consider employment. Generally speaking, research confirms that a job applicant's race influences how recruiters evaluate her, even on paper. Just a few years ago, economists at the University of Chicago and Harvard created and sent out close to five thousand résumés in response to employment ads in the areas of sales, customer service, and administrative support.[13] Using birth records, they gave half of the résumés a white-sounding name and the other half a black-sounding name. The names they chose should look familiar to you: the title of their published paper was "Are Emily and Greg more employable than Lakisha and Jamal?"

The economists set up separate voice mail boxes for their white and black fake applicants, and found that résumés with white names averaged a callback for every ten submissions. It took black applicants an average of fifteen résumés to get a call. You might think that sounds like a small difference, but try telling that to the job seeker who has to be 50 percent more proactive to get up to the same level of lukewarm response as everyone else. The researchers found that having a "white" name yielded just as many callbacks as listing an additional eight years of experience on the résumé.

How to account for this disparity? Again, the WYSIWYG response would be that human resources departments across the United States are full of hateful and intolerant people. But ponder the situation more carefully. Anyone who's ever evaluated résumés can tell you that they all start to look pretty similar pretty quickly—it's a subjective process in which even the most superficial of differentiating characteristics makes a big difference. Like formatting and font. Word choice. Spelling errors. Or even a name.

In fact, when you think about it, the résumé study is basically the IAT in action. It's the same setup: individuals with too little time to make too many evaluations about too many people. Instead of research respondents bombarded with word lists, it's managers bombarded with résumés. Under such circumstances—successive judgments made with little opportunity to scrutinize each one—our preexisting default associations make a big difference. Your thighs can already attest to that.

Alas, even when we have time to weigh our decisions, we're still not immune to category-based sentiment and expectation. Sticking to the realm of employment, disparities by race aren't limited to the paper trail of résumé evaluation. Face-to-face interviewing also looks very different depending on the color of the faces involved.

Consider a study from Princeton in which white participants were asked to interview a series of high school students in order to identify the strongest candidate for an academic team competition.[14] Each of the interviewers was given a list of fifteen questions to use to assess two candidates, one white and one black. The order of the two interviews was determined at random. And unbeknownst to the interviewers, *they* were actually the ones being observed the whole time, as members of the research team assessed their verbal and nonverbal performance from behind a one-way mirror.

The differences in how these interviewers interacted with the white and black applicants were readily apparent. They spent a longer time with white candidates—33 percent longer, to be precise. They sat several inches closer to white applicants, and even leaned in more during the course of the interview. Interviewers also made fewer speech errors when talking with the white applicant, as they were noticeably less likely to repeat themselves, hesitate, or stutter than they were when talking to the black applicant.

There was nothing in the profile of these interviewers to suggest that they were hateful individuals with intolerant attitudes. These were ordinary people. But their behavior changed enough between sessions to create very different experiences for white and black candidates. Perhaps they had lower expectations for the black applicants. Or maybe they were a tad more nervous during the interracial conversations. One thing's for sure, though: the changes in interviewer demeanor didn't result from differences in how the candidates themselves approached the interview. We know this because the "applicants" were actually students trained by the researchers to act in a uniform, rehearsed manner, right down to the angle at which they faced the interviewer and how much eye contact they maintained.

Again, the interviewers weren't out to torpedo the black candidates. But that's exactly what they did. It becomes just that much harder to nail the interview when the person you're talking to is disengaged, cold, or anxious. In fact, in a second study, the researchers changed things up and this time trained a set of interviewers. Half were instructed to conduct interviews in the manner of the white applicant sessions from the initial study—by sitting close, taking more time, and so on. The others were trained in the less immediate, more detached style of the previous black applicant sessions. The Manchurian interviewers were then sprung on unsuspecting white Princeton students.

These student volunteers were told that they were helping Career Services train new interviewers, and that they should treat the session like a real job interview. How did the "candidates," all white students, fare? As you'd expect, those randomly assigned to an engaged, friendly interviewer outperformed those interviewed in a less personal style. Indeed, had you watched the interviewees on video, you would've been convinced that the first group was just a more qualified, impressive, and interpersonally savvy set of people. Even though they weren't—even though the only real distinction was which interviewer they were assigned to.

In reality, of course, we don't get assigned to warm and cold interviewers at random. Reality is even less fair. Some of us regularly get interviewed by people who are open, relaxed, engaged, and willing to take the time to look for our strengths. And some of us aren't that lucky.

In other words, don't give in to the "so what?" response to your thigh-slapping performance. Category-based associations make a difference in the real world, and not just for employment issues. It's precisely this sort of stereotyped association that leads police officers in training simulations to have an easier time recognizing that a white suspect is unarmed than a black suspect.[15] That accounts for physicians with high-bias IAT scores being less likely to think that a black patient who presents with chest pains is in need of anticlotting thrombolytics.[16] That explains why the more bias people exhibit on an IAT-like measure, the more closed-off their body posture is during an informal conversation with someone of another race.[17]

In spite of your best efforts and deeply held convictions, you're not as fair-minded a person as you think you are. Few if any of us are.

MANAGING BIAS

We play a lot of games in my house. Yes, we have the obligatory basement Wii, but even more of our time is devoted to old standbys: meandering about Gum Drop Mountain, stuck in a perpetual loop of chutes and ladders, mixing it up with the old maid. Like my father decades before me, I've developed a penchant for falling asleep on the living room rug during these sessions—sometimes while waiting for my turn to come up, but just as often right in the middle of reading a question or calling a bingo number. So I spend a good chunk of these enjoyably lazy afternoons with my kids trying to think of creative ways to ward off the nap that lingers tantalizingly in the ether.

One strategy I've developed is to play conventional games unconventionally. Take, for example, Guess Who? This is the game where you're supposed to use as few yes/no questions as possible to figure out which of the dozens of plastic faces in front of you is the target face your opponent is holding. The obvious questions are those about gender or eye color or facial hair or clothing. Rather quickly, though, I start to find these unsatisfying, not to mention coma-inducing. So I like to sprinkle in the unexpected.

Instead of asking, "Is it a woman?" I'll try, "Does the person have ovaries?" I figure this way it's a game, but it's also an anatomy lesson.

Even better, I'm quite fond of the unanswerable question, such as, "Does the person feel fulfilled at work?" "Does she prefer red or green grapes?" Or, "Does he have commitment issues?"

I started doing this for fun—asking questions they can't really understand, much less answer, has proven to be an easy way to get a laugh out of my kids. Little did I suspect, though, that my own scientific research would soon come to show that many of us employ a similar strategy of dancing around the obvious when we navigate the sometimes choppy waters of real-life social interaction. Particularly when it comes to race.

After reading about our automatic tendencies toward in-group preference, categorization, and stereotyping, it's only natural to wonder, *What can we do about it?* One increasingly popular tactic these days seems to be to maintain that you don't even notice group differences to begin with. Such strategic efforts to appear color blind can be observed anywhere from the race-neutral elementary school curriculum that renders students surprised to find out later that Martin Luther King was black[18] to the facetious Stephen Colbert, who has on more than one occasion asked a talk show guest if she's African American because he doesn't "see color."

The assumption underlying this strategic color blindness is *if I don't even notice race, then I can't be a racist.* And so your coworker describes the new guy at the office by saying, "Oh, he's about my height, broad-shouldered, mid-forties, dresses well, smiles a lot," omitting the diagnostic fact that he's talking about one of only a handful of black men in the entire building. Or maybe race is mentioned, but only at the very end, in a stage whisper after first looking around to see who else is listening.

In other words, many people today gravitate toward the idea that talking about race is no different than admitting to your spouse that you think someone else is attractive: nothing good can possibly come of it. Instead, we search for creative ways to avoid the topic, even when it's relevant. So has emerged the mentality that total avoidance of race is the way to make a good impression— or, at least, the way to avoid making a bad one.

Does the strategy work? In a word, no.

In a series of studies in my lab at Tufts, colleagues and I have assessed the social consequences of such efforts to appear color blind.[19] And we've done so by using my favorite trick of playing conventional games unconventionally. In this research, we asked people to play a grown-up version of Guess Who? Our first step was to take a series of photos of adults so we could create a thirty-two-face array. Next, we recruited pairs of people to play our version of the game, giving them the regular instructions to ask as few yes/no questions as possible in identifying the target photo.

The pictures in the array always varied on several dimensions, just like in the kids' game. Specifically, there were three characteristics by which the photos were split on exactly fifty-fifty terms: background color, gender, and race. Half of the faces were on red backgrounds and half were on blue. Half were of women and half were of men. Half were unambiguously white faces and half were unambiguously black. This made for three particularly useful questions when playing: ask if the target photo has a red (or blue) background, for instance, and you cut down the remaining possibilities by half.

Indeed, almost every single adult in this research asked their partner the obvious question about background color. Same for gender. But a funny thing happened with race. When white people played the game with a white partner, they asked about race close to 95 percent of the time. But with a black partner, this number dropped to 63 percent—and in some versions of the game, considerably lower.

What were the consequences of this effort to dodge race? For one, it led to less efficient communication and poorer performance. It takes more questions to identify the target when you dance around the obvious.

Even more problematically, the color-blind strategy actually made a negative social impression. We showed silent video clips from the study to people who knew nothing about the research, asking them to evaluate the nonverbal behavior on display. They told us that the game players seemed less friendly and more distracted when going out of their way to avoid race. Too focused on not saying the wrong thing, these individuals came off as preoccupied and disingenuous. Ironically, when you try too hard to make a good impression, you run the risk of just the opposite.

So, as I've already suggested, we don't need our teachers needlessly harping on distinctions like gender in the classroom when doing so serves no concrete objective. And, no, we don't need our juries talking about race when assessing the physical damage a two-hundred-plus-pound assailant can cause. But going too far in the other direction by insisting that social categories don't even exist is hardly the answer. Bending over backward to maintain the façade of color blindness causes more problems than it solves.

Because let's face it: none of us are socially color blind, despite what the tongue-in-cheek talk show host would have you believe. The data have spoken: we notice race more quickly than we sneeze. Just as it's an oversimplification to think that discrimination always comes from hate, so is it naïve to believe that we can avoid bias by refusing to admit that we notice group differences in the first place.

WHAT, THEN, is a fair-minded and well-intentioned person to do?

Well, one lesson of this chapter is that you need not pretend that social categories don't exist in order to address social ills like conflict, prejudice, and discrimination. Doing so usually just makes things worse.

The next time you're in the produce section and your child points at a fellow shopper to exclaim, "Mommy, look—that man's face is a different color," remember that you don't have to shush her or make a panicked getaway to the frozen aisle. She's recognizing difference, not passing judgment. Talking about race isn't the same as pointing out a bad toupee.

And when you happen upon a more substantive discussion about group difference, don't just try to change the subject. Hear everyone out, even if you disagree. Refrain from automatically dismissing their position as "playing the race card."

Actually, we're long overdue to drop that phrase from the lexicon entirely. It's a mindless excuse to preempt uncomfortable conversations, a knee-jerk response to any attempt to discuss inequity. I'll say this for *Crash*: the movie may have offered an oversimplified take on discrimination, but at least it was willing to have the conversation. In the end, that's why people and critics liked it so much—it provided a chance to discuss that which many of us habitually shy away from. As the Guess Who? study demonstrates, constantly avoiding the reality in front of us isn't actually that much fun. Such mental gymnastics are onerous, distracting, and ultimately counterproductive.

And when you next find yourself interacting with someone of a different background, don't expend all your mental energy worrying about what not to say or not to do. What you recognize as your own anxiety born from good intent looks to others like lack of interest, disengagement, or the effort to hide something.

Instead, devote yourself to proactive, positive social efforts. Force yourself to maintain eye contact. Smile. Nod. Ask questions and then listen intently to the responses. Act naturally instead of trying to play it safe by clamming up. Research is clear: approaching interactions with the goal of promoting a positive outcome is far more effective than focusing on preventing a bad outcome.[20] It's much harder to make a good impression when all your mental energy is tied up trying to avoid a bad one.

In short, interracial interactions are just like any other daily experience: how you frame them makes a big difference. Life's a lot more fun—and things go more smoothly—when you think of diverse settings and conversations about race as learning opportunities rather than potential minefields.

Perhaps the most important lesson of this chapter, though, is to move past thinking about bias in strictly WYSIWYG terms. These days, everyone is much too caught up in avoiding the label "racist." The actor uses an epithet when pulled over by police, the comedian makes an ill-advised attempt at racial humor, the politician makes a remark that sounds like it came out of the nineteenth century . . . whatever the race-related controversy du jour, initial response is always the same: "I'm not a racist." Then the discussion inevitably heads in that direction, toward the question of whether or not this is a bigoted person.

So we're forced to wade through what passes for supporting evidence in these debates, like the touting of good intentions, past philanthropy, or even just having a few black friends. But this type of argument about who's a "racist" is tilting at windmills. The debate never gets anywhere because it's a dispositional term too loaded for anyone to admit to but too ethereal to ever pin conclusively on someone else.

It's high time to stop the fruitless arguments about who is and isn't a racist (or any other type of -ist, for that matter). We all are.

We all break down the people we see into distinct social categories. We're all impacted by stereotypes. We have automatic preferences for and against certain groups. We're more comfortable with in-groups than out-groups. The real question isn't whether or not you're an -ist. Rather, it's are you willing to make the effort to go beyond your default tendency of relying on category-based associations? And does the situation you're in leave you with enough cognitive energy to do so?

By no means do I suggest that you celebrate discrimination or remain complacent in its face. But it is OK to recognize that bias is part of human nature. It's actually liberating to admit it. If we'd all get over our denial that the way we see each other contributes to inequity, we could actually get to work on making the world a fairer place. And we might even loosen up and enjoy social interactions a bit more while we're at it.

Because the conclusion that bias has automatic aspects doesn't mean we're inevitably at its mercy. The IAT and measures like it assess implicit or nonconscious thoughts about different social groups—thoughts that can influence us when we don't realize we have to stand guard against them. This means that simply recognizing that you carry around such associations goes a long way toward dampening their effects. All the more reason for you to accept rather than avoid the conclusion that we all have biases: by doing so, you turn the implicit into the explicit, sapping the power of those preconceived notions lurking silently within.

So don't be afraid to ask yourself tough questions like, *how might my reaction have changed if the person in question had been less similar to me? Or would this incident have seemed different had the people involved been members of my own group?* Make the effort to shake yourself out of the rut of default assumption. Force yourself to ponder those expectations we usually don't acknowledge.

You can also proactively structure situations in ways that make discrimination less likely. There are out-and-out bigots who will act on any opportunity to make life difficult for certain others, but most of us want to be fair most of the time—the key is providing yourself with sufficient resources so that you don't have to cut cognitive corners. Like having ample time to make decisions. Or obtaining additional, individuating information about each person you're evaluating to prevent dependence on the superficial.

And take note of the simple research finding that you're most likely to rely on stereotypes when you're tired, overworked, or frustrated. In fact, "morning people" get more biased as the day wears on, and vice versa for "night people."[21] Thus, anything that helps you think clearly and feel comfortable also leaves you less prone to discriminate. Once again, learn to appreciate that the seemingly minor aspects of daily context have a major impact on how we think and act.

But none of this should surprise you anymore. You've been reading about the power of situations for more than two hundred pages now. You already know that the continuum of human capacity is remarkably broad—that just as we quickly fall head over heels in love, we also slip all too easily into the mind-set of bias. More often than not, it's context and not some immutable personality type that dictates which direction we go.

Remember, not all discrimination is born from animus; a good heart is not a fail-safe against inequity. In hate as in love, what you see is not always an accurate reflection of what, deep down, you get.

EPILOGUE

I LIED TO YOU. IN THE VERY FIRST PAGES OF THE
book, no less.

It wasn't an earth-shattering fabrication, but even if it was just
minor deception, I feel like I should come clean. So here goes.

Remember my opening story about hotel vouchers and the
Newark airport? My epic battle of wits with Marta, the seemingly
cold-blooded customer service representative? Well, while every
detail in that anecdote was true, I confess to having omitted a
crucial fact.

Yes, I told Marta that my wife was pregnant, a disclosure that
tipped the balance of the negotiations in our favor. And, yes, my
wife reacted to our free hotel room with superstitious concern: we
really had agreed not to tell anyone about our first pregnancy until

after three months had safely passed. But what I conveniently left out of the story is that there was no pregnancy at the time. OK, *someone* at the Newark airport was probably pregnant that night, but I had nothing to do with it—I swear. The jinx my wife was worried about was a future, still-hypothetical one.

I told Marta we were expecting simply to exploit a loophole in airline policy. And I didn't think twice about it. While I fancy myself an honest guy, the big, bad company was sticking it to us without remorse. By my mental calculus—admittedly aided by generous processes of self-perception and a healthy portion of rationalization—I figured that my dishonesty just evened the score.

In my first draft of the book, I admitted from the start that my successful navigation of Newark had included a flat-out lie. It struck me as a compelling way to illustrate the moral of the introduction, namely, that while understanding the power of situations doesn't inevitably make you a "better" person in a moral sense, it does render you a more *effective* person in a variety of pursuits.

When I circulated the draft, however, the opening concerned a few people. In fact, I believe my editor's exact question was, *Do you really want to introduce yourself to the readers by advocating for lying?* A fair point, I admit.

After all, this is a book that explores our tendency to use snippets of behavior to form lasting beliefs about the type of person someone is. I've already detailed how quickly we categorize and judge people upon meeting them, and how such conclusions, once reached, continue to influence expectations. So I'll concede that enabling a first impression of me as a liar might not have been the best idea. Instead, I decided to tell my story truthfully but leave out part of the punch line. Until now.

But I'm not confessing here for honesty's sake or to unburden a guilty conscience. I already told you: I don't feel bad about my lie to Marta. I'm doing it because this convoluted story about my story—my lying about my lying—offers a worthwhile lesson as well. It illustrates, once again, the importance of thinking closely about the contexts you're in (as well as those that you create).

OK, so there's nothing *that* remarkable about an editor and author ruminating on the nuances of a book's opening pages. It's part of their job descriptions, right? That they do so regularly simply confirms that we are indeed capable of thinking long and hard about the small social nuances that make a big difference—the mundane aspects of situations that have a dramatic impact on how we think and act. Indeed, many of us do this every day for a living, whether in publishing or in other fields like marketing, politics, education, or sales.

Too infrequently, though, do we conduct similar analyses of framing and context in other walks of life, from our ordinary interactions with strangers to our most intimate relationships with friends and loved ones. Instead, as you now know, we rely on assumptions about human nature to simplify and sanitize the unpredictability around us. We write off apathetic or antisocial acts as the work of dispositional miscreants. We cling to a view of the self as an independent agent unswayed by others. Time and again we convince ourselves that brief exposures to public behavior allow us to "really know someone," only to get burned by the boy-next-door-turned-serial-killer or the moralizing politician caught with his pants down.

The objective of this book has been to shake up your assumptions. To prompt you to take notice of the situational influences on human nature that too often remain hidden in plain sight. Just as the author agonizes over his introductory words in an effort to set the proper tone—or the advertising professional tweaks her campaign for maximum persuasive impact—so can your daily life benefit from closer analysis of what really makes people tick.

Once you start paying attention to the power of ordinary situations, there's no going back. By recognizing the true influences on social thought and behavior, you can't help but change the way you actually think and behave. As I alluded to in the opening chapter, it's a lot like learning the secret to a magic trick or the ending to an M. Night Shyamalan movie: knowing what to look for gives you new insight the second time you watch it.

Just think—the next time you're in a busy house or office and the phone rings, will you be as comfortable as you once were sitting by idly and assuming that someone else will answer it? Will you be as quick to agree with the columnist or TV talking head who blames the latest crisis on a few incorrigibly bad apples? Or as likely to explain an apparent gender difference in terms of "boys just being boys"?

I know that I see and interact with the world very differently for having studied situations. Sure, I find telemarketers as aggravating as the next guy, but I try not to take it out on them personally. They're just trying to earn a paycheck. When you stop to think about it, how miserable must it be to have repeated conversations all workday long with people who curse your very existence? By the same token, I know that they think that the longer they keep me on the phone, the more likely they are to get my money. Thus, I have no qualms about violating the social norm that usually prevents me from hanging up on someone in mid-sentence.

In the end, I recognize that it's the situation—not some predisposition for rudeness—that turns these individuals into the contemptible intrusions we all complain about openly. But I've also determined that their willingness to forsake the unwritten rule of not phoning during dinnertime frees me from any reciprocated concerns about the guidelines of civilized discourse.

On a regular basis, I hear similar stories from my students of years past. Some epiphanies are longer and some shorter, some mundane and some more profound. They share a common theme, though, of seeing the world differently after realizing just how much situations really matter.

Like Jill, who now works in finance, and had to figure out how to change her coworkers' problematic habit of completing paperwork incorrectly. So she thought back to what she had learned about how mindless conformity can be and used that knowledge to solve the problem, as she related in an e-mail:

> *My colleague was getting frustrated because she had sent several e-mails explaining how to fill out the two relatively simple forms, and no one could manage to complete them correctly . . . we decided to try taping up sample filled-in forms and ever since, we haven't had a problem. . . . Generally speaking, I try to keep in mind that rather than depending on the individuals executing the project to behave a*

certain way, I should design the steps to steer them in the direction of
behaving how I'd like them to.

Or Lauren, now training for a marathon, who checked in with the
following story of her persistence in the face of an ambiguous
potential emergency:

> *So I was taking a long run on Monday and stopped at a light after a*
> *few miles. I was catching my breath and glanced around when I*
> *noticed that the Metro bus display, instead of showing the route num-*
> *ber and destination, was flashing "EMERGENCY" and then "CALL*
> *POLICE." I looked around and saw to my dismay that no one else*
> *seemed to be disturbed, and I found myself thinking "do they know*
> *something I don't?" I thought about our class and the likelihood that*
> *no one would do anything since the bus had passengers, appeared to*
> *be following a normal route, and didn't appear to be on the verge of*
> *bursting into flames, but I decided I should do something . . . I didn't*
> *have a phone, so I stopped a woman who was crossing the street and*
> *she agreed and called 911. I continued on my run so I'm not sure what*
> *happened. . . . But I was glad I decided to stop someone.*

Or Samantha, now an elementary school teacher, who tells me that
she forces herself to include race in her lesson plans, even though
it's a difficult topic to address:

> *Most of the classes I have taught have had a vastly white majority.*
> *I find it difficult to talk about race in these situations—be it part*
> *of the academic or social emotional curriculum. However, despite my*

own discomfort, I don't stop myself from doing it. I have imple-
mented a unit on slavery in a 4th grade classroom, and just today
began a discussion about the sit-in movement in the south with my
2nd graders. . . . I guess what I learned is that what I am feeling is
my own discomfort, not necessarily anyone else's, and that avoiding
discussion of race doesn't make issues of race in our culture magically
disappear. In fact, it makes it worse.

Or Justin, a student who uses a wheelchair and finds himself newly
sensitive to the effects of social expectation:

As you might already know, people are usually rather uncomfortable
around people in wheelchairs (myself included ironically enough).
Knowing that they are uncomfortable, I might not act as open and
receptive which in turn makes others less willing to talk and interact
with me. This creates a self-fulfilling prophecy. Since I now recognize
this thanks to class, I am trying to use this to my advantage by trying
to be more open and outgoing and have it work the opposite way. And
while this is hard for me, I think that it is slowly working.

And on and on: from those who report getting less aggravated
with fellow drivers to those who have developed better strategies for successfully soliciting favors from others; from those who
have started to use Facebook snooping to make it seem like they
have something in common with a prospective dating partner to
those who have convinced the rest of the extended family to pick
out presents for a pending arrival *before* the baby's sex becomes
public knowledge.

Once you know to keep an eye out for it, the power of situations is everywhere you look.

AND, YET, SOMETIMES we still manage to look right past it. . . .

With my daughter in her car seat, we were less than a mile from morning preschool drop-off. The only remaining obstacle was the rotary. Perhaps you know it as a traffic circle or roundabout. Or maybe, if you're also four years old, "the round-and-round." It's one of those quirks that's supposed to make Boston charmingly idiosyncratic. Seven years after moving to town, I'm still waiting for this particular charm to kick in, especially during rush hour.

As we crept toward the maelstrom, we passed time by counting the cars in front of us, as usual. The countdown went smoothly before stalling out at three.

"Why did we stop, Daddy?" she asked after a beat.

"I'm not sure, honey," I replied. "The red car at the front of our line isn't moving right now."

This happens sometimes at the rotary. So I gave the red Nissan three cars up the benefit of the doubt at first. Twenty seconds maybe. It was a reasonable amount of time to wait for an opening before he'd have to take matters into his own hands and lead us into battle, traffic be damned. True, the signs read in big, block letters: "STATE LAW: DRIVERS YIELD TO ROTARY TRAF-FIC." But everyone knows these warnings are to be taken lightly, much like admonitions about mattress tags and key duplication.

I wasn't the only one who started honking. I may have been the first, but I wasn't the only one. Initially, I genuinely believed the clarion call might embolden Red Nissan—would let him know that those of us lined up behind him had faith in his ability to lead our charge. By the third or fourth honk, though, the cacophony I started had grown unmistakably aggressive. We were powerless behind Red Nissan, left with no choice but to wait for him to grow a pair, and it was starting to grate on us.

What kind of person just sits there with all these cars lined up behind him? What was he waiting for, an engraved invitation? What the hell, our horns wondered aloud, was wrong with Red Nissan?

"What's all that noise?" came a little voice from behind me.

I took a deep breath. "People are honking because the guy in the red car needs to learn how to drive," I explained as calmly as I could.

"You mean he didn't go to preschool when he was little?" she replied earnestly.

"His dad probably drove too slowly to get him there on time," I offered in return.

From my vantage point downhill and several cars back, I didn't have the clearest view. But now Red Nissan seemed to be gesticulating wildly, as if trying to defend his ineptitude through the medium of mime. Still, the honking continued.

Boy, this guy was a lost cause, I thought to myself. It's a miracle he's able to dress himself each morning. Now we were going to be late, and I just know these are the minutes I'm going to want back on my deathbed.

Finally, mercifully, we started to inch forward again. My daughter asked me another question, but I didn't really hear her. I was too agitated. I started to wonder what Red Nissan did for a living, praying that he wasn't a pharmacist or air traffic controller, hoping that he had channeled his impotent personality into a less impactful occupation, like restroom attendant or U.S. senator.

"Daddy, you didn't answer my question," my daughter piped up.

"Sorry, honey," I replied, as we eased into the rotary. "Ask me again."

"Why did those cars all have blue flags on them?"

I paused. "Say what?"

"All the cars going through the round-and-round had blue flags. And their lights were on, but it's not nighttime."

"Oh," I said, slumping down in my seat. The combined weight of insight and regret simultaneously landed on my shoulders. "That's called a funeral procession," I explained quietly. "You have to wait to let those go by."

You see, even people who study situations for a living still revert to bad habits in the mindless midst of the daily grind. When you're tired, busy, distracted, or just running on autopilot, you're that much more likely to let down your guard and fall back on old assumptions—it becomes all too easy to revert to looking past the context that's right in front of your eyes.

So while reading this book is a good start toward seeing human nature more clearly, my parting advice to you is to continue to force yourself to think about the impact of situations in your life, at least once a day. And make sure to learn from your mistakes. You know, like honking at mourners.

Fast-forward a few days from my regrettable performance at the rotary. I'm circling a full parking lot while late for an appointment. Suddenly, I catch a glimpse of a man climbing into his car two rows over. I speed to the spot and mark my territory via turn signal. Mesmerized by the sound of my own blinking, a few moments pass before I notice that he shows no signs of backing out. I try to wait patiently, but he's giving no cause for hope—no lights going on, no reach for the seat belt, nothing.

The delay is starting to get ridiculous. How can he be so deliberate when he sees me waiting here? But tempted as I am, I can't bring myself to honk. Chagrined by my misguided effort to break up the funeral procession earlier in the week, I start to wonder whether there might be a reasonable, situational cause for his inaction. Maybe he's taking an important call on his cell phone. Maybe he's waiting for someone to join him. Before my ruminations progress too far, though, they're interrupted by the sound of a car down the row vacating a space that I quickly claim.

Forty-five minutes later, I walked back to the parking lot to find my antagonist talking to a tow truck driver. Clearly, it had been car trouble that kept him from pulling out, not indifference to his fellow man. Even more surprising was that I knew the guy—he's the father of one of my daughter's classmates. The person I almost honked at wasn't some anonymous motorist—wasn't just Green Toyota—he was someone with whom I'd shared a handful of friendly conversations. A man I'd be crossing paths with several mornings a week for months to come. A man, I'll note, who cuts such an impressive figure that his left leg probably weighs as much as my entire body.

I shuddered as I imagined the fate I had narrowly averted. I could hear that little voice emerging from my backseat, or perhaps from my conscience, asking, "What's all that noise? Why are you honking this time? And why is Charlie's daddy coming at us with a tire iron?"

Mental note: add self-preservation to the list of positive outcomes brought about by appreciating the simple yet elegant conclusion that situations matter.

ACKNOWLEDGMENTS

Acknowledgments are boring for 99 percent of those who read them. I know this. I recognize that the vast majority of you will skim the following, if you look at it at all. But appreciate *my* situation: this is my first book. So I don't see how I can pass up the chance to thank in print those who have helped me get to this point. And, hey, at least I put this section at the very end so you didn't have to wade through it before getting to the good stuff.

As I wrote in the dedication, this book wouldn't have been possible without my colleagues. To my fellow social psychologists, I thank you once more for your consistently engaging and provocative research, as well as for letting me borrow it briefly to tell my story here—even if you didn't know that you had granted such permission until now. I hope I've done justice to your work.

Of course, my family deserves great thanks and recognition. I already acknowledged my wonderful wife and daughters, the illustrious Sommers Ladies, and they're the tip of the iceberg. Mom and Dad, thank you for your unwavering support, in terms emotional, academic, and financial, and for setting examples of how to balance commitments to both profession and family. Same goes for my always supportive mother-in-law and father-in-law (note to copy editor: yes, that last sentence is correct as written). And to my siblings nonpareil—Ben, Zach, Melissa, and

Charles—thank you for giving me ample practice when it comes to intellectual debate on mundane topics as well as low-brow arguments regarding the intellectual. Such skills came in handy when writing this book.

I'd also like to thank the entire community at Tufts. This book has been shaped by eight years' worth of conversations and interactions with Tufts students—some of the most impressive students you'll find in any classroom the world over. Your challenging questions and surprising observations are part of what make coming to work each day so much fun. That fun is also attributable to my departmental colleagues. In particular, I thank Nalini Ambady for encouraging me to start writing and for taking the time to read drafts and offer comments. And Keith Maddox, Lisa Shin, and Heather Urry for helping me waste time in amusing ways when such diversion was needed, as well as for giving me justifiable grief anytime I'd drop a phrase like "my agent" into regular conversation.

Speaking of which . . . I owe a tremendous debt of gratitude to my agent, the great Dan Lazar. We academic types have a hard time admitting when we don't know something, but I will fess up—I knew nothing about writing, much less publishing a book, a few years ago. Luckily, Dan knows it all. So, Dan, thanks for taking on a harebrained email query straight out of *Book Proposals for Dummies* and helping to turn it into something with a chance of finding a publisher. To my editor, Jake Morrissey, thanks for picking up where Dan left off, working with me to shape these ideas into a book with a chance of finding an audience. And to everyone at Writer's House—including Stephen Barr—and Riverhead—including Ali Cardia and Sarah Bowlin—who has (or will yet) devote their time and efforts to this project, I offer my sincerest appreciation as well.

A special acknowledgment to my high school English teachers, Pat Dunn and Bob Patterson, who taught me that writing could be fun and could even have personality. Thank you for that, for letting me find my own writing voice through trial and error, and for telling me when to

ACKNOWLEDGMENTS 291

shut up because that voice was disturbing the rest of the class. To Mrs. Dunn's current students, on the off chance that she ever shows you excerpts of this book—and a greater literary honor I cannot fathom—I inserted a few good vocab words for you to circle and look up before class (in particular, check out "sartorial" in Chapter 4). To Mr. Patterson, we all miss you.

Finally, dozens of other people have encouraged and guided me throughout the writing process and in the years leading up to it, sometimes without knowing that they were doing so. Far too many, in fact, to list them all here, from the colleagues and blog readers who said, "Hey, you should write a book someday," to the friends who suggested that I use as my subtitle "A Thinly Veiled Effort to Get on *The Daily Show*." But I owe particularly notable thank-yous to the following individuals: Saul Kassin, Steve Fein, Phoebe Ellsworth, Dan Ariely, Susan Pioli, Cameron Hughes, Pat Shin, Robbi Behr, and Mike Howard. And, because all great things are closed out by these two words: Mariano Rivera.

February 2011
Medford, Massachusetts

NOTES

Prologue

1. Alexander and Bruning (2008).

Chapter 1. WYSIWYG

1. This is not a textbook. If you were hoping for an exhaustive compendium of author names, methodological details, and statistical analyses, you're going to be disappointed. However, you can expect several of the studies discussed herein to be described in the same depth as the Stanford quiz show study in this chapter. Still other empirical results are summarized more succinctly in the effort to maintain the momentum of the narrative, but in all cases, the chapter end notes and bibliographies provide sufficient detail to allow you to look up and explore any research study further should you want to. For starters, regarding the Stanford quiz show study: Ross, Amabile, and Steinmetz (1977).

2. Castro Study: Jones and Harris (1967).

3. For news coverage of Marty Tankleff's arrest, trial, and eventual release: http://topics.nytimes.com/topics/reference/timestopics/people/t/martin_tankleff/index.html.

4. See Leo and Ofshe (1998) for more details.

5. Mock juror study with coerced confession: Kassin and Sukel (1997).

6. For a detailed review of our tendency to overestimate the correspondence of behavior and personality, its causes, and its effects: Gilbert and Malone (1995).

7. Texas videotape study: Gilbert, Pelham, and Krull (1988).

8. On evaluating friends versus strangers: Prager and Cutler (1990).

9. For more on this actor/observer difference: Jones and Nisbett (1972).

10. Fundamental Attribution Error: Ross (1977).

11. Fish study: Masuda and Nisbett (2001).

12. For much more on holistic and analytic thought across cultures: Nisbett et al. (2001).

13. Exploration of cross-cultural differences in the development of the WYSI-WYG mentality: Miller (1984).

14. For more details, including translated text from the letters in question: http://www.jfklibrary.org.

15. Khrushchev letter: State Department Publication 10338.

16. On relationship-enhancing attributions: Bradbury and Fincham (1992).

17. For a detailed and engaging read on several of these specific strategies: Cialdini's *Influence* (2008).

Chapter 2. Help Wanted

1. Coverage of the Bulger murder and subsequent trial available at http://www.guardian.co.uk/uk/bulger; see also Morrison (1998).

2. Good Samaritan study: Darley and Batson (1973).

3. Mall helping study: Baron (1997).

4. Restaurant gratuity study: Strohmetz et al. (2002).

5. Imaginary groups study: Garcia et al. (2002).

6. Intercom study: Darley and Latané (1968).

7. Death of Ignacio Mendez: http://www.nytimes.com/1999/06/18/nyregion/dead-man-found-on-train-was-visitor-from-delaware.html.

8. Smoke study: Latané and Darley (1968).

9. For review of Ringlemann and the general literature on social loafing: Karau and Williams (1993).

10. For review of research on urban locations and helping: Levine et al. (1994).

11. Michigan study of nature and cognitive functioning: Berman et al. (2008).

12. Milgram (1970), p. 1463.

13. Analysis of the *Times* article and other coverage of the Genovese murder: Manning, Levine, and Collins (2007).

14. As used in public discourse, this phrase is actually a misnomer. "Good Samaritan" laws refer to legal protections that shield from liability those individuals who make reasonable efforts to rescue another person in need. A requirement to assist others in need is actually referred to as the "duty to rescue" in legal circles.

15. Cialdini (2008), pp. 116–17.

16. Bra-size and hitchhiking study: Guéguen (2007).

17. AIDS perception study: Dooley (1995).

CHAPTER 3. GO WITH THE FLOW

1. For more on the murder of Christa Worthington, subsequent investigation, and trial: http://topics.nytimes.com/topics/reference/timestopics/people/w/christa_worthington/index.html.

2. For much, much more on conversational norms: Grice (1975).

3. On research findings related to ostracism (and the link to pain): Williams (2007).

4. Line judging study: Asch (1955).

5. At least, when the group in question meets certain criteria, such as including a diversity of opinions and individuals making independent judgments: Surowiecki (2004).

6. Visual perception and conformity study: Sherif (1935).

7. Cross-cultural examination of Asch conformity effects: Bond and Smith (1996).

8. NYU chameleon effect studies: Chartrand and Bargh (1999).

9. Soda favor study: Regan (1971).

10. Extra credit and lowballing study: Cialdini et al. (1978).

11. Copy machine study: Langer et al. (1978).

12. For more on Lynndie England: http://www.marieclaire.com/world-reports/news/latest/lynndie-england-1.

13. Gibson (1992), p. 79.

14. From: http://www.guardian.co.uk/world/2009/jan/03/abu-ghraib-lynndie-england-interview.

15. For more on the obedience studies: Milgram (1974); Blass (2004).

16. Milgram (1963).

17. Updated version of Milgram study: Burger (2009).

18. For more on this "banality of evil": Arendt (1963); Zimbardo (2007).

19. Milgram (1963), p. 371.

20. http://www.blimpyburger.com/ordering.htm.

21. For much more on groupthink and the Bay of Pigs: Janis (1972).

22. Janis (1972), p. 40.

23. Trick-or-treating study: Diener et al. (1976).

24. "Team of Rivals" cabinet: Goodwin (2005).

25. For review of research on minority influence: Wood et al. (1994).

Chapter 4. You're Not the Person You Thought You Were

1. Twenty Statements Test: Kuhn and McPartland (1954).

2. On distinctiveness and identity: McGuire, McGuire, Child, and Fujioka (1978).

3. McGraw (2001).

4. University of Michigan nylon stocking and construction noise studies: Nisbett and Wilson (1977).

5. Nisbett and Wilson (1977), p. 244.

6. Ansolabehere and Iyengar (1995).

7. Kassin and Sommers (1997).

8. Lieberman, Thomas, Finerman, and Dorey (2003).

9. Malleability of life satisfaction studies: Schwarz, Strack, Kommer, and Wagner (1987); Schwarz and Clore (1983).

10. Gilbert (2005).

11. Republicans study: Stapel and Schwarz (1998).

12. *Charlie's Angels* study: Kenrick and Gutierres (1980).

13. On social comparison, including the circumstances under which we're most likely to engage in it: Festinger (1954).

14. Adrenaline and emotion study: Schachter and Singer (1962).

15. For this comparison of sayings across cultures, and for a thorough review of cultural differences in self-concept: Markus and Kitayama (1991).

16. Japanese and American Twenty Statements Test comparison: Kanagawa, Cross, and Markus (1991).

17. On the reduced fixation on others' personalities in Asian cultures: Miller (1984).

18. "Asshole" study and culture of honor: Cohen et al. (1996).

19. Regional homicide rates: Cohen et al. (1996).

20. For much more on the "better-than-average-effect": Dunning (2005); Kruger and Dunning (1999).

21. Name letter studies: Pelham, Mirenberg, and Jones (2002).

22. Sports fan studies and basking in reflected glory: Cialdini et al. (1976).

23. For a review of downward social comparison, see Wood (1989).

24. For review of self-serving thought processes like this one: Mezulis et al. (2004).

25. On the adaptive nature of positive illusions: Taylor and Brown (1988).

26. Penn study of depression and perceived control: Alloy and Abramson (1979).

27. Hong Kong study: Hong et al. (1999).

28. Stanford pen pal study: Aronson et al. (2002).

Chapter 5. Mars and Venus Here on Earth

1. For more on gender and aggression: Archer (2004).

2. For one such study of gender difference in personal ads: Davis (1990).

3. For more on parents evaluating their newborn sons and daughters: Karraker et al. (1995).

4. Transcript of Summers's remarks: www.president.harvard.edu/speeches/summers_2005/nber.php.

5. On Harvard's job offer record under Summers's leadership: www.boston.com/news/local/articles/2005/01/17/summers_remarks_on_women_draw_fire/.

6. Michigan gender and math study: Spencer, Steele, and Quinn (1999).

7. Math test performance in gender-mixed versus all-female settings: Inzlicht and Ben-Zeev (2003).

8. Commercials and math performance study: Davies et al. (2002).

9. Swimsuit and math test study: Fredrickson et al. (1998).

10. On the effects of hearing genetic explanations for the math gender gap: Dar-Nimrod and Heine (2006).

11. The impact of teachers' math anxieties on student performance: Beilock et al. (2010).

12. On gender and different forms of aggression: Crick and Grotpeter (1995).

13. For review of gender, provocation, and aggression: Bettencourt and Miller (1996).

14. Princeton study of gender anonymity and aggression: Lightdale and Prentice (1994).

15. For review of gender difference in spatial skills: Voyer et al. (1995).

16. Infant shape rotation study: Moore and Johnson (2008).

17. Menstruation and spatial skill study: Hausmann et al. (2000).

18. German study of empathy and mental rotation: Ortner and Sieverding (2008).

19. Canadian video game study: Feng et al. (2007).

20. European testosterone study: Eisenegger et al. (2010).

21. For more on the role of context in boys' underperformance in academic domains such as reading and writing: Kleinfeld (2009); Tyre (2008).

22. On "Good morning, boys and girls": Bigler (2005).

CHAPTER 6. LOVE

1. On Westgate: Festinger et al. (1950).

2. Condo study: Ebbeson et al. (1976).

3. Marriage licenses in Columbus, Ohio: Clarke (1952).

4. Mere exposure to words and Chinese character studies: Zajonc (1968).

5. Mere exposure in the classroom: Moreland and Beach (1992).

6. On average features and beauty: Langlois et al. (1994).

7. "Can I buy you a drink?" study: Hendrickson and Goei (2009).

8. "Get to know you" study: Curtis and Miller (1986).

9. Virginia studies of secret relationships (and footsie): Wegner et al. (1994).

10. Shared experiences and attraction studies: Pinel et al. (2006).

11. On couples and attractiveness matching: Murstein (1972).

12. Capilano Bridge studies: Dutton and Aron (1974).

13. Florida State solicitation studies: Clark and Hatfield (1989).

14. Updated solicitation study: Schützwohl et al. (2009).

15. Northwestern speed-dating study: Finkel and Eastwick (2009).

16. On gender differences in sexual jealousy: DeSteno and Salovey (1996).

17. For much more on the emotional, cognitive, and mental effects of loneliness: Cacioppo and Patrick (2008).

18. For much more on the psychology of our need for social affiliation: Schachter (1959).

CHAPTER 7. HATE

1. Race and death penalty in Georgia: Baldus et al. (1990).

2. Race and death penalty in Philadelphia: Baldus et al. (1998).

3. Prototypicality and death penalty: Eberhardt et al. (2006).

4. Dot estimation and financial allocation study: Tajfel et al. (1971).

5. Dot estimation and social memory study: Howard and Rothbart (1980).

6. Colorado study of race, gender, and brain activity: Ito and Urland (2003).

7. For review of the "own-race bias": Meissner and Brigham (2001).

8. University of Texas at El Paso study: MacLin and Malpass (2001).

9. On the IAT: Greenwald et al. (1998); Nosek et al. (2007); http://implicit.harvard.edu/implicit/.

10. For more on these statistics and the general influence of race on media depictions: Entman and Rojecki (2001).

11. Race and media coverage of crime: Dixon and Linz (2000); Entman and Rojecki (2001).

12. Tufts nonverbal behavior and television characters study: Weisbuch et al. (2009).

13. Résumé study: Bertrand and Mullainathan (2004).

14. Princeton interviewing studies: Word et al. (1974).

15. Police simulation study: Correll et al. (2002).

16. Physicians and IAT study: Green et al. (2007).

17. Nonverbal behavior in interracial conversations: Dovidio et al. (2002).

18. For more on this example and color blindness in schools: Schofield (2007).

19. Strategic color blindness studies: Apfelbaum et al. (2008); Norton et al. (2006).

20. On these goals of prevention and promotion, as well as interracial interaction more generally: Shelton and Richeson (2006).

21. Stereotyping and circadian rhythm: Bodenhausen (1990).

BIBLIOGRAPHY

PROLOGUE

Alexander, M., and J. R. Bruning. *How to Break a Terrorist: The U.S. Interrogators Who Used Brains, Not Brutality, to Take Down the Deadliest Man in Iraq*. New York: Free Press, 2008.

CHAPTER 1. WYSIWYG

Bradbury, T. N., and F. D. Fincham (1992). Attributions and behavior in marital interaction. *Journal of Personality and Social Psychology* 63: 613–28.

Cialdini, R. B. *Influence: Science and Practice*, 5th ed. Boston: Allyn & Bacon, 2008.

Gilbert, D. T., and P. S. Malone (1995). The correspondence bias. *Psychological Bulletin* 117: 21–38.

Gilbert, D. T., B. W. Pelham, and D. S. Krull (1988). On cognitive busyness: When person perceivers meet persons perceived. *Journal of Personality and Social Psychology* 54: 733–40.

Jones, E. E., and V. A. Harris (1967). The attribution of attitudes. *Journal of Experimental Social Psychology* 3: 1–24.

Jones, E. E., and R. E. Nisbett. The actor and the observer: Divergent perceptions of the causes of the behavior. In E. E. Jones, D. E. Kanouse, H. H. Kelley, R. E. Nisbett, S. Valins, and B. Weiner, eds., *Attribution: Perceiving the Causes of Behavior*. Morristown, NJ: General Learning Press, 1972.

Kassin, S. M., and H. Sukel (1997). Coerced confessions and the jury: An experimental test of the "harmless error" rule. *Law and Human Behavior* 21: 27–46.

Leo, R. A., and R. J. Ofshe (1998). The consequences of false confessions: Deprivations of liberty and miscarriages of justice in the age of psychological interrogation. *Journal of Criminal Law and Criminology* 88: 429–96.

Masuda, T., and R. E. Nisbett (2001). Attending holistically vs. analytically: Comparing the context sensitivity of Japanese and Americans. *Journal of Personality and Social Psychology* 81: 922–34.

Miller, J. G. (1984). Culture and the development of everyday social explanation. *Journal of Personality and Social Psychology* 46: 961–78.

Nisbett, R. E., K. Peng, I. Choi, and A. Norenzayan (2001). Culture and systems of thought: Holistic versus analytic cognition. *Psychological Review* 108: 291–310.

Prager, I. G., and B. L. Cutler (1990). Attributing traits to oneself and to others: The role of acquaintance level. *Personality and Social Psychology Bulletin* 16: 309–19.

Ross, L. The intuitive psychologist and his shortcomings: Distortions in the attribution process. In L. Berkowitz, ed., *Advances in Experimental Social Psychology*, Vol. 10 (pp. 173–220). New York: Academic Press, 1977.

Ross, L., T. M. Amabile, and J. L. Steinmetz (1977). Social roles, social control, and biases in social perception. *Journal of Personality and Social Psychology* 35: 485–94.

http://www.jfklibrary.org

http://topics.nytimes.com/topics/reference/timestopics/people/t/martin_tankleff/index.html

Chapter 2. Help Wanted

Baron, R. A. (1997). The sweet smell of . . . helping: Effects of pleasant ambient fragrance on prosocial behavior in shopping malls. *Personality and Social Psychology Bulletin* 23: 498–503.

Berman, M. G., J. Jonides, and S. Kaplan (2008). The cognitive benefits of interacting with nature. *Psychological Science* 19: 1207–12.

Cialdini, R. B. *Influence: Science and Practice*, 5th ed. Boston: Allyn & Bacon, 2008.

Darley, J. M., and C. D. Batson (1973). "From Jerusalem to Jericho": A study of situational and dispositional variables in helping behavior. *Journal of Personality and Social Psychology* 27: 100–108.

Darley, J. M., and B. Latané (1968). Bystander intervention in emergencies: Diffusion of responsibility. *Journal of Personality and Social Psychology* 8: 377–83.

Dooley, P. A. (1995). Perceptions of the onset controllability of AIDS and helping judgments. *Journal of Applied Social Psychology* 10: 858–69.

Garcia, S. M., K. Weaver, G. B. Moskowitz, and J. M. Darley (2002). Crowded minds: The implicit bystander effect. *Journal of Personality and Social Psychology* 83: 843–53.

Guéguen, N. (2007). Bust size and hitchhiking: A field study. *Perceptual and Motor Skills* 105: 1294–98.

Karau, S. J., and K. D. Williams (1993). Social loafing: A meta-analytic review and theoretical integration. *Journal of Personality and Social Psychology* 65: 681–706.

Latané, B., and J. M. Darley (1968). Group inhibition of bystander intervention in emergencies. *Journal of Personality and Social Psychology* 10: 215–21.

Levine, R. V., T. S. Martinez, G. Brase, and K. Sorenson (1994). Helping in 36 U.S. cities. *Journal of Personality and Social Psychology* 67: 69–82.

Manning, R., M. Levine, and A. Collins (2007). The Kitty Genovese murder and the social psychology of helping: The parable of the 38 witnesses. *American Psychologist* 62: 555–62.

Milgram, S. (1970). The experience of living in cities. *Science* 167: 1461–68.

Morrison, B. *As If.* London: Granta, 1998.

Strohmetz, D. B., B. Rind, R. Fisher, and M. Lynn (2002). Sweetening the till: The use of candy to increase restaurant tipping. *Journal of Applied Social Psychology* 32: 300–309.

http://www.blimpyburger.com/ordering.htm

http://www.guardian.co.uk/uk/bulger

CHAPTER 3. GO WITH THE FLOW

Arendt, H. *Eichmann in Jerusalem: A Report on the Banality of Evil.* New York: Viking Press, 1963.

Asch, S. E. (1955). Opinions and social pressure. *Scientific American* 193: 31–35.

Blass, T. *The Man Who Shocked the World: The Life and Legacy of Stanley Milgram.* New York: Basic Books, 2004.

Bond, R., and P. B. Smith (1996). Culture and conformity: A meta-analysis of studies using Asch's (1952b. 1956) line judgment task. *Psychological Bulletin* 119: 111–37.

Burger, J. M. (2009). Replicating Milgram: Would people still obey today? *American Psychologist* 64: 1–11.

Chartrand, T. L., and J. A. Bargh (1999). The chameleon effect: The perception-behavior link and social interaction. *Journal of Personality and Social Psychology* 76: 893–910.

Cialdini, R. B., J. T. Cacioppo, R. Bassett, and J. A. Miller (1978). Lowball procedure for producing compliance: Commitment then cost. *Journal of Personality and Social Psychology* 36: 463–76.

Diener, E., S. F. Fraser, A. L. Beaman, and R. T. Kelem (1976). Effects of deindividuation variables on stealing among Halloween trick-or-treaters. *Journal of Personality and Social Psychology* 33: 178–83.

Gibson, J. T. Factors contributing to the creation of a torturer. In P. Suedfeld, ed., *Psychology and Torture: The Series in Clinical and Community Psychology* (pp. 77–88). Washington, DC: Hemisphere, 1992.

Goodwin, D. K. *Team of Rivals: The Political Genius of Abraham Lincoln.* New York: Simon & Schuster, 2005.

Grice, H. P. Logic and conversation. In P. Cole and J. Morgan, eds., *Syntax and Semantics,* Vol. 3. New York: Academic Press, 1975.

Janis, I. *Victims of Groupthink.* Boston: Houghton Mifflin, 1972.

Langer, E., A. Blank, and B. Chanowitz (1978). The mindlessness of ostensibly thoughtful action: The role of "placebic" information in interpersonal interaction. *Journal of Personality and Social Psychology* 36: 635–42.

Milgram, S. (1963). Behavioral study of obedience. *Journal of Abnormal and Social Psychology* 67: 371–78.

Milgram, S. *Obedience to Authority: An Experimental View*. New York: Harper & Row, 1974.

Regan, D. T. (1971). Effects of a favor and liking on compliance. *Journal of Experimental Social Psychology* 7: 627–39.

Sherif, M. (1935). A study of some social factors in perception. *Archives of Psychology* 27: 187.

Surowiecki, J. *The Wisdom of Crowds*. New York: Random House, 2004.

Williams, K. D. (2007). Ostracism. *Annual Review of Psychology* 58: 425–52.

Wood, W., S. Lundgren, J. A. Oullette, S. Busceme, and T. Blackstone (1994). Minority influence: A meta-analytic review of social influence processes. *Psychological Bulletin* 115: 323–45.

Zimbardo, P. *The Lucifer Effect: Understanding How Good People Turn Evil*. New York: Random House, 2007.

http://topics.nytimes.com/topics/reference/timestopics/people/w/christa_worthington/index.html

http://www.marieclaire.com/world-reports/news/latest/lynndie-england-1

http://www.guardian.co.uk/world/2009/jan/03/abu-ghraib-lynndie-england-interview

CHAPTER 4. YOU'RE NOT THE PERSON YOU THOUGHT YOU WERE

Alloy, L. B., and L. Y. Abramson (1979). Judgment of contingency in depressed and nondepressed students: Sadder but wiser? *Journal of Experimental Psychology: General* 108: 441–85.

Ansolabehere, S., and S. Iyengar. *Going Negative: How Political Advertisements Shrink and Polarize the Electorate*. New York: Free Press, 1995.

Aronson, J., C. B. Fried, and C. Good (2002). Reducing the effects of stereotype threat on African American college students by shaping theories of intelligence. *Journal of Experimental Social Psychology* 33: 113–25.

Cialdini, R. B., R. J. Borden, A. Thorne, M. R. Walker, S. Freeman, and M. R. Sloan (1976). Basking in reflected glory: Three (football) field studies. *Journal of Personality and Social Psychology* 34: 366–75.

Cohen, D., R. E. Nisbett, B. F. Bowdle, and N. Schwarz (1996). Insult, aggression, and the southern culture of honor: An "experimental ethnography." *Journal of Personality and Social Psychology* 70: 945–60.

Dunning, D. *Self-Insight: Roadblocks and Detours on the Path to Knowing Thyself*. New York: Psychology Press, 2005.

Festinger, L. (1954). A theory of social comparison processes. *Human Relations* 7: 117–40.

Gilbert, D. *Stumbling on Happiness*. New York: Vintage Books, 2005.

Hong, Y., C. Chiu, C. Dweck, D. M. S. Lin, and W. Wan (1999). Implicit theories, habits, and coping: A meaning system approach. *Journal of Personality and Social Psychology* 77: 588–99.

Kanagawa, C., S. E. Cross, and H. R. Markus (1991). "Who am I?" The cultural psychology of the conceptual self. *Personality and Social Psychology Bulletin* 27: 90–103.

Kassin, S. M., and S. R. Sommers (1997). Inadmissible testimony, instructions to disregard, and the jury: Substantive versus procedural considerations. *Personality and Social Psychology Bulletin* 23: 1046–54.

Kenrick, D. T., and S. E. Gutierres (1980). Contrast effects and judgments of physical attractiveness: When beauty becomes a social problem. *Journal of Personality and Social Psychology* 38: 131–40.

Kruger, J., and D. Dunning (1999). Unskilled and unaware of it: How difficulties in recognizing one's own incompetence lead to inflated self-assessments. *Journal of Personality and Social Psychology* 77: 1121–34.

Kuhn, M. H., and T. S. McPartland (1954). *American Sociological Review* 19: 68–76.

Lieberman, J. R., B. R. Thomas, G. A. M. Finerman, and F. Dorey (2003). Patients' reasons for undergoing total hip arthroplasty can change over time. *Journal of Arthroplasty* 18: 63–68.

Markus, H. R., and S. Kitayama (1991). Culture and the self: Implications for cognition, emotion, and motivation. *Psychological Review* 98: 224–53.

McGraw, P. C. *Self Matters: Creating Your Life from the Inside Out*. New York: Simon & Schuster, 2001.

McGuire, W. J., C. V. McGuire, P. Child, and T. Fujioka (1978). Salience of ethnicity in the spontaneous self-concept as a function of one's ethnic distinctiveness in the social environment. *Journal of Personality and Social Psychology* 36: 511–20.

Mezulis, A. H., L. Y. Abramson, J. S. Hyde, and J. L. Hankin (2004). Is there a universal positivity bias in attributions?: A meta-analytic review of individual, developmental, and cultural differences in the self-serving attributional bias. *Psychological Bulletin* 130: 711–47.

Miller, J. G. (1984). Culture and the development of everyday social explanation. *Journal of Personality and Social Psychology* 46: 961–78.

Nisbett, R. E., and T. D. Wilson (1977). Telling more than we can know: Verbal reports on mental processes. *Psychological Review* 84: 231–59.

Pelham, B. W., M. C. Mirenberg, and J. T. Jones (2002). Why Susie sells seashells by the seashore: Implicit egotism and major life decisions. *Journal of Personality and Social Psychology* 82: 469–87.

Schachter, S., and J. Singer (1962). Cognitive, social, and physiological determinants of emotional state. *Psychological Review* 69: 379–99.

Schwarz, N., and G. L. Clore (1983). Mood, misattribution, and judgments of well-being: Informative and directive functions of affective states. *Journal of Personality and Social Psychology* 45: 513–23.

Schwarz, N., F. Strack, D. Kommer, and D. Wagner (1987). Soccer, rooms and the quality of your life: Mood effects on judgments of satisfaction with life in general and with specific life-domains. *European Journal of Social Psychology* 17: 69–79.

Stapel, D. A., and N. Schwarz (1998). The Republican who did not want to become president: Colin Powell's impact on evaluations of the Republican Party and Bob Dole. *Personality and Social Psychology Bulletin* 24: 690–98.

Taylor, S. E., and J. D. Brown (1988). Illusion and well-being: a social psychological perspective on mental health. *Psychological Bulletin* 103: 193–210.

Wood, J. V. (1989). Theory and research concerning social comparisons of personal attributes. *Psychological Bulletin* 106: 231–48.

Chapter 5. Mars and Venus Here on Earth

Archer, J. (2004). Sex differences in aggression in real-world settings: A meta-analytic review. *Review of General Psychology* 8: 291–322.

Bettencourt, B. A., and N. Miller (1996). Gender differences in aggression as a function of provocation: A meta-analysis. *Psychological Bulletin* 119: 422–47.

Beilock, S. L., E. A. Gunderson, G. Ramirez, and S. C. Levine (2010). Female teachers' math anxiety affects girls' math achievement. *Proceedings of the National Academy of Sciences* 107: 1860–63.

Bigler, R. S. (2005). "Good morning, boys and girls": When a simple greeting engenders stereotypes. *Teaching Tolerance* 28: 22–23.

Crick, N. R., and J. K. Grotpeter (1995). Relational aggression, gender, and social-psychological adjustment. *Child Development* 66: 710–22.

Dar-Nimrod, I., and S. J. Heine, (2006). Exposure to scientific theories affects women's math performance. *Science* 20: 435.

Davies, P. G., S. J. Spencer, D. M. Quinn, and R. Gerhardstein (2002). Consuming images: How television commercials that elicit stereotype threat can restrain women academically and professionally. *Personality and Social Psychology Bulletin* 28: 1615–28.

Davis, S. (1990). Men as success objects and women as sex objects: A study of personal advertisements. *Sex Roles* 23: 45–50.

Eisenegger, C., M. Naef, R. Snozzi, M. Heinrichs, and E. Fehr (2010). Prejudice and truth about the effect of testosterone on human bargaining behaviour. *Nature* 463: 356–59.

Feng, J., and I. Spence, and J. Pratt (2007). Playing an action video game reduces gender differences in spatial cognition. *Psychological Science* 18: 850–55.

Fredrickson, B. L., T. Roberts, S. M. Noll, D. M. Quinn, and J. M. Twenge (1998). That swimsuit becomes you: Sex differences in self-objectification, restrained eating, and math performance. *Journal of Personality and Social Psychology* 75: 269–84.

Hausmann, M., D. Slabbekoorn, S. H. M. Van Goozen, K. T. Cohen-Kettenis, and O. Güntürkün (2000). Sex hormones affect spatial abilities during the menstrual cycle. *Behavioral Neuroscience* 114: 1245–50.

Inzlicht, M., and T. Ben-Zeev (2003). A threatening intellectual environment:

Why females are susceptible to experiencing problem-solving deficits in the presence of males. *Psychological Science* 11: 365–71.

Karraker, K. J., D. A. Vogel, and M. A. Lake (1995). Parents' gender-stereotyped perceptions of newborns: The eye of the beholder revisited. *Sex Roles* 33: 687–701.

Kleinfeld, J. (2009). The state of American boyhood. *Gender Issues* 26: 113–29.

Lightdale, J. R., D. A. Prentice (1994). Rethinking sex differences in aggression: Aggressive behavior in the absence of social roles. *Personality and Social Psychology Bulletin* 20: 34–44.

Moore, D. S., and S. P. Johnson (2008). Mental rotation in human infants: A sex difference. *Psychological Science* 19: 1063–66.

Ortner, T. M., and M. Sieverding (2008). Where are the gender differences? Male priming boosts spatial skills in women. *Sex Roles* 59: 274–81.

Spencer, S. J., C. M. Steele, and D. Quinn (1999). Stereotype threat and women's math performance. *Journal of Experimental Social Psychology* 35: 4–28.

Tyre, P. *The Trouble with Boys*. New York: Crown, 2008.

Voyer, D., S. Voyer, and M. P. Bryden (1995). Magnitude of sex differences in spatial abilities: A meta-analysis and consideration of critical variables. *Psychological Bulletin* 117: 250–70.

http://www.boston.com/news/local/articles/2005/01/17/summers_remarks_on_women_draw_fire

http://www.president.harvard.edu/speeches/summers_2005/nber.php

Chapter 6. Love

Cacioppo, J. T., and W. Patrick, *Loneliness: Human Nature and the Need for Social Connection*. New York: W. W. Norton, 2008.

Clark, R. D. III, and E. Hatfield (1989). Gender differences in receptivity to sexual offers. *Journal of Personality and Human Sexuality* 2: 39–55.

Clarke, A. C. (1952). An examination of the operation of propinquity as a factor in mate selection. *American Sociological Review* 27: 17–22.

Curtis, R. C., and K. Miller (1986). Believing another likes or dislikes you: Behaviors making the beliefs come true. *Journal of Personality and Social Psychology* 51: 284–90.

DeSteno, D. A., and P. Salovey (1996). Evolutionary origins of sex differences in jealousy? Questioning the "fitness" of the model. *Psychological Science* 7: 367–72.

Dutton, D. G., and A. P. Aron (1974). Some evidence for heightened sexual attraction under conditions of high anxiety. *Journal of Personality and Social Psychology* 4: 510–17.

Ebbeson, E. B., G. L. Kjos, and V. J. Konecni (1976). Spatial ecology: Its effects on the choice of friends and enemies. *Journal of Experimental Social Psychology* 12: 508–18.

Festinger, L., S. Schachter, and K. Back. *Social Pressures in Informal Groups*. New York: Harper & Brothers, 1950.

Finkel, E. J., and P. W. Eastwick (2009). Arbitrary social norms influence sex differences in romantic selectivity. *Psychological Science* 20: 1291–95.

Hendrickson, B., and R. Goei (2009). Reciprocity and dating: Explaining the effects of favor and status on compliance with a date request. *Communication Research* 36: 585–608.

Langlois, J. H., L. A. Roggman, and L. Musselman (1994). What is average and what is not average about attractive faces? *Psychological Science* 5: 214–20.

Moreland, R. L., and S. Beach (1992). Exposure effects in the classroom: The development of affinity among students. *Journal of Experimental Social Psychology* 28: 255–76.

Murstein, B. I. (1972). Physical attractiveness and marital choice. *Journal of Personality and Social Psychology* 22: 8–12.

Pinel, E. C., A. E. Long, M. J. Landau, K. Alexander, and T. Pyszczynski (2006). Seeing I to I: A pathway to interpersonal connectedness. *Journal of Personality and Social Psychology* 90: 243–57.

Schachter, S. *The Psychology of Affiliation*. Stanford, CA: Stanford University Press, 1959.

Schützwohl, A., A. Fuchs, W. F. McKibbin, and T. K. Schakelford (2009). How willing are you to accept sexual requests from slightly unattractive to exceptionally attractive imagined requestors? *Human Nature* 20: 282–93.

Wegner, D. M., J. D. Lane, and S. Dimitri (1994). The allure of secret relationships. *Journal of Personality and Social Psychology* 66: 287–300.

Zajonc, R. B. (1968). Attitudinal effects of mere exposure. *Journal of Personality and Social Psychology* 9: 1–27.

CHAPTER 7. HATE

Apfelbaum, E. P., S. R. Sommers, and M. I. Norton (2008). Seeing race and seeming racist? Evaluating strategic colorblindness in social interaction. *Journal of Personality and Social Psychology* 95: 918–32.

Baldus, D. C., C. A. Pulaski, and G. Woodworth. *Equal Justice and the Death Penalty: A Legal and Empirical Analysis.* Boston: Northeastern University Press, 1990.

Baldus, D. C., G. Woodworth, D. Zuckerman, N. A. Weiner, and B. Broffitt (1998). Racial discrimination and the death penalty in the post-Furman era: An empirical and legal overview, with recent findings from Philadelphia. *Cornell Law Review* 83: 1638–1770.

Bertrand, M., and S. Mullainathan (2004). Are Emily and Greg more employable than Lakisha and Jamal? A field experiment on labor market discrimination. *American Economic Review* 94: 991–1013.

Bodenhausen, G. V. (1990). Stereotypes as judgmental heuristics: Evidence of circadian variations in discrimination. *Psychological Science* 1: 319–22.

Correll, J., B. Park, C. M. Judd, and B. Wittenbrink (2002). The police officer's dilemma: Using ethnicity to disambiguate potentially threatening individuals. *Journal of Personality and Social Psychology* 83: 1314–29.

Dixon, T. L., and D. Linz (2000). Overrepresentation and underrepresentation of African Americans and Latinos as lawbreakers on television news. *Journal of Communication* 50: 131–54.

Dovidio, J. F., K. Kawakami, and S. L. Gaertner (2002). Implicit and explicit prejudice and interracial interaction. *Journal of Personality and Social Psychology* 82: 62–68.

Eberhardt, J. L., P. G. Davies, V. Purdie-Vaughns, and S. L. Johnson (2006). Looking deathworthy: Perceived stereotypicality of Black defendants predicts capital-sentencing outcomes. *Psychological Science* 17: 383–86.

Entman, R. M., and A. Rojecki. *The Black Image in the White Mind: Media and Race in America.* Chicago: University of Chicago Press, 2001.

Green, A. R., D. R. Carney, D. J. Pallin, H. N. Long, K. L. Raymond, L. I. Iezzoni, and M. B. Banaji (2007). Implicit bias among physicians and its prediction of thrombolysis decisions for Black and White patients. *Journal of General Internal Medicine* 22: 1231–38.

Greenwald, A. G., D. E. McGhee, and J. L. K. Schwartz (1998). Measuring individual differences in implicit cognition: The implicit association test. *Journal of Personality and Social Psychology* 74: 1464–80.

Howard, J. W., and M. Rothbart (1980). Social categorization and memory for in-group and out-group behavior. *Journal of Personality and Social Psychology* 38: 301–10.

Ito, T. A., and G. R. Urland (2003). Race and gender on the brain: Electrocortical measures of attention to the race and gender of multiply categorizable individuals. *Journal of Personality and Social Psychology* 85: 616–26.

MacLin, O. H., and R. S. Malpass (2001). Racial categorization of faces: The ambiguous race face effect. *Psychology, Public Policy, and Law* 7: 98–118.

Meissner, C. A., and J. C. Brigham (2001). Thirty years of investigating the own-race bias in memory for faces. *Psychology, Public Policy, and Law* 7: 3–35.

Norton, M. I., S. R. Sommers, E. P. Apfelbaum, N. Pura, and D. Ariely (2006). Colorblindness and interracial interaction: Playing the political correctness game. *Psychological Science* 17: 949–53.

Nosek, B. A., A. G. Greenwald, and M. R. Banaji. The Implicit Association Test at age 7: A methodological and conceptual review. In J. A. Bargh, ed., *Social Psychology and the Unconscious: The Automaticity of Higher Mental Processes* (pp. 265–92). New York: Psychology Press, 2007.

Schofield, J. W. The colorblind perspective in school: Causes and consequences. In J. A. Banks and C. A. McGee Banks, eds., *Multicultural Education: Issues and Perspectives* (pp. 271–95). New York: Wiley, 2007.

Shelton, J. N., and J. A. Richeson. Interracial interactions: A relational approach. In M. P. Zanna, ed., *Advances in Experimental Social Psychology*, Vol. 38 (pp. 121–81). San Diego, CA: Elsevier Academic Press, 2006.

Tajfel, H., M. G. Billig, R. P. Bundy, and C. Flament (1971). Social categorization and intergroup behaviour. *European Journal of Social Psychology* 2: 149–78.

Weisbuch, M., K. Pauker, and N. Ambady (2009). The subtle transmission of race bias via televised nonverbal behavior. *Science* 326: 1711–14.

Word, C. O., M. P. Zanna, and J. Cooper (1974). The nonverbal mediation of self-fulfilling prophecies in interracial interaction. *Journal of Experimental Social Psychology* 10: 109–20.

http://implicit.harvard.edu/implicit

INDEX

Sam Sommers is an award-winning psychology professor at Tufts University. His research has been covered by *Good Morning America*, NPR, *Harper's*, the *Washington Post*, and the *Los Angeles Times*. He lives near Boston with his wife and two daughters.

To arrange a speaking engagement for the author, please contact the Penguin Speakers Bureau at speakersbureau@us.penguingroup.com.